SCM STUDYGUIDE TO CHURCH HISTORY

SCM STUDYGUIDE TO CHURCH HISTORY

Stephen Spencer

scm press

© Stephen Spencer 2013

Published in 2013 by SCM Press
Editorial office
3rd Floor
Invicta House
108–114 Golden Lane,
London
EC1Y 0TG

SCM Press is an imprint of Hymns Ancient & Modern Ltd
(a registered charity)
13A Hellesdon Park Road
Norwich NR6 5DR, UK

www.scmpress.co.uk

British Library Cataloguing in Publication data

A catalogue record for this book is available
from the British Library

978-0-334-04645-5

Typeset by Regent Typesetting
Printed and bound by
CPI Group (UK) Ltd

Contents

Preface

There is renewed interest in Christian history. The recent television series by Diarmaid MacCulloch and his book *A History of Christianity: The First Three Thousand Years* reflected this and encouraged it. Jonathan Hill, Robert Bruce Mullin, Stephen Backhouse and Miranda Threlfall-Holmes have also recently published accessible and attractive surveys of a vast subject. Yet, there is still a need for a one-volume introduction to the study of the history of the institution of the Church, looking at the development of its corporate life especially within the Western setting, with attention to some of the key texts. This volume seeks to fill the gap.

The chapters that follow build on my two earlier SCM Studyguides. The first, *Christian Mission*, described the broad nature of God's saving purpose in history and especially its manifestation in Christian mission through the centuries. The rich diversity of the ways the Church has participated in the *missio Dei* emerged clearly from that survey. The second, *Anglicanism*, looked at what that mission has meant for the individual disciple, especially within one denominational tradition, that of Anglicanism. It traced different ways that scripture, tradition and reason have guided the Christian life. This third volume looks at what Christian mission has meant for the corporate life of the Church, especially as the Church has participated in the cross currents of human history and its surprising variety of organizational forms. I am grateful to Natalie Watson and SCM Press for giving me the opportunity to write about these interrelated topics in an extended way. I need to point out that there are points of contact between the stories told in the three volumes, and figures such as Augustine, Luther and John Wesley, and some of the things they wrote, appear in more than one place.

I am grateful to Stephen Platten, the Bishop of Wakefield, for granting me some study leave to complete this volume. I am again grateful to my wife Sally for reading through the entire book and making corrections.

Finally, I must again thank the ordinands of the Yorkshire Ministry Course for listening to and encouraging my teaching on all these topics. This volume is dedicated to them in gratitude for all they have given me.

1

Studying Church History

Why Study Church History?

The study of history helps us to live our lives in the present. This is because, as Rowan Williams has written,

> history is a set of stories we tell in order to understand better who we are and the world we're now in; as a written affair, it is never just a catalogue of things that happen to have happened. It is bound to be making judgements about the importance of what it deals with, and often – always? – has some element of moral judgement not far below the surface. We start telling the story to get a better definition of who we are or of what the subject is that we're describing: history helps us define things. Good history makes us think again about the definition of things we thought we understood pretty well, because it engages not just with what is familiar but with what is strange. It recognizes that 'the past is a foreign country' as well as being *our* past. (Williams 2005, p. 1)

The study of church history, then, is a way of exploring and rediscovering an understanding of what the Church is today. As texts are examined and evidence assessed, it is usual to find that inherited notions and images, such as the Church as a state institution, with hierarchies and laws and civil power, can give way to other more fluid images, such as the Church as a movement of ideas or association of friends. It is a discipline that can uncover strange and unsavoury aspects of the Church's life, as in the history of the Crusades, as well as inspirational and uplifting episodes, as in the rise of different monastic orders, in which men and women have turned their back on worldly riches to seek God in the desert or slum. The study of church history forces us to re-think and re-define what

Jesus' followers, an assorted group of men, women and children from across the centuries, might actually be.

How to Study Church History?

History cannot be the attempt to create a complete account of all that happened, a meta-narrative that answers all questions and settles all disputes. This would require an encyclopedic coverage of all aspects of the subject as well as the ability to see history from every point of view, which only God can have! But nor can history just be the detailed study of specific episodes or personalities with no attempt to place them within the bigger picture. This would result in the reader getting lost in a jungle of detail. Broad patterns of development and meaning need to be traced. We need a map of the whole within which to locate the specific parts.

But we also need to recognize the limitations of such maps because they can only be drawn from one point of view. They are the view from one location on the planet, at one point in time, with all the limitations and unfinished business that that implies. The historian needs to acknowledge how other perspectives are also valid and also deserve to be recognized. In this way, history itself is never finished: the publication of scholarly books on episodes and people is always an invitation for other studies to be written from different and complementary perspectives, to add to and enrich our understanding of what has gone on.

History depends on the work of others. The monographs and surveys of historians provide 'secondary literature' which give orientation and a point of departure as we begin our own reading and research. But behind these books lie the 'primary sources', those documents, records, artefacts and buildings that come from the period itself. The student of history needs to 'read' and become familiar with all of these, because they provide the raw data of history. They reveal how the past is 'a foreign country' but they also allow that past to be rediscovered in new and fresh ways.

But primary sources need interpreting. The reader needs always to ask *who* are the author or authors, what their point of view may have been, and why they were producing the document or artefact in the first place. Then a critical perspective can be acquired, one which allows the historian to gain a sense of perspective on what they are studying and so be able to begin to weigh and evaluate its meaning and importance.

This Studyguide

Church history is obviously a vast subject and it is easy to get lost in the woods of detail. A specific line of enquiry is needed to give shape and direction to the study, one that also allows the bigger mapping exercise to take place. This Studyguide will explore one question that is both specific and general in its scope, a question coming from those involved in the 'emerging church' and 'fresh expressions' movements in different parts of the Western world at this time. The question comes out of the contrast between these new congregations which often meet in places like gyms, schools, pubs and clubs, and traditional church building-based congregations, and it is this: what kind of body *is* the Church? Traditional congregations have assumed that their pattern of corporate life provides the answer, with regular Sunday services, leadership structures, membership roll and authorized financial arrangements. The new 'emerging churches', on the other hand, are seeking different or 'fresh' ways of being the Church, ways that change the inherited pattern in a range of fundamental ways. For example, they may not meet on Sundays, they may not work with a structured approach to leadership and they may not have anything resembling a membership roll or budget or annual accounts. Are they still churches? What is actually required to be a real Church? Is it necessary, for example, for a church to have an existence at one remove from the society or community in which it is found, or can it just be one facet of that wider life, as when a school or hospital employs a chaplaincy team to minister to the whole institution? Does a church need a legal constitution or to be financially independent or have its own building? In other words, can a church be part and parcel of a wider society and therefore be integrated and identified with it, or is it a body that needs to exist in its own right and therefore needs to stand apart from that society in important respects?

This is a question about the organizational form of the Church. Helen Cameron has recently studied and written about this topic, drawing on the recently established discipline of organizational studies. In *Resourcing Mission* (2010), she provides an answer, which is not one answer but five. She identifies five genres or cultural forms of organization that are widespread in the range of churches found in contemporary Western society. Her forms can be summarized as:

1 *Public utility*: providing an essential service; covering the country; without a membership but having legal officers.
2 *Voluntary association*: having a definite membership; with set procedures for members to run the association themselves and with an agreed aim.
3 *Friendship group*: a voluntary and informal body; the aim is fellowship.
4 *Third-place meeting*: occurring within a public space (e.g. café, pub); constrained by the limits of that space; with a shared aim which can be changed by agreement.
5 *Network resource*: providing support to a group of people who already have a shared and stated aim.

> (based on Cameron 2010, pp. 24–37, see also Cameron et al. 2005)

The fundamental contrasts between the different forms can be seen in this list. For example, if a church is a public utility that serves a whole population, it cannot be a voluntary association with a membership list. Churches will ultimately be one or the other, though they may have elements that recall other forms. But the terminology that Cameron uses is clearly drawn from a twenty-first-century setting. To use this framework in church history will require some adaptation. In this Studyguide, the following slightly different set of terms will emerge from our survey: the Church as a state institution (for 1); voluntary association (as in 2); devotional circles (for 3); meetings or cells within a wider community (for 4); ordered network (for 5). In addition to these five, we will occasionally find the Church being a community, as in a self-sufficient commune, or, more extremely, as in a sect. This can be labelled as number 6.

Is one form right and the others wrong? Each has had its place, but as our survey unfolds, judgements about the appropriateness of each form in their changing social and religious settings will emerge, for moral judgement cannot be avoided in historical study, as Rowan Williams pointed about above. In different language, it can be said that church history and ecclesiology are intimately related.

The history of the Church shows a fascinating interaction of Church and society, at global, national and local levels, with different forms of church life emerging and then disappearing again. It is an interaction that has gone through several discernible phases of development over the centuries and in different places. We shall examine a set of 'moments' in this unfolding story, moments that clearly illustrate the major phases and, together, build up an overview.

But the chapters that follow will not attempt to provide a complete or final account of that story. There is not enough space and, more importantly, to attempt such a thing would be to attempt to produce the kind of metanarrative of history that was criticized above. Instead, they will assemble information about some of the key events and personalities, quote some of the key statements and let a theologian or church leader from each era express what is distinctively new about its self-understanding. Each chapter will ask further questions about the contemporary application of what has been uncovered. Readers will be encouraged to go further into the subject by doing their own research and taking the debate forward in different ways. Hence lists of further reading will be included at the end of each chapter.

The Studyguide also has a Western bias, especially in the later chapters, because this is of most relevance to the intended readership, who are those participating in the life and ministry of Western and especially English-speaking churches. It will provide them with their own family history, as it were. Other traditions and branches of the Church have much to teach, but in an introductory volume like this the priority must be to answer the question 'who do you think *you* are?'

A Framework

First of all it is necessary to introduce Christian history as a whole, which is the setting for the more specific subject of church history. The next few pages will provide a panoramic canvas on which to explore the changing forms of the Church. A tried and tested way to do this is to sub-divide the two millennia of Christian history into its major phases or eras and present a portrait of each in turn. This Studyguide follows Hans Küng's sub-division in his well-known *Christianity: Its Essence and History* (English translation 1995). Küng divides the history into six major eras: Jewish Christian or Apostolic; Hellenistic; Medieval Catholic; Reformation; Enlightenment Modern; and Postmodern. This book will broadly follow these divisions except that the longest of his eras, the 1,000 years of Medieval Catholic Christianity from Constantine to the medieval period, will be covered by three chapters rather than one, making eight chapters in all. Furthermore the subdivision of the last two eras will be slightly different. Küng brackets together the Enlightenment and the modern era, lasting from the mid-seventeenth to the early twentieth century, with his final era being the current or 'postmodern' age. But there is still considerable debate as to whether a postmodern age can clearly be distinguished from the modern age. For historians it seems too soon to be making a hard and fast distinction (though not, perhaps, for missiologists: see Spencer 2007). This Studyguide makes a slightly different division, with the seventeenth and eighteenth centuries receiving their own chapter under the title 'Churches of the Enlightenment', and the nineteenth and twentieth centuries receiving a chapter with the title 'Churches in the Modern Era'. These pages will not venture into the twenty-first century or enter the debate about whether postmodernity exists.

Palestinian origins

The first Christians inhabited three different worlds. They came from a Jewish Palestinian background with the worldview of first-century Palestinian Judaism. This was dominated by eschatology, and specifically by the belief that the end of the age was near, a time of war and floods and death. The ardent hope and expectation was that a messiah would then appear, as described in the book of Daniel (e.g. 7.13, 12.1–4), who would throw off Roman oppression and usher in a new age of liberation and prosperity for the people of Israel.

But they also lived within a world of trade and commerce, which generally used the Greek language as the medium of communication and which was heavily influenced by Greek ways of thinking and communication. Finally they were also under the authority of the Romans, who were the superpower of the day, controlling and colonizing many parts of the Mediterranean world and whose soldiers commonly taxed and demanded bribes from ordinary citizens.

Jewish Christians saw Jesus as the long expected messiah and many believed that he would return with power within a generation (e.g. 1 Thess. 4.15ff.). They were filled with a sense of urgency that this was the final hour. They believed they were to go out to as many people as possible to alert and prepare them for the coming of the messiah and the end of the age. The days were short, the end times were near, and destruction was just around the corner. It was imperative to get people to turn to the Lord so that they would repent, get their lives in order and be ready for his coming. In 1 Corinthians 7.29–33 we are given a glimpse of how this worldview affected the life of the first Christians in the Jewish diaspora: they were not to be over-concerned with everyday affairs of the world but were to be ready for the end.

The question to be faced in the next chapter, from a number of angles and in greater detail, is how all this shaped the nature and form of the Church itself.

Within the Hellenistic world

As Christianity spread beyond Palestine and around the Mediterranean world it came to be dominated more and more by Greek language and culture. This was the world of trade and commerce, under the control of the Roman Empire but using the Greek language as the medium of communication. Language draws on culture and learning for its vocabulary, and Greek language drew on Greek learning and philosophy. In this, the influence of Plato and Neoplatonism should not be underestimated. This was an outlook that did not see reality in linear terms, as an extended story with a beginning in the past, a present and a future that was still awaited. Instead it saw the visible and material world as a set of changing and ephemeral reflections of an eternal and unchanging world. The real world is the world of the forms, which are eternal realities found in such things as truth, goodness, beauty and virtue. Our visible world reflects these to a greater or lesser extent, and the purpose of human life is to gain understanding and knowledge of these things and so be freed from the shackles of earthly existence.

All of this had a profound influence on the Church and the way it understood the Kingdom. Beginning in the latter part of the first century, a shift of emphasis began to occur, away from expectation that the Kingdom would come in the near future, to one of believing the Kingdom could be accessed here and now, through wise teaching and worship. A shift from a futurist eschatology to a realized eschatology began to occur. This is seen in John's Gospel, where judgement and eternal life are sometimes described as being *already present* in the world (e.g. 5.21–4). It continued with the Apologists such as Justin Martyr, who described how Christianity was in deep accord with Greek learning and philosophy, and continued with the brilliant and creative Alexandrian theologian Origen. It also accounts for why the early Church invested so much time and energy in developing the Creeds. The reason is that if access to the eternal life of the Kingdom is gained through right understanding, it is crucial that the Church has a correct definition and description of what this right understanding might be. The development of orthodoxy (right *understanding*) replaced the earlier Jewish emphasis (from the Prophets) on orthopraxis (the right *practice* of justice and righteousness).

This Hellenistic phase of Christianity continued with the development of the Orthodoxy of Byzantium, in which the Liturgy became the central expression of Christian discipleship. It saw the development of the catechumenate, a forty-day period of preparation for baptism at the Easter Vigil. This was the origin of the season of Lent.

Catholic Christianity from Constantine

The next era had its roots in the conversion of the Roman Emperor Constantine in the year 312. He rose to power through the defeat of his brothers who had been co-rulers of the Empire. During his rise to power he became committed to the Christian religion, which he legalized in the year 312. It quickly became established as the religion of the Empire. Constantine took control of the affairs of the Church and called the bishops to his winter palace at Nicea in Asia Minor (modern-day Iznik in Turkey). There he made the bishops agree on a creedal statement which became the basis of the Nicene Creed. The bishops and the emperor's officials were now to work together, supporting and strengthening the work of both. The Nicene canons show the Church becoming an arm of the Roman government. This shows a marriage of Church and state, that would later be called Christendom.

The alliance would remain a dominant reality in both East and West for a thousand years. While the Hellenistic and Byzantine Church would lose ground to Islam in the East (finally resulting in the fall of Constantinople in 1453), the Western Church would gain in strength. After the collapse of the Roman Empire, the papacy replaced the emperor as the supreme authority in the Church, and gained immense influence. Christianity came to be seen as a unity of the spiritual and temporal, in a fixed hierarchy with the popes and the kings at the top of the pyramid and the peasants at the bottom. A moment that symbolized all this was the crowning of the Frankish king Charlemagne by Pope Leo III in

800. Leo gave divine sanction to Charlemagne's rule over the whole of central Europe, from France in the West to Germany in the East, while Charlemagne undertook to uphold and strengthen the Papacy's mission to Christianize all the peoples of Europe. In the later Middle Ages, however, rivalry between pope and kings would be intense, with the pope occasionally having the upper hand but the kings more often subjecting him to their will. As the nation states of Western Europe gained in unity and commercial power in the later Middle Ages this became more and more the case.

Reformation

The next era in the West is linked with the Reformation of the sixteenth century. This began as a movement of church reform initiated by the German monk Martin Luther and his doctrine of justification by grace through faith. Luther came to see that the whole structure of Church and state is secondary to the way believers are saved and enter God's kingdom. He came to see that justification occurs when a believer simply accepts and trusts in Christ's saving atonement on the cross. This occurs through the individual having faith in the unseen God rather than through incorporation into the sacramental life of the Church. A new emphasis developed on the individual and their invisible relationship with God. Furthermore, the words of scripture, which contain the promise of justification, take priority over everything else and create the Church itself: 'God's word cannot be without God's people, and conversely, God's people cannot be without God's word. For who would preach the word, or hear it preached, if there were no people of God? And what could or would God's people believe, if there were no word of God? ('On the Councils and the Church', in McGrath 1999, pp. 202–3)

The Reformation saw the pulpit replace the altar as the focus of worship and of church architecture; it also resulted in a de-clericalization of the priesthood and the removal of shrines and devotions to the saints especially to the Blessed Virgin Mary. Many of the kingdoms and churches of northern Europe rejected the authority of the pope, becoming independent national churches under their own monarch. The marriage of Church and state continued, but with the monarch now clearly in control of the affairs of the Church, though still with no authority to preach or celebrate sacraments. There was a sharper distinction between the earthly and the heavenly, the kingdoms of this world and the kingdom of God. An important and wide-ranging change in the nature of the Church occurred, one that is the subject of Chapter 7.

The Enlightenment era

The post-Reformation era begins with advances in science in the late seventeenth century, represented above all by Sir Isaac Newton's re-definition of the laws of physics. European society was becoming increasingly impressed with the ability of the human mind to measure, map and understand the physical world in which we live. Human reason seemed to be the measure of all things, and this is why this period is often called the Age of Enlightenment or the Age of Reason. It showed that many believed they were no longer dependent on supernatural revelation and they became suspicious of medieval thought as stifling. There was a new belief in progress, which was now leaving behind the traditions of the Middle Ages, the Church and the feudal order of society. Immanuel Kant, the greatest philosopher of the Enlightenment, defined the range and scope of human reason, placing religion beyond its scope and thereby inadvertently beginning the process of religion's marginalization in modern Europe.

There were political consequences to all of this. A new individualism implied the rise of democratic ideals and the overthrow of the monarchies. Revolution beckoned, with the American War of Independence (1775–83) and the French Revolution (1789) putting this new thinking into practice. This age saw the rise of the democratic ideal, in which the autonomous individual would control the government of the nation.

But another consequence of the scientific breakthroughs was the rise of technology, for example the great inventions that created Lancashire's cotton industry: Watt's steam engine, Kay's flying shuttle, Hargreaves's spinning jenny, Cartwright's power loom (all between 1733 and 1785). These paved the way for the rise of industrialization, resulting in major social changes as rural populations moved to the new factories in the cities, first in Britain and then in Germany.

Enlightenment thought had a massive impact on Protestantism. While many Protestants remained committed to the Christianity of the Reformation era, others in a more liberal tradition came increasingly to see Christianity governed by philosophical thought ('reason'), where supernatural elements were played down or reinterpreted and sin regarded as a kind of ignorance and seen as something that is in principle solvable. William Law, an Anglican writer on prayer, demonstrated this new confidence in human reason when he stated that 'Reason is our universal law that obliges us in all places and at all times; and no actions have any honour, but so far as they are instances of our obedience to reason' (*Serious Call* XXIV).

In this period, the churches sponsored educational initiatives within their missionary work. One early example is Thomas Bray founding the 'Society for Promoting Christian Knowledge' in 1698 'to promote and encourage the erection of charity schools in all parts of England and Wales ... promoting Christian knowledge both at home and in the other parts of the world by the best methods that should offer'. It is the emphasis on schools and knowledge, rather than on churches and worship, that makes this quotation typical of its age. Chapter 8 charts the impact of all this on the nature of the Church itself.

Modernity

The nineteenth century saw the European powers engage in extensive commercial expansion overseas, carrying Western culture, philosophy and education to many points around the globe. The Age of Reason became the Age of Empire, in which European nations harnessed technology and industrialization for a scramble for global domination. This led to increasing competition between them, and the next step along this road was inevitably war. In the First World War the so-called enlightened European powers proceeded to kill a whole generation of their young men on the battlefield with their new found technology. Out of these tragic events came the Versailles Treaty, the humiliation of Germany and the rise of Nazism. Out of those events came, of course, the Holocaust, the Second World War and the dropping of the atomic bombs on Hiroshima and Nagasaki.

These traumatic events destroyed the Enlightenment belief in human progress founded on reason and technology. While technology continued to develop with great speed in the twentieth century, it was now regarded with a certain degree of suspicion in Western thinking. After the Second World War arose a number of anti-technology movements, among them opposition to the atomic bomb, to unchecked industrial growth and to the genetic engineering of crops.

Another key development in the modern era was mass immigration into Western societies from the Indian sub-continent, Africa and parts of Asia. This resulted in the forming of plural societies, with different religions, cultures, languages and customs rubbing shoulders with each other in most of the larger European cities. And this included not only the arrival of non-Christian religions but other forms of Christianity from the southern hemisphere.

These two developments gave rise to a new way of thinking within modernity in which there was an abyss between the rational and the subjective aspects of humanity. This lead to both dimensions developing in isolation from one another. But in late modernity there was a new searching beyond the old certitudes, including a new willingness to revisit the despised zones of the spiritual and religious as roots of healing.

As a whole

There are at least two important qualifications to this subdivision of Christianity into six distinct eras. The first is that the characteristic beliefs and practices of each era are not limited to that era but continue to be expressed in later eras. So, for example, the apocalyptic worldview of the earliest period is found in later periods of the Church's life, such as among the Anabaptists of the sixteenth century and various sects of the modern period including the Seventh Day Adventists, the Jehovah's Witnesses and the Plymouth Brethren. The beliefs and practices of the Hellenistic Church are still to be found within the Orthodox tradition in many parts of Eastern Europe and Russia. The outlook of the medieval Roman Catholic Church can still be found in many parts of the Roman Catholic world today. The outlook of the Protestant Reformers has been influential in subsequent centuries, such as in the seventeenth-century Pietism of the Moravians and eighteenth-century Evangelical revivals in Britain and New England through figures such as John Wesley and George Whitfield, though with an increased recognition of the importance of inward feeling alongside justification by faith.

A second qualification is that it is important also to recognize significant continuity running through each of the eras. This is found in the way over the centuries Christians have always recognized Jesus as Lord and Saviour. Hans Küng summarizes this continuity as 'the abiding substance of faith in which Jesus is believed to be the Christ, the decisive event of revelation' (Küng 1995). This substance of faith includes implications for the practice of the Church, such as the way the Bible and sacraments have always been at the heart of worship, though with varying emphases on one or the other.

This chapter began with the question 'What kind of body is the Church?' Helen Cameron suggested five possible answers to this question, and I have added a sixth. The question now becomes 'Which of these six have actually appeared in Christian history and which have been the dominant ones?' The survey above has sketched an evolving and involved history with at least six major eras between the first and the twentieth centuries. What form or forms has the Church taken within these different eras?

Discussion Questions

Is it necessary to study church history?
Can the work of historians be impartial?
What makes a church a church?

Bibliography and Further Reading

Backhouse, Stephen (2011), *The Compact Guide to Christian History*, Oxford: Lion Hudson.

Cameron, Helen (2010), *Resourcing Mission: Practical Theology for Changing Churches*, London: SCM Press.

Cameron, Helen, Philip Richter, Douglas Davies and Frances Ward (2005), *Studying Local Churches: A Handbook*, London: SCM Press.

Cross, F. L. and E. A. Livingstone (eds) (2005), *The Oxford Dictionary of the Christian Church*, 4th edn, Oxford: Oxford University Press.

Hill, Jonathan (2007), *The History of Christianity*, Oxford: Lion Hudson.

Küng, Hans (1995), *Christianity: Its Essence and History*, London: SCM Press.

McGrath, Alistair (3rd edn, 1999), *Reformation Thought: An Introduction*, Oxford: Blackwell.

Mullin, Robert Bruce (2008), *A Short World History of Christianity*, Louisville, KY: Westminster John Knox Press.

Spencer, Stephen (2007), *SCM Studyguide Christian Mission*, London: SCM Press.

Williams, Rowan (2005), *Why Study the Past?*, London: Darton, Longman and Todd.

2

The Apostolic Church: Meeting or Community?

The earliest phase of the Church's life is associated with those followers of Jesus who after Pentecost became missionary preachers and teachers of the gospel message or, as they are usually called, 'apostles'. This is the period between Jesus' death in about 33 and the year 66 or thereabouts, when these apostles had either been killed or had died or had stopped preaching because of old age. This short period was especially formative of the life of the Church and deserves its own chapter.

Birth in Jerusalem

Sources

The main source of information about this first phase of the Church's life is the Acts of the Apostles. A problem immediately presents itself, because it was not written by one of the apostles but by Luke and has its own version of events. The author is writing from a particular point of view and wishes to emphasize the work of the Holy Spirit in the growth of the Church and the acceptance of Gentiles as its full members. Paul is the central figure of Acts, and the second half of the book charts the progress of his preaching mission from Palestine across the ancient world to its capital, Rome. The book ends with the gospel message being received in Rome. The fact that it omits the death of Paul shows the selective nature of the story that it tells. It probably leaves out other important events. It therefore needs to be handled with care by the historian.

The other major source of information is the letters of Paul. The earliest of these is generally recognized to be 1 Thessalonians, written to the church at Thessalonika in Greece. He wrote it after recently visiting the church, possibly the visit mentioned in Acts 17.1–9, possibly during his stay at Corinth mentioned in Acts 18.1–18. The immediate reason for writing was the return of Timothy to Paul after Timothy's visit to the church (1 Thess. 3.6). This all means it was written some 18–20 years after Jesus' death. It gives a vivid insight into the earliest phase of Christianity.

The next letter to be written is likely to have been Paul's letter to the church in Galatia, probably written when Paul was staying at Ephesus (Acts 19.1–20). This would have been around the year 54. He stayed at Ephesus for three months, and the letter shows he was in dispute with some Jewish Christians who were saying that Gentile Christians should be circumcised and so become Jews. This group are called the Judaizers. The letter is written to argue why this is wrong and it presents the first extended insight into Paul's developing theology. His letter argues that the church should open its doors to Gentiles without condition. This argument is expanded and enriched in his letter to the Romans written a few years later. The letters to the Corinthian church show Paul's response to a number of other contentious issues and are a rich source of information about the life and beliefs of the apostolic Church. But the fact that all his letters are written in response to current controversies rather than as general presentations of his theology means that they need to be seen as partial rather than comprehensive in the story they tell.

Timeline

37BC–4AD	King Herod the Great
4	Tetrarchy of Herod's sons under Rome (though Judea under a Roman 'Prefect')
4–66	Varieties of Judaism in Palestine, many messianic, some separatist (like the Essenes of the Qumran community)
33	Death and resurrection of Jesus in Jerusalem and Galilee, leading to birth of the Church at Pentecost
c.37	Conversion of Paul

c.40	Division between Hebrews and 'Hellenists' (cf. Acts 6)
c.49	Council of Jerusalem (Acts 15; see also Gal. 2.1–10)
c.50–c.60	Writing of Paul's letters
c.60–c.90	Writing of Synoptic Gospels
64	Nero's persecution
66–70	First Jewish revolt
c.67	Paul and Peter executed in Rome
70	Destruction of Jerusalem
70–73	Siege of Masada where the Zealots had taken refuge in Herod's fort
80–90	Probable expulsion of Christians from synagogues ('18 Benedictions' throughout Palestine)
c.100	Council of Jamnia (of Rabbis) and settling of Hebrew/ OT Canon

Pentecost

Acts and the fourth gospel agree that it was the receiving of the Holy Spirit in the hearts and lives of the disciples that transformed them from being a frightened and traumatized group (e.g. John 20.19; Mark 16.8) into becoming confident and passionate advocates of Jesus' message (Acts 2.1–4; John 20.22). They were now apostles: as the Father had sent him, so Jesus was sending them into the world (John 20.21).

Acts associates this event with the Jewish festival of Pentecost, a festival that took place 50 days after the Passover festival (*penta* means fifty). It was a commemoration of the giving of the law to Moses on Mount Sinai and the creation of the Covenant between God and his people. Palestinian Jews were required to travel to Jerusalem on this day. The description in Acts of the rush of violent wind and tongues of fire recalls the thunder, lightning, cloud and fire on Sinai when Moses was there (Exod. 19.16–19). It also recalls the time when Elijah met God on Mount Horeb with the earthquake and fire. Elijah had renewed the commitment of the people to the Covenant. So, in a related way, these events at Pentecost were renewing the life of Israel. Peter's speech makes clear that the dramatic happenings were fulfilling the words of the prophet Joel about the ending of the age and the coming of God's kingdom:

> But Peter, standing with the eleven, raised his voice and addressed them: 'Men of Judea and all who live in Jerusalem … this is what was spoken through the prophet Joel:
>> "In the last days it will be, God declares,
>> that I will pour out my Spirit upon all flesh,
>> and your sons and your daughters shall prophesy,
>> and your young men shall see visions,
>> and your old men shall dream dreams … The sun shall be turned to darkness and the moon to blood, before the coming of the Lord's great and glorious day.
>> Then everyone who calls on the name of the Lord shall be saved."
> …
> Repent and be baptized every one of you in the name of Jesus Christ so that your sins may be forgiven; and you will receive the gift of the Holy Spirit. For the promise [of Joel] is for you …'
> And he testified with many other arguments and exhorted them, saying 'Save yourselves from this corrupt generation.' (Acts 2.14–40; cf. Gen. 6.9)

Time was short, then, and the need for repentance was pressing. The people gathered in Jerusalem must escape destruction by believing in the Lord Jesus. Pentecost was also the fulfilling of the words of John the Baptist that God would send the Holy Spirit to 'baptize' his people with fire (Matt. 3.1; Mark 1.8; Luke 3.16).

Acts therefore shows how for the first believers the sending of the Holy Spirit was a major turning point: it was the renewing of the Jewish law and the Covenant, showing continuity between Judaism and Christianity, but in such a way that it was also the start of something new, the coming together of those now able to really live the life of God's kingdom. And, as the speaking in many languages shows, this was now not only for Jesus' own race but for people of all languages. The apostles were to welcome all nations into their common life, as

Jesus himself had instructed (Acts 1.8). This would fulfil the prophecy of Isaiah (e.g. 49.6, 22).

The Day of Pentecost is generally regarded by Christians as the birth of the Church. But the accounts in John and Acts raise an important question for church historians: was this the birth of a new religious organization? The uncontrollable role of the Holy Spirit suggests it was more like the start of a movement, where vision and inspiration were propelling the followers of Jesus forward, rather than anything more concrete like the setting up of a new institution. Furthermore the emphasis on continuity with Judaism implied by Acts shows that this event was happening within the organizational and institutional life of the Jewish nation (even though outsiders were being welcomed in). It seems that at first this event was all about the creation of a movement of renewal within a wider society, rather than the creation of a new organization or society or community itself.

Is this true of the apostolic Church as a whole? What are we really dealing with in this first crucial phase of the Church's life? Let us examine how it lived and evolved over the next few decades, looking at a number of different features of its corporate life, asking whether it was primarily a fluid movement of ideas and inspiration or the coming into being of a new organization or community with its own independent life?

Common Life

Worship

Acts shows how the Temple in Jerusalem remained the focus of worship for the believers after the Day of Pentecost. It was the main centre of Jewish worship, for there was only one such Temple, and Jews from foreign lands, such as Hellenists who spoke Greek, came from around the Mediterranean world to attend the main annual festivals (such as the Passover and Pentecost: see Acts 8.27–8, 20.16). The Temple itself was divided into sections, the inner courts being for Jews only and the outer court being open to Gentile worshippers. The Christian believers went to the Temple to pray at the hour of prayer, which is three o'clock in the afternoon (see Acts 3.1; see also Luke 18.10). The apostles also engaged in teaching in the Temple, such as when Peter and John were arrested by the priests and the Sadducees (Acts 4.1–3). At other times, 'signs and wonders' were done by the apostles in the Temple and at Solomon's Portico (5.12). Even after being arrested they would go back to the Temple to preach (5.17–21). Sometimes believers would go to the Temple for ritual purification, which would involve making a sacrifice, as when Paul visited Jerusalem later in his ministry (21.26). The Temple clearly remained at the heart of the apostolic Church for some decades. This shows deep continuity between the faith of the Church and Judaism.

The other place of worship was the home. Worship here became centred around 'the breaking of bread', which is mentioned in connection with the Jerusalem church (Acts 2.42, 46) and as taking place in other places (e.g. 20.7), where it began to be connected with the first day of the week. This was when the Christians expressed their unity and joy in the risen Lord. In 1 Corinthians 11.23–6, we see that it was when they remembered Jesus' instruction to them at the Last Supper to 'do this in remembrance' of him. Paul shows that they had begun to follow a set pattern, though people were still bringing their own food to eat as part of the event, keeping it all quite informal. Paul shows it was not only a fellowship meal or an Agape (love feast), but a proclamation of Jesus' death (11.26). In a charged way, then, it was bringing that death into the present, not just pointing to it in the past. This was like Jewish rites performed in the home during the Passover festival, which not only remembered the escape from Egypt but dramatically re-lived and re-presented it in the present. In Hebrew, this re-living was called *zikharon* and in Greek *ammanesis*. The Church adopted this Jewish form of worship but re-focused it on the death of Christ. But the meal was not seen as a sacrifice (believers were still offering sacrifices in the Temple): this would only come later when the Church had become separated from Judaism after the destruction of the Temple. Continuity with Judaism is again apparent in the genesis of this rite.

Sharing of goods

In Acts 2.44–6, we are given the striking information that the believers had all things in common and would sell their possessions and give the proceeds to the group as a whole. 'There was not a needy person among them, for as many as owned lands or houses sold them and brought the proceeds of what was sold.

They laid it at the apostles' feet, and it was distributed to each as any had need'
(Acts 4.34–5). Those who lied about how much they gave could expect harsh
judgement (5.1–11). Was this a form of proto-Communism, a setting up of a
new society of equality and common ownership, in contrast to the capitalist
society of first-century Jerusalem? In Paul's first letter to the Thessalonians, we
are given sharp insight into the mind-set of the first Christians which suggests
a different rationale for common ownership:

> For this we declare to you by the word of the Lord, that we who are alive, who
> are left until the coming of the Lord, will by no means precede those who have
> died. For the Lord himself, with a cry of command, with the archangel's call
> and with the sound of God's trumpet, will descend from heaven, and the dead
> in Christ will rise first. Then we who are alive, who are left, will be caught up
> in the clouds together with them to meet the Lord in the air; and so we will
> be with the Lord for ever. Therefore encourage one another with these words.
> (1 Thess. 4.15ff)

The apostolic Church, then, believed that Jesus would return with power within
the current generation and so fulfil the Jewish eschatological expectation of the
return of the Messiah.

1 Corinthians 7.29–33 offers a glimpse of how this worldview affected the everyday life of the first Christians in the Jewish diaspora: they were not to be over-
concerned with everyday affairs of the world but were to be ready for the end.

There was therefore no need to keep property and investments for the long
term: the believers could sell their possessions to look after one another while
awaiting the end of the age. This made them similar to the Qumran community,
who lived near the Dead Sea and held everything in common while expecting the end of the age to dawn soon. But the believers did not live as a separate community: they were happy to keep living in Jerusalem among the wider
population.

Jesus did not return and there is evidence that the Jerusalem church suffered
the consequences of having sold their property. Paul hints in Galatians that
they had become very poor and at the end of Romans he indicates that he was
organizing a collection for the Church (Rom. 15.26; see also 1 Cor. 16.1–3). The
policy of having everything in common did not, unfortunately, give long-term
financial security. But it is another example of how the apostolic Church was
caught up within an eschatologically expectant Judaism and should be viewed as

a movement of renewal within the Jewish nation rather than as a new religious community.

Leadership

What kind of leadership is found in the Jerusalem church? The book of Acts seems to present Peter as taking the lead at the beginning. He calls for the appointment of a new twelfth disciple (1.15–22); he was the first to speak on the Day of Pentecost (2.14–41); he heals the lame man and explains its meaning to the people at Solomon's Portico (3.12–26); he defends John and himself before the Council (4.8–12); he takes the lead in questioning Ananias and Sapphira (5.3–11); his shadow is recognized as having healing properties (5.15); and he is mentioned as holding a special position in relation to the other apostles (5.29).

Yet, after Peter's speech on the Day of Pentecost the crowd approach not only him but all the apostles (2.37). This implies that authority did not rest with Peter on his own but with the twelve as a group. In the third chapter, we find Peter working closely with John and both are recognized as having authority (e.g. 3.11, 4.13). Money gained from the sale of houses and land is given to the apostles as a whole (4.35). Signs and wonders are done among the people 'through the apostles' (5.12). There is therefore a strong collective dimension to the leadership of the apostolic Church, with Peter emerging as more of a representative figure than a designated leader in his own right. There is no evidence of a regulated leadership structure but apparently a more spontaneous one, like the kind of leadership that emerges among a group of friends who set off on some adventure together.

The situation changes with the persecution of the Jerusalem church following the death of Stephen. Acts reports that 'all except the apostles were scattered throughout the countryside of Judea and Samaria' (8.1–4). The apostles send out Peter and John to the new believers at Samaria (8.14): this shows that Peter and John were seen more as ambassadors than presidents. This is confirmed in the following chapter where Peter is found having a roving role, going 'here and there among all the believers' (9.32). Within a short time he is mixing with new Gentile believers, especially after his vision at Joppa and his encounter with the Roman centurion Cornelius at Caesarea. This results in criticism of Peter by those believers who believe Gentiles should first be circumcised and become Jews before joining the Church. This indicates that he is beginning to lose his position as a representative leader of the Church. After his arrest in Jerusalem and dramatic release from prison he has to leave the city quickly and has to ask those he meets to give the news of his release 'to James and to the believers' (12.17). This shows that James was now being seen as the representative leader. This was not James the apostle, because he had already been put to death by Herod, but was probably James 'the brother of the Lord' (Mark 6.9; see also 1 Cor. 15.7; Gal. 1.19), to whom leadership of the Jerusalem church seems to pass. This shows that Peter is not only supplanted but a dynastic dimension to leadership is becoming established, with the brother of the Lord stepping forward. This is confirmed by the account in Acts 15 of the meeting or council in Jerusalem to resolve the dispute between those who wanted believers to be circumcised and those who did not. Peter is now presented not as presiding over the meeting but as one of the advocates supporting non-circumcision. It is James who sums up the debate and then lays down a ruling, that Gentile believers need not be circumcised but should observe Jewish food laws (Acts 15.19–21). A new kind of leadership, based on a different type of authority, is being implied in these verses.

A few years later, when Paul returns to visit the church in Jerusalem, he goes 'to visit James; and all the elders were present' to give an account of all that he had been doing (21.18). Again, Peter is not mentioned. So the early spontaneous and collective form of leadership seems to have evolved into a more dynastic pattern, with a blood relation of Jesus taking on a directive role. This shows the continuing embeddedness of the Church within Jewish society.

Outside Jerusalem, it seems Peter still retained a pre-eminent authority. When the Gospels came to be written, first by Mark and then Matthew and Luke, probably some 30 years after these events, he is presented as the leader of the disciples and the 'rock' upon whom the Church would be built (Mark 8.29; Matt. 16.18). On the other hand, there is no evidence that he somehow governed the world-wide Church. The kind of leadership that he exercised would have been of a piece with his and John's work in Samaria, where they had 'testified and spoken the word of the Lord ... proclaiming the good news to many villages' (Acts 8.25). In modern language, his role seems to have been that of a leading missionary rather than executive director. Paul confirms this with his description of Peter as being 'entrusted with the gospel for the circumcised' (Gal. 2.7, though curiously this seems to contradict Acts 15.7, where Peter describes himself as being the one 'through whom the Gentiles would hear the message of the good news and become believers').

Division and Expansion

Acts emphasizes unity and common purpose in the apostolic Church but there is also evidence of widening division. Even before the issue over admission of Gentiles, there was division between the 'Hebrews' and the 'Hellenists' in Acts 6. The 'Hebrews' were probably indigenous Jews from Judea and Galilee, who spoke Aramaic and Hebrew and included some who had known Jesus. The Hellenists would have been Jews from further afield whose native tongue was Greek and who had come to Jerusalem to worship in the Temple. It is not clear what the grievance was. Recent scholarship suggests the Hellenist widows were not receiving the preaching of the word when they sat together in their meeting place in the city (see Collins 2009). This would explain why the seven who were appointed to minister to them were preachers such as Stephen and Philip. At any rate, the apostles chose men with Greek names, indicating they were ordaining Greek ministers for the Greek widows. This orderly response to the division seems to have paid off as the Church continued to grow in size including believers from among the Temple priests (7.7).

But one of the Hellenists, Stephen, publicly announced that the Temple was now redundant (7.48) and that the whole Jewish nation was 'uncircumcised' and therefore condemned. This radical view was bound to exacerbate the divisions, not only within the Church but between the Church and the Jewish leaders in the city. Stephen paid the ultimate price for this. The great persecution that followed his death seems to have been directed especially against his fellow Hellenists because Philip is mentioned as one of those who had to flee (8.5) and others are described as travelling beyond Palestine to Greek-speaking cities (11.19), although the Hebrew-speaking apostles remained in Jerusalem (8.1). This was the start of what would eventually be a terminal division in the Church between those who saw following Christ as a renewal movement within Judaism, and those like Stephen who were beginning to see that the movement would take them out of this society and into something new. However, Stephen's total dismissal of Judaism was not permanently influential: Paul's view that Christianity was a fulfilment of Judaism became much more widely accepted (Paul remained committed to Judaism, as is shown when he had his Greek companion Timothy circumcised so that he could help with preaching to Jews in various cities: 16.3). But an important split had begun to reveal itself.

It is also important to note that the term 'Christian' itself was not used in Jerusalem. It was only coined when the Church reached Antioch in Syria where Gentiles started to join the fellowship in some numbers (11.26). There was now a need for a name for these people who were followers of Christ but who were not necessarily Jews, and the term that was coined was 'Christians'. The 'Hebrews', on the other hand, would continue to see themselves as part of Judaism and, as we have already observed, were adopting a more traditionally dynastic form of leadership under James.

The next moment of tension occurred when Herod Agrippa attacked the Church. Agrippa, a puppet of the Romans, was briefly put in charge of Jerusalem in the 40s. He was unpopular with the Jewish nationalists and may have been courting their popularity by attacking the Church. The Church was known to have connections with Gentiles and therefore be under suspicion by the nationalists. Mounting tension within the Church is indicated by the existence of the circumcision party who criticized Peter for his acceptance of Cornelius and other Gentiles in Caesarea (11.2–3). They are described by Paul as 'certain people' who 'came from James' (Gal. 2.12). They are probably the same group who are described as 'the sect of the Pharisees' in Acts 15.5. They were now sending delegations to Antioch to make the Church insist on circumcision for the new Gentile believers. Paul, by now a staunch advocate of the Christians, became the target of their attacks. Paul himself reports that at one point Peter wavered in his support for the Gentiles and withdrew from them 'for fear of the circumcision faction' (Gal. 2.12). 'And the other Jews joined him in this hypocrisy, so that even Barnabas was led astray by their hypocrisy' (Acts 2.13). Paul reports that he had to confront Peter 'before them all' and point out his inconsistency and hypocrisy in living with the Gentiles at one point and withdrawing from them at the next (2.14).

Clearly the division was coming to a head and the meeting at Jerusalem reported in Acts 15 had to find a solution. At that meeting, as we have seen, James arbitrated between the two points of view and ruled that the Gentiles were not to be forced to be circumcised, but were to be asked to observe basic Jewish food laws. This was a decisive moment. The Jerusalem church was beginning to accept that the followers of Jesus were now becoming a movement that went beyond Judaism. It was a movement creating something new, exactly what as yet not very clear. Paul would spend the next 20 years working out and writing about what this was and what it meant for the Judaism that had nurtured their faith. But it was a ruling that would make the position of the Jerusalem church increasingly difficult, as it came more and more under suspicion from Jewish nationalists who themselves were becoming more and more opposed to mixing with Gentiles. Armed rebellion against Roman rule would break out in 66 AD, and the Jerusalem church would have flee to Pella in Palestine in 68 AD, just before the Romans responded to the rebellion by destroying Jerusalem in 70 AD.

The complete parting of Judaism and Christianity still lay in the future. What emerges clearly from Acts and Paul's letters is that the Christian Church in this first phase of its life was a spontaneous movement of renewal from within Judaism, lacking a clear centralized leadership structure. It attracted Gentile believers in increasing numbers and so began to pull in two different directions, with tension and sometimes dispute. Wonderful things were happening, such as people being healed, lives being turned around and bonds forged across continents, but it was a movement of ideas and inspiration among people that had debate and argument at the heart of its life, a sign of vigour and potential. It was not, at that point, a clearly defined institution with obvious boundaries between those who were in and those who were not, but something more nebulous.

Expansion beyond Palestine

Did the Church become more of an organized community in its own right as it spread beyond Jerusalem and Palestine? Acts describes the church at Antioch as being one of the first to become established. Antioch was located in the Roman province of Syria and was a cosmopolitan city, with Greek-speaking Gentiles and Jews from across the Eastern Mediterranean basin. Evidently some believers from Cyprus and Cyrene (in North Africa) spoke to non-Jewish Greeks about Christ, and large numbers became believers (11.21). This was not planned by any central leadership. It was so surprising that the Jerusalem church decided to send Barnabas (who was also originally from Cyprus: see Acts 4.36) to find out what was going on. When he arrived and saw what was happening, he realized that he needed help and went to fetch Paul from Tarsus. Furthermore, Acts 13 reveals that this church did not have one obvious leader but a group of prominent 'prophets and teachers', drawn from a cosmopolitan mix of believers. So it clearly had a spontaneous and vigorous life of its own, which Acts attributes to the direction of the Holy Spirit. It then sent Barnabas and Paul away on a preaching mission to other cities (13.3, see also, for example, 16.6), which turned into Paul's three great missionary journeys. There was little that was pre-planned in all of this.

It is likely that the eschatological expectation mentioned above was as strong among the new Gentile believers as Jewish believers: they must all have accepted that time was short and that the message of Jesus must be relayed across the ancient world as quickly as possible. Paul's missionary journeys, which form the main subject matter of the second half of the book of Acts, make sense as an urgent response to this expectation. Paul himself in his letters, as we have seen, shows how dominant this expectation was in his own thinking.

The meeting or council of Jerusalem may have made life more difficult for the Jerusalem church but it released the brakes of a Gentile mission. Acts reports that following the meeting Paul and Barnabas decided to revisit the new churches beyond Palestine and see how they were doing (15.36). They could not agree on who to take with them, and so parted company, but this in itself shows a new confidence and energy in both of them.

Self-understanding: *Ekklesia*

What, then, was the emerging form of the apostolic Church? Was it, as is often assumed, the coming into being of a new community with its own independent life? Or was it something else, an entity within the life of an already existing wider community? To help answer this, the ways in which the believers described their corporate life can be examined.

'The Way'

In a number of places the book of Acts uses an evocative phrase to describe the believers as a whole: it calls them 'the Way' (9.2, 18.25, 19.9, 22.4, 24.22). This title recalls Jesus' own teaching about being 'the way' (John 14.6); it recalls the ministry of John the Baptist who was to prepare 'the way of the Lord' (Mark 1.2; Matt 3.3; Luke 3.4). It also recalls the teaching of the prophets Isaiah and Malachi whom John quotes (Isa. 40.3; Mal. 3.1). The fact that the first believers called themselves the Way shows they believed they were fulfilling the teaching of John the Baptist, who himself fulfilled the prophecies of Isaiah and Malachi and others. In Isaiah 'the Way' is the place where the Lord will come to bring salvation to the people of Israel (Isa. 40.1–2). The believers would have seen themselves as preparing people for the return of Christ in power and glory.

This title therefore shows the continuity between the life of the Church and the religion of Israel. It shows how they believed their life was beginning to fulfil what had been foretold by the prophets. The Qumran community, a strict religious group living in the desert near the Dead Sea, had a similar expectation, but unlike the believers saw a need to go and live as a self-sufficient community on their own.

Ekklesia

The word 'church' in the English New Testament is a translation of the Greek word, *ekklesia*. This originally referred to the convened assembly of a city-state, the supreme legislative and judicial body in the classical days of the Greek city-states. In the *ekklesia*, every citizen had equal rights, including the right to make their voice heard. This classical usage is found in Acts 19.29–32 and 38–9. The other root of the word lies in the Septuagint, the Greek translation of the Hebrew scriptures. There *ekklesia* occurs as the normal, though not the only, translation of two Hebrew words, *qahal* and *edhah*. The first always refers to the actual meeting together of the people of Israel as they journeyed from Egypt to the Promised Land (e.g. Lev. 4.14). It is the process of assembling for whatever reason. *Edhah*, on the other hand, when used of the people of Israel, refers to the whole society, or those who represent it, whether they happen to be assembled or not (e.g. Exod. 12.3) (Preston 1997, p. 6).

In passing, it is worth noting that the English word 'church', like the Scots 'kirk', comes from a different root, *kuriakos*, 'belonging to the Lord', even though it is the normal translation of *ekklesia*. The French église, on the other hand, derives from *ekklesia* and was taken over directly into Latin and then into French.

The first Christians, who were mostly Jewish and not members of a Greek city state, would have primarily associated the word with the second root, from the Septuagint. They would have heard it used in the synagogues when the Septuagint Bible was read out. The fact that they chose to describe themselves with this word (e.g. Acts 8.1) shows at least two important things about their own self-understanding:

First, that they believed the Church is a meeting together of Christians (as in the *qahal* root of *ekklesia*). It is defined by their assembling together, which is therefore the essence of what it is about. In other words, living together as a community, or eating together, or worshipping together, do not make believers into a church: it is the simple act of meeting together, no more and no less. Their community, on the other hand, was the Jewish society in which they were already living. Such assembling together was very important to them, but it was just one activity among many others in their day-to-day lives within the wider Jewish community.

But, secondly, the Church is the whole assembly of Christians (as in the *edhah* root of *ekklesia*), not certain individuals or groups within it. In other words, it is composed not just of those who are meeting together at the moment, but of everyone who at one time or another has met with other Christians in this way. Such usage may be comparable to the way the Church of England once regarded all those who had been baptized to be part of itself, whether or not they had attended church in the last year, or ten years.

Paul's letters, the earliest written documents in the New Testament, show him developing the use of the word *ekklesia* and adding two more points to this basic ecclesiology. He begins by using the word to refer to specific local meetings of Christians: 'the church of the Thessalonians in God the Father and the Lord Jesus Christ' (1 Thess.1.1), 'the churches of Galatia' (Gal. 1.2), 'the church that is at Cenchreae' (Rom. 16.1), 'the church that is in the house of Prisca and Aquila' (Rom. 16.3), 'the churches of Asia' (1 Cor. 16.19), 'the church that is in the house of Nymphas' (Col. 4.15), 'the church in the house of Philemon' (Phil.1), etc. Here the word 'church' is being used for the meeting together of Christians in these places: it is the actual and specific meetings of Christ's followers in certain towns and regions. This is consonant with the *qahal* root of *ekklesia*.

But, then, more commonly, Paul shifts the emphasis and uses *ekklesia* to describe how it is God who meets with Christians in different places: 'the church of God which is in Corinth, those who are sanctified in Christ Jesus, called to be saints' (1 Cor. 1.2); 'the churches of God which are in Judaea in Christ Jesus' (1 Thess. 2.14); 'the Church of the living God, the pillar and buttress of the truth' (1 Tim. 3.15). In these passages two things are made clear:

First, the assembly is composed of those called into a special relationship with God in Jesus Christ. So the different churches are not so much meetings of Christians with each other as meetings between them and God, meetings that he has called. They belong to him. This shows that in the *ekklesia* the point was not simply for Christians to meet with each other but to respond to what God had done for them and to give collective praise and thanksgiving back to him.

Then, secondly, they are not so much many meetings as one meeting, a meeting that takes place in many different places. In other words, the local church is part of something much greater than itself, an assembly of all those called by God, whether or not they are meeting together at that moment (as in *edhah*). So the society that meets is not just a local *ekklesia*, but the universal *ekklesia* which is in a particular place. Paul can talk quite simply about 'the Church of God', the Church that he persecuted. There are many church meetings yet, really, one Church meeting between God and those who have responded to him. There is one universal Church absolutely, and the one universal Church is represented in a particular local church (Preston 1997, p. 8).

All of this implies, then, that at the beginning of its life the Church cannot be seen as a community in its own right. It is part and parcel of the Jewish community in Palestine and for this reason has trouble accepting non-Jews into its life, though does so after some argument and division. Furthermore, it understands itself in a specific way, to be a kind of meeting, but a meeting for anyone and everyone called by God in Jesus within the Jewish community and the Gentile world. It sees itself as including not just those who happen to be meeting that day but everyone who has been part of the meetings. And it sees itself as not many meetings but one meeting which is not primarily between Christians themselves but between God and those who have responded to him in the movement of his mission in the world. So a local church embodies this wider reality: it is a living sign of something worldwide, an assembly of every soul who has responded to the inspirational movement of God's mission in Christ.

Finally, on this basis, we can ask the key question of what is the organizational form of the apostolic Church. Returning to Cameron's list of such forms (see p. 4), it is the fourth form that presents itself, the 'Third-place meeting', which occurs 'within a public space (e.g. café, pub), constrained by limits of that space, a shared aim which can be changed by agreement'. While the apostolic Church probably did not meet in cafés or pubs, there is an important sense in which it met within an already existing religious and cultural public setting, that of first-century Judaism, and specifically the Jewish community of Jerusalem and Palestine. Furthermore many of the meetings were within the public spaces of the Temple precincts, as the believers met together to pray (Acts 2.46). The church was clearly 'constrained' by this location, as the division over admitting Gentiles shows. Furthermore it had a clear shared aim, which was to proclaim Christ and encourage repentance before his return. With these qualifications, then, the apostolic Church might appropriately be called a 'third place meeting', albeit one that took place in different places at different times.

But did the division between the Hebrews and Hellenists and the growth of the Church in the new setting of Antioch require a different form, one which might develop in the next phase of the Church's life?

Discussion Questions

What kind of leadership did Peter exercise in the apostolic Church?
Would you describe the Jerusalem church as a house church?
Do any churches today resemble the apostolic Church?

Bibliography and Further Reading

Chadwick, Henry (1993), *The Early Church*, revised edn, Harmondsworth: Penguin.
Collins, John N. (2009), *Diakonia: Re-interpreting the Ancient Sources*, Oxford: Oxford University Press.
Frend, W. H. C. (1984), *The Rise of Christianity*, London: Darton, Longman and Todd.
MacCulloch, Diarmaid (2009), *A History of Christianity: The First Three Thousand Years*, Ch. 3, Harmondsworth: Allen Lane.
Preston, Geoffrey (1997), *Faces of the Church: Meditations on a Mystery and Its Images*, Edinburgh: T & T Clark.

3

The Hellenistic Church: Sect or Association?

Into the Hellenistic World

As the first generation of Christians passed away, the Jerusalem church and the Jewish form of Christianity that it represented took some severe knocks. In Jerusalem, the Christian believers were regarded with suspicion and hostility by the nationalists because of their connections with Gentiles. This hostility reached intense levels after the outbreak of the Jewish rebellion against the Romans in 66 AD, and it is likely the believers fled from the city at that point, probably going east of the river Jordan. The Roman response to the Jewish revolt took some time to come, but when it did it was devastating. The Roman legions under Titus surrounded the city, breached its walls and destroyed it in 70. This included the destruction of the Temple, a profound blow for Judaism. The treasures of the Temple were looted and despatched to Rome. The Romans then turned their attention to the Zealots who had fortified themselves in Herod's mountain fortress in Masada in the Judaean wilderness. The Romans took three years to build a huge rampart up the side of the mountain so that their legionaries could climb over the walls and kill the Zealots. When they finally got into the fortress, they found that the Zealots had already committed mass suicide.

All of this forced the believers to decide whether they were still part of Judaism, or whether they should begin to see themselves as a body of people existing in their own right. Without the temple in which Jesus himself had worshipped and taught, the need to keep in touch with Judaism would have seemed less and less important.

There was also ongoing hostility towards the Church from the Jewish religious leadership after the destruction of the Temple. In 71, it is likely that the leaders of the Pharisees gathered at Jamnia (south of modern Tel-Aviv) to regroup and redefine post-Temple Judaism. This re-definition resulted in a second major blow to Jewish Christianity: the expulsion of Christians from synagogues, demonstrated in the publication of a Palestinian prayer to be added to the Amidah or Eighteen Benedictions said in all synagogues:

> And for apostates let there be no hope; and may the insolent kingdom be quickly uprooted, in our days. And may the Nazarenes and the heretics perish quickly; and may they be erased from the Book of Life; and may they not be inscribed with the righteous. (in Scott 2000, Appendix E)

Some Christian communities felt very bitter about this. Matthew's Gospel, with its harsh condemnation of the Jewish Pharisees and rabbis in chapter 23, probably reflects this bitterness.

A third blow to Jewish Christianity was the fact that the Lord had not returned. The apostles and their converts, as we have seen, had an intense expectation that Jesus would return 'with power' within their own generation (e.g. Acts 2.17; Mark 9.1). There is some evidence that the failure of Jesus to return in this way resulted in second-generation Christians being mocked and scorned. The writer of 2 Peter warns his readers to expect this:

> First of all you must understand this, that in the last days scoffers will come, scoffing and indulging their own lusts and saying, 'Where is the promise of his coming? For ever since our ancestors died, all things continue as they were from the beginning of creation! (2 Peter 3.3)

The letter then seeks to explain the delay of Jesus by quoting the Psalms in which 1,000 years are like one day for God: in other words God's time is not human time. 'The Lord is not slow about his promise, as some think of slowness, but is patient with you, not wanting any to perish, but all to come to repentance. But the day of the Lord will come like a thief, and then the heavens will pass away with a loud noise, and the elements will be dissolved with fire, and the earth and everything that is done on it will be disclosed' (2 Peter 3.4–10). This passage shows how the Church was beginning to adjust to the very different worldview of Greek culture which was dominant around the Mediterranean world.

What was this Hellenistic worldview? It drew a contrast with the Jewish linear view of history, from Abraham's call in the past to the future expectation of the coming of the Messiah with his new age of liberation. Instead, Hellenistic culture was broadly influenced by Platonism with its belief in the eternal forms and the unchanging nature of reality. The writer of 2 Peter describes this as the belief that 'all things continue as they were from the beginning of creation'. The temporal world that we see, touch, hear and smell is, then, only a world of appearances: the life and death of plants, animals and even human beings masks another and more durable world, of the eternal forms, of realities like truth, beauty, and goodness, and these are unchanging. We gain access to these eternal realities through gaining knowledge and wisdom, and then our understanding is enlarged and enriched, and we can achieve a union with this divine world.

To understand this point of view it is necessary to go back to Plato himself (427–347 BC), the disciple and recorder of Socrates, who was the pre-eminent influence on Hellenistic culture. A passage from his dialogue Timaeus sums it up:

> If the heart of man has been set on the love of learning and true wisdom and he has exercised that part of himself above all, he is surely bound to have thoughts immortal and divine, if he shall lay hold upon truth, nor can he fail to possess immortality in the fullest meaning that human nature admits; and because he is always devoutly cherishing the divine part and maintaining the guardian genius that dwells with him in good estate, he must needs be happy above all. (Charlesworth 2002, p. 19)

In this passage, it is significant that union with the divine and immortality is seen as being achieved not at some future day of judgement, but in the here and now, through learning and the acquisition of wisdom. In Plato's philosophy generally, the divine is portrayed as an immortal and ever-present reality, contrasted with the material world which changes and decays, a world of dust and ashes and of mere appearances that are passing away. In opposition to Greek mythology, which portrayed heroism, glory in battle and strength as the supreme virtues, Socrates and Platonism generally presented learning, knowledge, wisdom and belief as the key to immortality and happiness.

The allegory of the cave, from Plato's *Republic* (Part 7.7), is a famous portrayal of this point of view, where the material and visible world is equated with transient shadows on the walls of the cave which shackled prisoners spend their day watching. We are those prisoners. The real world, of the eternal forms, is equated with what is outside the cave and bathed in bright sunshine. It is through philosophy that a prisoner is freed from their shackles and enabled to move out of the shadows and into the sunshine of the real and eternal world.

In the first century, this philosophical worldview became generally disseminated around the ancient world as Neoplatonism and began to influence the early Christian community when it moved out of the confines of Palestinian Judaism and into cosmopolitan cities such as Caesarea, Antioch in Syria and Ephesus in Asia Minor. It was highly influential in the major centres of learning in the ancient world, such as Alexandria in Egypt as well Athens and Ephesus. Judaism had already been engaging with Platonism, not least through the Jewish philosopher Philo (c.20–50 AD) in Alexandria. It is possible to see the influence of Platonic language and ways of thinking in the Book of Wisdom in the Apocrypha:

> The beginning of wisdom is the most sincere desire for instruction, and concern for instruction is love of her, and love of her is the keeping of her laws, and giving heed to her laws is assurance of immortality, and immortality brings one near to God; so the desire for wisdom leads to a kingdom. (6.17–20)

Timeline

c.35–c.107	Ignatius of Antioch
c.60–c.120	Writing of Gospels
64	Nero's persecution
66–70	First Jewish revolt; destruction of Jerusalem
c.85–160	Marcion
c.100–c.165	Justin Martyr
c.112	Persecution of Christians; Pliny's letter to Trajan
c.120	Gnosticism flourishes
c.130–c.200	Irenaeus of Lyon

c.160	Montanism begins
c.184–254	Origen
c.250–c.336	Arius
270	Anthony in the desert; the beginnings of monasticism
284	Emperor Diocletian and the great persecution
c.300–373	Athanasius
306	Constantine rises to power as one of the emperors
312	Battle of Milvian Bridge: Constantine becomes Western Emperor
313	Edict of Milan: Christians can worship in public and own property
325	Council of Nicea
c.330–c.395	Basil of Caesarea, Gregory of Nazianzus, Gregory of Nyssa

Persecution and Devotion

The weakening and eventual disappearance of the Jerusalem church was by no means the end of the Church as a whole. By the 60s, it had spread far and wide around the Mediterranean world, not least through Paul's missionary journeys. The New Testament shows it spreading from Samaria to Syria, Antioch and Tarsus in the north. From there, it spread to the different regions of Asia Minor (what we call Turkey) and across the Aegean to the Greek city states. Paul addressed his longest letter to the church in Rome, showing how it was already established on the Italian peninsular before he arrived to preach and teach. There were churches on Cyprus and Malta and to the south of Palestine, in Alexandria in Egypt and possibly in Arabia.

The New Testament and later writings indicate that Christianity first spread as an urban religion, in the cities, rather than to the rural areas. It has been estimated that by 100 AD there were about 7,500 Christians out of the known world's estimated population of 60 million. These were dotted throughout the Roman Empire, with some beyond the Eastern borders such as in Edessa. Then, with a growth rate of 40 per cent per decade, in 200 there were probably around 220,000 Christians, and in 300 probably in the region of 6 million (Stark 1997, p. 6).

But this phenomenal growth took place against the backdrop of persecution, a persecution which ironically became a source of encouragement and identity for the early Church: as Tertullian would famously say, 'the blood of martyrs is the seed of the Church'. This persecution must be the starting point in any survey of the key features of the second- and third-century Church.

The first state sponsored persecution was that of the Emperor Nero in Rome in 64. Fire had spread through the city destroying a large number of districts, and the insecure Nero needed a scapegoat. He chose the Christians and had large numbers rounded up. Tacitus, a Roman writer and politician, reports that many Christians were fed to the wild animals in the Coliseum, while others were crucified and then burnt. It is not known if Peter and Paul perished in this persecution, but it seems likely. A consequence of the persecution was that Christianity came to be regarded with suspicion by the Roman ruling classes and for more than a century 'the church was condemned to the life of a suspected and unpopular Judaistic sect that had no legal standing' (Frend 1984, p. 110).

More detail about the persecution and the response of the Christians is revealed in a letter of 111 to the Emperor Trajan from the Roman governor of Bithynia (in Asia Minor), Pliny the Younger (c.62–c.115). It provides a number of revealing insights into how the Christians lived and also how the authorities responded to them. The letter begins with a description of how Pliny was rounding them up, trying them and then executing them:

> Meanwhile, in the case of those who were denounced to me as Christians, I have observed the following procedure: I interrogated these as to whether they were Christians; those who confessed I interrogated a second and a third time, threatening them with punishment; those who persisted I ordered executed. For I had no doubt that, whatever the nature of their creed, stubbornness and inflexible obstinacy surely deserve to be punished. There were others possessed of the same folly; but because they were Roman citizens, I signed an order for them to be transferred to Rome ... They asserted, however, that the sum and substance of their fault or error had been that they were accustomed

to meet on a fixed day before dawn and sing responsively a hymn to Christ as to a god, and to bind themselves by oath, not to some crime, but not to commit fraud, theft, or adultery, not falsify their trust, nor to refuse to return a trust when called upon to do so. When this was over, it was their custom to depart and to assemble again to partake of food – but ordinary and innocent food. Even this, they affirmed, they had ceased to do after my edict by which, in accordance with your instructions, I had forbidden political associations. Accordingly, I judged it all the more necessary to find out what the truth was by torturing two female slaves who were called deaconesses. But I discovered nothing else but depraved, excessive superstition. (Epistle X. xcvi)

This passage reveals not only the severity of the persecution but also the peaceful and unthreatening life of the Christians. They were not actively rebelling against the Roman state but were honest and law-abiding people. They met together to worship and to eat but otherwise were ordinary members of society. Their only crime for which they were being punished was to refuse to worship the emperor or other official Roman deities.

Persecution became a recurrent feature of the Church's life. Ignatius Bishop of Antioch was martyred in Rome in 107. Polycarp, the Bishop of Smyrna (modern-day Izmir in Turkey), was burnt and stabbed to death around the year 156. The account of his death in the *Martyrdom of Polycarp* had a lasting influence on the early Church. Justin Martyr, despite his efforts to show the reasonableness of Christianity (more on p. 39), was beheaded in Rome around 165. An intense campaign of persecution took place under the Emperor Marcus Aurelius (161–80). This may have been because the Empire was under attack from Parthians in the east and German tribes in the north and also faced plague and revolts in Syria and Egypt, and the peaceful but non-conforming Christians made good scapegoats for all of this. A letter from the Christians of Lyons and Vienne (itself the earliest evidence of the Church in what is now called France) is preserved in Eusebius' history of the Church. The letter dates from 177. It seems there was a riot in the city and the Christians were blamed. Around 50 were arrested and taken to the amphitheatre to be tortured and killed, including the 90-year-old Bishop Pothinus. One of the most brutal killings was of a slave girl called Blandina. The account of her death also reveals the way martyrdom came to be regarded with great veneration in this early period of the Church's life:

Blandina was hung up fastened to a stake, and exposed, as food to the wild beasts that were let loose against her; and through her presenting the spectacle of one suspended on something like a cross, and through her earnest prayers, she inspired the [other Christian prisoners] with great eagerness: for in the combat they saw, by means of their sister, with their bodily eyes, Him who was crucified for them, that He might persuade those who trust in Him that every one that has suffered for the glory of Christ has eternal communion with the living God. When none of the wild beasts at that time touched her, she was taken down from the stake and conveyed back to prison.

After all these, on the last day of the gladiatorial shows, Blandina was again brought in along with Ponticus, a boy of about fifteen years of age. These two had been taken daily to the amphitheatre to see the tortures which the rest endured, and force was used to compel them to swear by the idols of the heathen; but on account of their remaining steadfast, and setting all their devices at nought, the multitude were furious against them, so as neither to pity the tender years of the boy nor to respect the sex of the woman. Accordingly they exposed them to every terror, and inflicted on them every torture, repeatedly trying to compel them to swear. But they failed in effecting this; for Ponticus, encouraged by his sister, so plainly indeed that even the heathens saw that it was she that encouraged and confirmed him, after enduring nobly every kind of torture, gave up the ghost; while the blessed Blandina, last of all, after having like a noble mother encouraged her children, and sent them on before her victorious to the King, trod the same path of conflict which her children had trod, hastening on to them with joy and exultation at her departure, not as one thrown to the wild beasts, but as one invited to a marriage supper. And after she had been scourged and exposed to the wild beasts, and roasted in the iron chair, she was at last enclosed in a net and cast before a bull. And after having been well tossed by the bull, though without having any feeling of what was happening to her, through her hope and firm hold of what had been entrusted to her and her converse with Christ, she also was sacrificed, the heathens themselves acknowledging that never among them did woman endure so many and such fearful tortures. (Eusebius, *History of the Church*, Book 5, Chapter 1)

Persecution would continue intermittently in the third century, sometimes with great severity, especially under the emperors Septimius Severus in 199, Decian in 249–51, Valerian in 258 and finally and terribly with Diocletian from 303 to 304.

Despite this, or possibly because of it, the Church continued to grow and to worship with faithfulness and devotion in its own special way. The following definitive and moving account of that worship comes from Justin Martyr (c.100–c.165), probably written in about the year 150:

> And on the day called Sunday, all who live in cities or in the country gather together to one place, and the memoirs of the apostles or the writings of the prophets are read, as long as time permits; then, when the reader has ceased, the overseer verbally instructs, and exhorts to the imitation of these good things.
>
> Then we all rise together and pray, and, as we before said, when our prayer is ended, bread and wine and water are brought, and the overseer in like manner offers prayers and thanksgivings, according to his ability, and the people assent, saying Amen; and there is a distribution to each, and a participation of that over which thanks have been given, and to those who are absent a portion is sent by the deacons.
>
> And they who are well to do, and willing, give what each thinks fit; and what is collected is deposited with the overseer, who provides for the orphans and widows and those who, through sickness or any other cause, are in want, and those who are in bonds and the strangers sojourning among us, and in a word takes care of all who are in need.
>
> But Sunday is the day on which we all hold our common assembly, because it is the first day on which God, having wrought a change in the darkness and matter, made the world; and Jesus Christ our Saviour on the same day rose from the dead (Justin Martyr, *Apology* I.67).

Right Believing

The general influence of Platonism on the theological outlook of the Church is fundamentally important. In the same way that it influenced certain Jewish writings (as noted above), so its influence can be detected from later New Testament writings onwards. It is seen in the way they shift their presentation of eschatology away from the expectation of a future judgement and salvation at the *parousia* (which was prominent in 1 Thess. and Matt. 25, for example), to an assertion that this judgement and salvation are already a present reality. This is the shift from a future eschatology to a realized eschatology, in line with Platonism's emphasis on the divine being an ever-present reality behind the appearances of this world. John's Gospel presents one of the first examples of this with its emphasis on what Christ has already accomplished and what he offers here and now:

> Those who believe in him are not condemned; but those who do not believe are condemned *already*, because they have not believed in the name of the only Son of God. And this is the judgement, that the light *has* come into the world, and people loved darkness rather than light because their deeds were evil. (5.18–19, italics mine)

> Very truly, I tell you, anyone who hears my word and believes him who sent me has eternal life, and does not come under judgement, but *has* passed from death to life. Very truly, I tell you, the hour is coming, *and now is here*, when the dead will hear the voice of the Son of God, and those who hear will live. (5.24–5, italics mine)

Furthermore, in one of the key verses of the Gospel and one of the most famous verses in the New Testament, it is the interior virtue of belief rather than the practice of righteousness and justice (which are supreme virtues within the Hebrew scriptures, as in Amos 5.24) which is presented as the heart of Christian living and the gateway to eternal life: 'For God so loved the world that he gave his only Son, so that everyone who believes in him may not perish but may have eternal life' (John 3.16).

All of this shows the start of a major shift in Christian thinking, the first such shift in the history of the Christian movement, from one mainly influenced by Hebrew ways of thinking to one increasingly influenced by Hellenistic ways of thinking.

The Apologists, who were Greek-speaking theologians, show the next stage in this development. One of the first and most influential was Justin Martyr, who was born into a pagan family and converted to Christianity as a young man. He taught in Ephesus and Rome, where he opened a Christian school, and published his two *Apologies*, in which he sought to show that Christianity was a true philosophy, better able than any other to express the nature of reality. He developed the doctrine of the 'generative' or 'germinative' Word (*logos*), who had sown the seed of truth in all people and who had become incarnate in Christ in order to teach all people the whole truth. Justin Martyr was positing a fundamental continuity between Greek and Roman philosophy and Christ, using the terminology of the one to describe the other: if you knew one, you were on the way to knowing the other. He also employed a number of ideas from the Neoplatonism of Philo to interpret and explain the Hebrew scriptures.

Among the subsequent church fathers Clement of Alexandria (c.150–c.215) was influential, becoming head of the Christian catechetical school in Alexandria in 190. The school taught scholars about the ways that Christianity was the true philosophy. It also trained new converts (catechumens) before their baptism. Clement showed that Christianity was not only in accord with Greek philosophy but was its best example. He also taught that Christianity required moral discipline and the fulfilling of duties in everyday life. Clement is regarded by many historians as the first intentional theologian and ethicist.

Origen (c.185–254) was a student of Clement and succeeded him as head of the Catechetical school in Alexandria. Probably the most prolific and brilliant of early theologians, he interweaved Neoplatonism with Christian thought. He was educated in neo-Platonic philosophy in the Alexandrian tradition and wrote the following letter to his former student Gregory Thaumaturgus, at around 230:

> I wish to ask you to extract from the philosophy of the Greeks what may serve as a course of study or a preparation for Christianity, and from geometry and astronomy what will serve to explain the sacred scriptures, in order that all that the sons of the philosophers are wont to say about geometry and music, grammar, rhetoric, and astronomy, as fellow-helpers to philosophy, we may say about philosophy itself, in relation to Christianity. ('Letter to Gregory')

In his works, many of which are now lost, Origen presented a fundamental and creative reinterpretation of the Christian faith in terms of Greek philosophy, and his treatise *On First Principles* is the first systematic theology. He also interpreted the stories of the Bible allegorically, showing how they carried a meaning which needed to be unlocked from the text of scripture through the application of a key. This was a deeper, philosophical meaning. In all of this, we see the explaining of the Christian faith to a Greek culture, with an emphasis on the way

Christianity expresses eternal truth. Greek philosophy is positively evaluated as a 'school-master' that can lead the Greeks to Christ.

What impact did this change of outlook have on the beliefs of the Church? There is clearly a fundamental shift taking place. In the Apostolic period, under the influence of Jewish beliefs, the Church saw itself as a meeting of people who believed preparing for the end of the age, repentance and righteous living were key to salvation (i.e. 'orthopraxis' or right living). Now, though, the Church was increasingly seeing itself as standing between a changing and ephemeral earth and an eternal and real heaven. The Christian faith was becoming defined and accepted as a set of beliefs about heaven, to be learnt and assimilated within the mind of the believer. Salvation was increasingly seen as the progress of the soul as it learnt and assimilated these doctrines and became united with the immortal wisdom of God (i.e. 'orthodoxy' or right thinking).

This is one reason, as already mentioned, why the development of creeds became centrally important for the Church. It was crucial that everyone knew the right doctrine so that they would have access to eternal life. The story of the development of the creeds is complex and protracted and took place in the next period, but we should note three key moments:

1   The Council of Nicea (325), which defined the being of God as 'three *hypostases* in one *ousia*' (often translated as 'three persons in one substance', the doctrine of the Trinity).
2   The first Council of Constantinople (381), which adopted the Creed of Nicea.
3   The Council of Chalcedon (451), which attempted to define with finality and clarity the nature of Christ as fully human and fully divine.

Self-understanding: From Ignatius to Cyprian

But many went further than Clement and even Origen. From about 120, Gnosticism (from the Greek word *gnosis*, knowledge) began to be very influential. This was an extreme form of Platonism, in which the visible world of matter and flesh was regarded as not just not real but positively evil, the creation of the 'Demiurge', an evil god. Salvation became a matter of escaping from the prison of matter and flesh and ascending into the pure eternal realm of knowledge. The believer must join a Gnostic (i.e. knowing) community before they could be inducted into this esoteric knowledge, which had had been secretly handed down by the apostles. There were many varieties of Gnostics and some were more extreme than others. One of the most influential Gnostic writers was Marcion (c.85–c.160), who denied that Christ was born of a woman: Jesus only appeared to be human and was purely of the eternal realm. This denial of the incarnation is called docetism and was common to many Gnostics. Marcion also rejected the Hebrew scriptures because of their claim that God was the creator of the material world: how could God create something that was fundamentally evil? Marcion also dismissed the original apostles because they were too Jewish to understand Jesus correctly!

Ignatius of Antioch

The rise of Gnosticism prompted some vigorous responses. The first was from Ignatius, Bishop of Antioch (c.35/50–c.107). In his hastily composed letters, impressively written while he was being escorted to Rome to be put to death in the Coliseum, he attacked the docetics who denied that Jesus had a body and only appeared as a human being. He affirmed the reality of the physical and material, not least the physical body of Christ. Then, in his Epistle to the Smynaeans, he made an important statement about where legitimate authority lies in this increasingly divided body of believers:

> See that you all follow the bishop, even as Jesus Christ does the Father, and the presbytery as you would the apostles; and reverence the deacons, as being the institution of God. Let no man do anything connected with the Church without the bishop. Let that be deemed a proper Eucharist, which is [administered] either by the bishop, or by one to whom he has entrusted it. Wherever the bishop shall appear, there let the multitude [of the people] also be; even as, wherever Jesus Christ is, there is the Catholic Church. It is not lawful without the bishop either to baptize or to celebrate a love-feast; but whatsoever he shall approve of, that is also pleasing to God, so that everything that is done may be secure and valid. (*Epistle to the Smynaeans*, Chapter 8)

Moreover, it is in accordance with reason that we should return to soberness [of conduct], and, while yet we have opportunity, exercise repentance towards God. It is well to reverence both God and the bishop. He who honours the bishop has been honoured by God; he who does anything without the knowledge of the bishop, does [in reality] serve the devil. Let all things, then, abound to you through grace, for you are worthy. (Chapter 9)

This is a very important statement. It shows that in response to division caused by Gnosticism the idea of a legitimate authority was developed. Ignatius describes three facets of this legitimate authority. First, it is to be centred not on charismatic prophets or preachers or Gnostic teachers but on bishops (literally 'overseers'), those who have oversight of the life of the Church and carry forward the oversight of the Apostles in the first century. Secondly, Ignatius shows, probably for the first time in Christian writings, that under the bishops there were now two other distinct orders of ministry: the presbyters (literally 'elders') and the deacons (literally 'ministers'). In the New Testament, the Greek words for bishops and presbyters were used interchangeably (e.g. Acts 20.17, 28; Titus 1.5, 7). But now there is a clear distinction and a sense of hierarchy, with the bishop as the one who presides over the presbyters and deacons. Thirdly, again probably for the first time, the epistle uses the word 'catholic' (literally 'of the whole' or universal) to describe the Church of Jesus Christ. It is a Church for all, and therefore for the whole world, and its authority will have this kind of scope. It is not just for those who have special knowledge. In later centuries the word 'Catholic' would become increasingly widely used as the Church faced up to the dangers of division posed by Gnosticism and other sects.

Irenaeus

The Bishop of Lyons, Irenaeus (c.130–c.200), developed this ecclesiology. He was from Anatolia in Asia Minor and was elected to be bishop in 178 (the year after the killing of the 48 martyrs). Here he encountered Gnosticism and became its great opponent. He opposed it at length in his treatise *Against Heresies* of 185. He disliked the way Gnosticism denigrated the material world in which Christ had become incarnate; he disliked its denial of his humanity; he hated the way it separated the Old and New Testaments; he believed God had been at work in the history of Israel before the coming of Christ; he disproved the notion that a secret apostolic tradition had been handed down; he argued that the Church's beliefs are quite open and the way they have been handed down can be clearly traced. He then built on Ignatius of Antioch's teaching and developed the idea of apostolic succession and the primacy of the see of Rome over the other dioceses of the Church:

> It is within the power of all, therefore, in every Church, who may wish to see the truth, to contemplate clearly the tradition of the apostles manifested throughout the whole world; and we are in a position to reckon up those who were by the apostles instituted bishops in the Churches, and [to demonstrate] the succession of these men to our own times ... [not least] that tradition derived from the apostles, of the very great, the very ancient, and universally known Church founded and organized at Rome by the two most glorious apostles, Peter and Paul; as also the faith preached to men, which comes down to our time by means of the successions of the bishops. For it is a matter of necessity that every Church should agree with this Church, on account of its preeminent authority, that is, the faithful everywhere, inasmuch as the tradition has been preserved continuously by those [faithful men] who exist everywhere. (*Against the Heresies* III.3.1–2)

In all of this, there was a growing conviction that the Church had a unifying structure, based on the succession of bishops from the apostles and centred on the see of Rome. The Church was not, in other words, just a movement of ideas and inspiration without any regulating infrastructure: it was an association deliberately derived from its founding fathers and regulated through reference to its founding see.

Marcion's rejection of the Old Testament also prompted Irenaeus to argue for the formation of the Christian canon of scripture, in which Hebrew scriptures would be bound together with gospels and apostolic letters. The final form of the canon would not be agreed in the West until 393, but the genesis of its development lies here in the second century.

Cyprian

Would other parts of the Church accept that the unity of the Church was derived from the see of Peter? The Church of North Africa, Latin speaking and centred on Carthage, provided support. Cyprian of Carthage (c.200–58) was the leading voice. He had been a pagan philosopher and converted to Christianity in about 246. He was elected Bishop of Carthage two years later. He led the Church through the traumas of the Decian persecution (249–58) and had to decide whether to re-baptize Christians who had renounced their faith in the face of persecution (he did). He would die a martyr in 258. In his treatise 'On the unity of the Church', written in the middle of the disunity brought about by the persecution, he makes a powerful plea for maintaining the unity of the Church through the episcopate derived from (though not ruled by) the see of Peter:

> The Lord speaks to Peter, saying, 'I say unto you, that you are Peter; and upon this rock I will build my Church …' And although to all the apostles, after His resurrection, He gives an equal power, and says, 'As the Father has sent me, even so send I you …' yet, that He might set forth unity, He arranged by His authority the origin of that unity, as beginning from one. Assuredly the rest of the apostles were also the same as was Peter, endowed with a like partnership both of honour and power; but the beginning proceeds from unity. And this unity we ought firmly to hold and assert, especially those of us that are bishops who preside in the Church, that we may also prove the episcopate itself to be one and undivided. Let no one deceive the brotherhood by a falsehood: let no one corrupt the truth of the faith by perfidious prevarication. The episcopate is one, each part of which is held by each one for the whole. The Church also is one, which is spread abroad far and wide into a multitude by an increase of fruitfulness. As there are many rays of the sun, but one light; and many branches of a tree, but one strength based in its tenacious root; and since from one spring flow many streams, although the multiplicity seems diffused in the liberality of an overflowing abundance, yet the unity is still preserved in the source. Separate a ray of the sun from its body of light, its unity does not allow a division of light; break a branch from a tree—when broken, it will not be able to bud; cut off the stream from its fountain, and that which is cut off dries up. Thus also the Church, shone over with the light of the Lord, sheds forth her rays over the whole world, yet it is one light which

is everywhere diffused, nor is the unity of the body separated. Her fruitful abundance spreads her branches over the whole world. She broadly expands her rivers, liberally flowing, yet her head is one, her source one; and she is one mother, plentiful in the results of fruitfulness: from her womb we are born, by her milk we are nourished, by her spirit we are animated. ('On the Unity of the Church', 5)

What, then, had the Church itself become in this period? The Roman authorities came to describe it as a 'Judaistic sect', but was this a fair description? A sect is defined by its intention to stand apart from the rest of society and to see itself as superior to that society in important respects. This was true of Marcion and many of the Gnostics. But Pliny's account of the Christians (see pp. 36–7) shows that they did not stand apart from society but were law abiding and morally upright people. Their only crime, for which they were punished, was not to worship the emperor or the other official Roman deities. This is hardly a portrait of a sect. Furthermore the response to Gnosticism by Ignatius of Antioch and Irenaeus of Lyons shows how the Church was committed to being an open and ordered association, in clear continuity with its Jewish roots but also learning to see itself as distinct from Judaism and standing on its own organizational feet. The see of Rome was to provide a reference point for the life and doctrine of other dioceses. As Cyprian argued, it was the source through which Christ's life and 'rays of light' shone into the whole world.

Could it then be called a community? The word 'community' is most commonly used of the people who live in a certain place, whether it is a village or region or nation. They are a community because they have this physical connectedness even though they have different beliefs and interests. It is true that the word can also be used to describe those who share a major interest or occupation, such as 'the legal community' or 'the racing community', but this use is through analogy: those who work in the legal profession, or those who go to races, are like a physical community. A community in its primary sense is the body of people who physically inhabit the same space, whether local, national or international.

Tertullian

Can this word be used to describe the Church in the second and third centuries? Tertullian of Carthage (c.155–222) was converted to Christianity through his encounter with Christians and the courage they showed in adversity. He was a brilliant polemicist and wrote extensively to explain and advocate the Christian faith. The following passage is very revealing of the way Christians lived their lives. But does it show that the Church was a community in the sense defined above?

> We are but of yesterday, and we have filled every place before you – cities, islands, fortresses, towns, market-places, even the camps, tribes, companies, palace, senate, forum – we have left nothing to you but the temples of your gods.
>
> I shall go on to demonstrate the peculiarities of the Christian society, so that, having refuted the evil accusations against it, I may point out its positive good. We are a body knit together by the sense of one belief, united in discipline, bound together by a common hope. We form an alliance and a congregation to assail God with our prayer, like a battalion drawn up for combat. This violence God delights in. We pray, too, for the emperors, for their ministers and all in authority, for the welfare of the world, for the prevalence of peace, for the delay of the final consummation ...
>
> But it is mainly the deeds of a love so noble that lead many to put a brand of infamy on us. 'See how they love one another,' they say, for they themselves are animated by mutual hatred. And they are angry with us, too, because we call one another brother; for no other reason, as I think, than because among themselves names of affinity are assumed only in a mere pretence of affection. But we are your brothers as well, by the law of our common mother nature ... We live with you, eat the same food, wear the same clothing, have the same way of life as you; we are subject to the same needs of existence. We are not Indian Brahmins or fakirs living in woods and exiling themselves from ordinary life ... We live in the same world as you: we go to your forum, your market, your baths, your shops, your workshops, your inns, your fairs and the other places of trade. We sail with you, we serve as soldiers with you, and till the ground and engage in trade ... (*Apology* 37, 39, 42)

If the Church cannot be described as a community in its own right, what other cultural form accords with Tertullian's vivid description? We are led to the specific notion of an association, for those who belong to an association belong to different geographical communities depending on where they live and work, but they choose to associate with like-minded people. The believers chose to meet together, to worship and eat and to pray for one another and support one another through adversities. It is therefore as a voluntary association, to use one of Cameron's organizational forms (see p. 4), that the Church can be described. And because at this stage of its life the believers were largely drawn from towns and cities, it is appropriate to describe the Church as an urban association, though one whose goal and aim is the life of heaven rather than just improving the life of the town or city.

The Church of the third century grew and developed in the face not only of persecution from the authorities and the challenge of re-thinking its faith in the face of Hellenistic culture but also of the challenging rise of Gnosticism and sectarianism. It evolved from being an assembly drawn from one community, to being something standing in its own right, a voluntary association. Cameron defined this as a body with a definite membership, set procedures for members to run the association themselves and an agreed aim. All these features can be seen above, with the agreed aim being that of opening the way from earth to heaven through Christ. Furthermore, it drew adherents from a large number of communities across the ancient world and aspired to be catholic, of the whole world for the whole world. It developed its own ministerial authority structure and sense of where that authority comes from. But it did not set itself up to be an alternative society or community: Tertullian is very clear that Christians belong to their surrounding communities as much as anyone else does. The thing they bring to those communities is 'the deeds of love'.

Discussion Questions

Is persecution necessary for church growth?

Was the Hellenistic Church right to emphasize right believing over right action?

Should all churches actively seek to be re-united with the See of Rome?

Bibliography and Further Reading

Chadwick, Henry (1993), *The Early Church*, revised edn, Harmondsworth: Penguin.
Charlesworth, Max (2002), *Philosophy and Religion: From Plato to Postmodernism*, Oxford: Oneworld.
Frend, W. H. C. (1984), *The Rise of Christianity*, London: Darton, Longman and Todd.
MacCulloch, Diarmaid (2009), *A History of Christianity: The First Three Thousand Years*, Ch. 4, Harmondsworth: Allen Lane.
Scott, J. Julius, Jnr (2000), *Jewish Backgrounds of the New Testament*, Ada: Baker Books.
Stark, Rodney (1997), *The Rise of Christianity*, San Francisco: Harper Collins.
Stevenson, J. and W. H. C. Frend (1987), *A New Eusebius: Documents illustrating the History of the Church to AD336*, London: SPCK.

The writings of the church fathers quoted in this chapter are available in English translation in A. Cleveland Coxe et al. (eds) (1994), *The Ante-Nicene Fathers* (1994), 10 vols, Peabody MA: Hendrickson Publishers. The translations quoted in this chapter are available online, for example at http://www.newadvent.org/fathers/.

4

From Constantine to Byzantium: A State Church?

The Fourth-Century Revolution

At the beginning of the fourth century a political event would take place which would have revolutionary consequences for the Church. The story begins with Emperor Diocletian (who ruled from 284 to 305). He was an army general who rose to power through the support of the legions. He had great administrative ability and divided the Empire into two provinces, East and West, and then 12 dioceses (a term later adopted by the Church in its own territorial organization). However, in 303, he turned against the Church in what became called the Great Persecution (and in the East 'the Era of Martyrs'). He believed the Christian faith undermined his own absolute and 'divine' power and he ordered that all churches should be torn down, Bibles burned and clergy tortured. There were a considerable number of martyrs (probably including the first British martyr Alban, a Roman soldier who volunteered to die in place of a priest). But subsequent events show that Diocletian was acting more out of desperation than calculation, for in 305 he abdicated and handed over the Empire to others, one of whom was Constantius Chlorus, the father of Constantine.

Constantine was another determined general and when Constantius died in 306, he was in York on a campaign with his legions: they immediately proclaimed him an emperor. He then set about gaining control of the Western Empire by engaging his brother and rival Maxentius in battle. They fought at the Milvian Bridge near Rome, and the Christian historian Eusebius (a contemporary and admirer of Constantine) described the events. He writes that on the day before the battle Constantine reported

> that about noon, when the day was already beginning to decline, he saw with his own eyes the trophy of a cross of light in the heavens, above the sun, and bearing the inscription, CONQUER BY THIS. At this sight he himself was struck with amazement, and his whole army also, which followed him on this expedition, and witnessed the miracle. (Eusebius Pamphilus of Caesarea, *The Life of the Blessed Emperor Constantine*, Chapters 28–31)

Then during the night 'in his sleep the Christ of God appeared to him with the same sign which he had seen in the heavens, and commanded him to make a likeness of that sign which he had seen in the heavens, and to use it as a safeguard in all engagements with his enemies'.

Constantine ordered a standard to be made, to be carried at the head of his army, incorporating the sign he had seen. This would be called the Labarum and like other standards carried a powerful symbolic message. Eusebius provides an embellished description, one that shows that Christianity had now acquired a new place in the Empire:

> Now it was made in the following manner. A long spear, overlaid with gold, formed the figure of the cross by means of a transverse bar laid over it. On the top of the whole was fixed a wreath of gold and precious stones; and within this, the symbol of the Saviour's name, two letters indicating the name of Christ by means of its initial characters, the letter P being intersected by X in its centre: and these letters the emperor was in the habit of wearing on his helmet at a later period. From the cross-bar of the spear was suspended a cloth, a royal piece, covered with a profuse embroidery of most brilliant precious stones; and which, being also richly interlaced with gold, presented an indescribable degree of beauty to the beholder. This banner was of a square form, and the upright staff, whose lower section was of great length, bore a golden half-length portrait of the pious emperor and his children on its upper part, beneath the trophy of the cross, and immediately above the embroidered banner.

The emperor constantly made use of this sign of salvation as a safeguard against every adverse and hostile power, and commanded that others similar to it should be carried at the head of all his armies. (ibid.)

Constantine also ordered that the shields of his soldiers be marked with the 'XP' symbol, and he then went on to win the battle and gain control of the Western Empire.

As he then took control of the life of the Western Empire, he brought Diocletian's persecution to an end. This was also seen in the Edict of Milan of 313, which allowed Christians to have legal ownership of their churches. He also granted legal toleration to all religions in the Empire. His family and court began to adopt the Christian faith in increasing numbers. In 324, he marched east to fight his other brother Licinius for control of the Eastern half of the Roman Empire. At the battle of Chrysopolis (324), near the Bosphorus, Constantine was victorious and became the undisputed head of the whole Roman Empire. He decided to rebuild the city of Byzantium on the banks of the Bosphorus and to name it after himself. This was the founding of Constantinople (which today is called Istanbul). It would become the new capital of the whole Roman Empire. He then turned his attention to leading and unifying the Church.

Constantine may have placed himself in the service of the Christian God because of the rapid spread of Christianity through the Roman Empire. He knew he would do himself no harm in gaining the support of an increasingly significant section of the population. His mother Helena was already a Christian and would later play a prominent part in founding churches, not least in the Holy Land which she visited in 326. In the words of the historian W. H. C. Frend, this represents a revolution for Christianity and the Empire: a transformation of its status from a hidden and persecuted minority to a visible and influential public body (Frend 1984, p. 474).

Timeline

c.300–373	Athanasius
306	Constantine rises to power as one of the emperors
311	Donatist schism begins in north Africa

312	Battle of Milvian Bridge: Constantine becomes Western Emperor
313	Edict of Milan: Christians can worship in public and own property
c.316–397	Martin of Tours
323	Eusebius' *Ecclesiastical History*
324	Constantine becomes emperor of whole Roman Empire (east as well as west)
325	Council of Nicea
340–397	Ambrose
354–430	Augustine
c.360–c.435	John Cassian
381	First Council of Constantinople
401–407	Pope Innocent I asserts primacy of Rome
410	Rome attacked by Alaric and the Goths
427	Augustine finishes *The City of God*
432	Beginning of Patrick's ministry in Ireland
451	Council of Chalcedon
455	The Vandals capture Rome
476	Odoacer deposes Romulus Augustulus: end of the Roman Empire in the West

The Establishing of the Church

When Constantine arrived in the East, he found the Greek churches bitterly divided between Bishop Alexander of Alexandria and his presbyter Arius over a theological dispute concerning the nature of Christ. Arius believed that 'the logos became incarnate by taking the place of the reason in the man Jesus so that Christ was neither fully God nor fully human, but a third something' (in Miles 2004, p. 71). Alexander denied this, arguing that Christ was a human being as well as divine.

Constantine could not tolerate his new power base, the Christian Church, being divided in this way. So he called a meeting of all the bishops at his summer residence at Nicaea, a few miles from Constantinople, in 325. Eusebius describes this first ecumenical council:

> In effect, the most distinguished of God's ministers from all the churches which abounded in Europe, Libya, and Asia were here assembled. And a single house of prayer, as though divinely enlarged, sufficed to contain at once Syrians and Cilicians, Phoenicians and Arabians, delegates from Palestine, and others from Egypt; Thebans and Libyans, with those who came from the region of Mesopotamia. A Persian bishop too was present at this conference … (ibid., Book 3.VII)

Constantine presided over the assembly. On the issue of whether Christ was fully human, the issue dividing the followers of Arius and the followers of Alexander, the majority of the 318 bishops agreed with Alexander. Arius and two supporters who did not sign the following Nicean formula were deposed and exiled:

> We believe in one God, the Father all-sovereign, Maker of all things visible and invisible; and in one Lord Jesus Christ, the Son of God, begotten of the Father, only-begotten, that is, from the substance (*ousia*) of the Father; God of God, Light of Light, true God of true God, begotten not made, of one substance (*homousion*) with the Father through whom all things were made, things in heaven and things on earth; who for us and for our salvation came down, and was enfleshed, and enhumaned, suffered, and rose on the third day, ascended into the heavens, is coming to judge the living and the dead; and in the Holy Spirit. (in Miles 2004, pp. 71–2)

The presence of the emperor's own troops outside the meeting hall may have helped to concentrate the minds of the bishops. Other new laws were passed which began to introduce a whole new way of governing and thinking about the Church. There were 20 canons regulating church discipline: bishops were not allowed to move from one diocese to another; they had to be consecrated by all the bishops of their province if possible and by not less than three; and the bishops of the provincial capitals (metropolitans) were given the right of veto.

All of this helped to establish a clear structure within the hierarchy of the Church and also centralized power in the hands of the bishops. Three bishops, of Rome, Alexandria and Antioch, were recognized as having a wider authority (Constantinople would soon be added to this list). Henry Chadwick comments that

> [t]he Nicene canons throw much light, therefore, on the developing organization and 'power structure' of the church. By 325 the Greek churches at least were accustomed to an organization based on the secular provincial system, and the unit normally conformed to that of the State. But what court of appeal could stand above a provincial council? ... In fact, as the fourth century advanced, it became increasingly the tendency for the final decisions about church policy to be taken by the emperor, and the group in the church which at any given time swayed the course of events was very often that which succeeded in obtaining the imperial ear. (Chadwick 1993, pp. 131–2)

Constantine also changed the wider law of the Empire. In general, he made the law more humane: he eased the effects of slavery; he instituted grants to support poor children so that fathers would not expose unwanted babies to the elements; he freed celibates and unmarried persons from special taxes; he protected the clergy and ordered that Sundays should become public holidays. He also became the patron of new church basilicas in Palestine, Rome and Constantinople. He did not, though, outlaw pagan religion. Many of his citizens continued to worship other gods, and Constantine allowed religious toleration.

The Church, then, was becoming firmly embedded within the political structure, in a position of power and wealth, but under a monarch who had authority over the Church as well as state. The Mediterranean world was now entering a completely new phase in its history, in which members of the 'race of Christians' would be playing a predominant role. Their interest and ideas were to prevail, and their leaders would direct affairs of the state, accompany the emperor on campaigns and act as his chief advisers at home. Indicative of the new state of affairs is the survival of the names of no less than 1,100 bishops and other clergy who lived in the reign of Constantine and his sons. The army, too, previously the symbol of the protecting power of the gods, now carried the sacred monogram on its shields (Frend 1984, p. 522).

While a later emperor, Julian (361–3) would try to reverse these developments and return Rome to being a pagan state, he was too late: in the three decades before he came to power, 'the Graeco-Roman world had taken a long and irreversible step toward its transformation into the Byzantine church-state' (ibid., p. 522).

Eusebius as Bishop of Caeserea and as already noted the first church historian and a great admirer of Constantine passed over Constantine's brutal treatment of the members of his own family and eulogized the emperor in an address delivered towards the end of his reign in 336:

> The only begotten Word of God reigns, from ages which had no beginning, to infinite and endless ages, the partner of his Father's kingdom. And our emperor ever beloved by him, who derives the source of imperial authority from above, and is strong in the power of his sacred title, has controlled the empire of the world for a long period of years. (in Stevenson 1987, p. 391)

This statement shows that while the emperor was no longer regarded as being a god, he was nevertheless seen by his supporters in the Church as having significant divine authority. It is a statement that demonstrates how far the Church itself had travelled in its self-understanding. Eusebius then goes on to describe the missionary implications of this imperial theology:

> Again, that Preserver of the universe orders the whole heaven and earth, and the celestial kingdom, consistently with his Father's will. Even so our emperor whom He loves, by bringing those whom he rules on earth to the only begotten and saving Word renders them fit subjects for his kingdom. (ibid., p. 391)

Here, then, the emperor was being given a mandate to use the power of the Empire to bring its diverse peoples into the Christian religion.

While Constantine allowed a plurality of religions in the Empire, later emperors would do as Eusebius suggested and try to make Christianity the only one. Furthermore, one form of that faith, the Catholic, would be enforced, an example being the treatment of the followers of Arius. As mentioned, he was a priest of Alexandria who came into conflict with his bishop over whether the Son existed eternally with the Father or, as he argued, from 'before the ages' but not eternally (so preserving the Platonic distinction between the eternal and the earthly). This teaching became very popular and two factions formed in the fourth-century Church, one supporting him and becoming known as Arianism, and the other led by Athanasius, which later became known as Orthodoxy. In 380 Emperor Theodosius I issued an edict making Orthodox Christianity the official religion and making any deviation from the Nicean formula illegal. In 381 he called the first Council of Constantinople, which placed the Bishop of Constantinople second in honour to the Bishop of Rome. It outlawed congregations that followed the teaching of Arius, confiscated property held by these and other heretical groups. Many pagan temples were destroyed or forcibly converted into churches. Orthodox Christianity was now not just a privileged religion but had come to be the established religion.

A similar push for uniformity can be seen in the official response to Donatism. The Donatists were a group within the Church in North Africa who had suffered under Diocletian's persecution and now were appalled that under Constantine some of their brethren who had become traitors to the faith had now rejoined the Church and even in some cases become bishops. The followers of Bishop Donatus could not accept this and formed themselves into a separate church with their own line of bishops. This schism began at Carthage and spread along the north African coast in the fourth century. The state responded by persecuting the Donatists in 317–21 and 346–8, with the collusion of the official church. Then, after Augustine was elected Bishop of Hippo in 396, he campaigned against the Donatists, arguing that the Catholic Church was for all people, sinners as well as saints. The validity of its ministry came not from the moral character of its ministers but from Christ himself. At the start of the fifth century the authorities again persecuted the Donatists, fining and imprisoning them (though this did not stamp them out).

All of this put a new gloss on the statement in the Nicean Creed (which was formally adopted at the Council of Constantinople of 381) that the Church is 'one' as well as 'holy', 'catholic' and 'apostolic': the Church was to be one as the Roman Empire was one, exercising authority over everyone within the Empire: there was to be one order, with Christ at the head and beneath him the emperor exercising a magisterial authority over the peoples of the earth. Implicit within this was a new understanding of mission: the Church was to come into an increasing alliance with the state, and together Church and state would do all they could to incorporate more and more people within its jurisdiction. The Church, in other words, was now to work for the creation of Christendom.

In the West, though, this would hardly get going before the Germanic tribes began to invade and take control of the Empire. In 410, Rome itself was attacked and sacked by Alaric and the Goths. The creation of Christendom would belong to a later era. In the east, however, such a marriage of Church and state would become the norm for the next 1,000 years. The Patriarch of Constantinople, appointed by the emperor, came to be seen as the most senior of the Eastern patriarchs because of his closeness to the emperor. In many ways, he had to do as he was bid by the emperor. The episcopal seat, in the great basilica of Saint Sophia, was next door to the emperor's throne in the imperial palace, showing its subservience to his authority.

Nevertheless there were some occasions when the emperor had to bow to the authority of the Church. When in 390 Theodosius killed over 7,000 citizens of Thessalonica in retribution for a riot against his authority, Bishop Ambrose of Milan (c.340–97) was outraged and castigated the emperor for being so harsh.

> I urge, I beg, I exhort, I warn, for it is a grief to me, that you who were an example of unusual piety, who were conspicuous for clemency, who would not suffer single offenders to be put in peril, should not mourn that so many have perished. Though you have waged battle most successfully, though in other matters, too, you are worthy of praise, yet piety was ever the crown of your actions. The devil envied that which was your most excellent possession. Conquer him whilst you still possess that wherewith you may conquer. Do not add another sin to your sin by a course of action which has injured many. (Ambrose, Letter 51 to Theodosius)

Theodosius publicly acknowledged his guilt and submitted to penance. This was the first time that an emperor bowed to the authority of the Church. It proved the truth of Ambrose's statement that 'The emperor is within the church, not above the church' ('Sermon Against Auxentius on the Giving Up of the Basilicas', 36). An alliance with the state was not to be confused with subservience to the state.

The Rise of Monasticism

The fourth century was not just about the Church acquiring privileged status and worldly power. There was another and remarkable development, one that took it in a completely different direction. This is the story of the rise of monasticism, when monks who up to now had lived alone, began to live together. The word 'monk' comes from the Greek *monos*, alone. But from now on there would be two kinds of monk: those who continued to live alone and would be called hermits or anchorites, and those who lived together in groups, who would be called cenobites.

Anthony of Egypt (c.251–356) is commonly regarded as the founder of this monasticism. From c.270, he began the journey from hermit to cenobite. His life was later publicized by Athanasius the Bishop of Alexandria in his *Life of St Anthony*:

Antony you must know was by descent an Egyptian: his parents were of good family and possessed considerable wealth, and as they were Christians he also was reared in the same Faith ... (Section 1)

After the death of his father and mother he was left alone with one little sister: his age was about eighteen or twenty, and on him the care both of home and sister rested. Now it was not six months after the death of his parents, and going according to custom into the Lord's House, ... and it happened the Gospel was being read, and he heard the Lord saying to the rich man (Matt. 19.21), 'If you would be perfect, go and sell that you have and give to the poor; and come follow Me and you shall have treasure in heaven.' Antony, as though God had put him in mind of the Saints, and the passage had been read on his account, went out immediately from the church, and gave the possessions of his forefathers to the villagers – they were three hundred acres, productive and very fair – that they should be no more a clog upon himself and his sister. And all the rest that was movable he sold, and having got together much money he gave it to the poor, reserving a little however for his sister's sake. (Section 2)

After placing his sister in the care of a convent Anthony visited a number of hermits and devoted himself to prayer, fasting and charitable works. He lived very simply, sleeping on a rush mat, and Athanasius describes how he engaged in spiritual warfare against the temptations of the devil. On one occasion, he lived among tombs and had an intense experience of being attacked by the devil, and he remained resolute and came out of the experience all the stronger. He then decided to go into the desert, for this was believed to be the home of evil spirits, to do battle with them. He was about 34 by this time and took up residence in a ruined fort:

> And so for nearly twenty years he continued training himself in solitude, never going forth, and but seldom seen by any. After this, when many were eager and wishful to imitate his discipline, and his acquaintances came and began to cast down and wrench off the door by force, Antony, as from a shrine, came forth initiated in the mysteries and filled with the Spirit of God … he persuaded many to embrace the solitary life. And thus it happened in the end that cells arose even in the mountains, and the desert was colonised by monks, who came forth from their own people, and enrolled themselves for the citizenship in the heavens. (Section 14)

Anthony therefore started a movement that would spread from Egypt across North Africa and to Syria and Asia Minor. The monks would sometimes come to be taught by him, showing his position as the leader of this new monasticism.

During the rest of his life he alternated between seeking solitude (through going to areas where he was not known) and travelling to cities such as Alexandria to teach the Christian churches and oppose Arianism. This was when Athanasius came across him:

> And the fame of Antony came even unto kings. For Constantine Augustus, and his sons Constantius and Constans the Augusti wrote letters to him, as to a father, and begged an answer from him. But he made nothing very much of the letters, nor did he rejoice at the messages, but was the same as he had been before the Emperors wrote to him. (Section 81)

Frend provides the following commentary on all of this:

> Antony's motives were partly religious, to live entirely by literal obedience to Scripture, but there was also a social motive. Athanasius, who wrote a life of Antony, says that he despairingly asked 'Why do the rich grind the faces of the

poor?' Hard work for his own subsistence needs was his practice. He himself had been a failure in early life and had little use for the ways of secular society. His settlement of ascetics in the mountains became a refuge for those fleeing from the extortions of tax collectors, whose 'grumbles' he records. This social motive was combined with an ascetic tradition that reached back to the dawn of Christianity, to John the Baptist, and to Jesus' example of seeking out a solitary place for prayer in the mountains or wilderness. Almost for the first time in three centuries the Lord's commands were being accepted literally by Christ's followers. (Frend 1984, p. 423)

When the Emperor Diocletian seized power in 284, the Church was still over-whelmingly an urban institution. Anthony and his followers, along with other Christians in North Africa, helped to create the new phenomenon of a non-urban monastic Christianity, in which their heroic battles with demons in the deserts won over subsistence farmers who had up to now lived lives dominated by pagan superstition.

Elsewhere, Frend writes that the rise of the monastic movement would eventu-ally lead to the total disintegration of rural paganism in the entire Greco-Roman world. And following Frend, David Bosch has commented that

> [w]hen Christianity became the official religion of the Empire and persecu-tions ended, the monk succeeded the martyr as the expression of unqualified witness and protest against worldliness. Since the fourth century the history of the church on the move, particularly in the East, was essentially also the history of monasticism. In fact, from the very beginning of monasticism, the most daring and most efficient missionaries were the monks. (Bosch 1991, p. 202)

But what about the Church in Western Europe? The earliest phases of monasti-cism here involved figures like Martin of Tours (c.316–97), who after serving as a soldier in the Roman legions converted to Christianity and established a hermitage near Milan. He then moved to Poitiers where other hermits gathered around him inspired by his charisma and teaching. He preached extensively in the rural regions of central and western Gaul. He was then called to become Bishop of Tours but resisted at first. Then, in 372, he was asked to visit the city to prepare a very sick woman for her death, which he did, and after arriving there was pressurised to become bishop by the Christian community. He did not, however, change his way of life: he refused to live in the city and settled in a small cell a short distance from Tours, beyond the Loire. Some other hermits joined him there, and thus was gradually formed a new monastery, which grew and became known as Marmoutier or, in Latin, Majus Monasterium.

Martin's biographer, Sulpitius Severus, describes the spartan lifestyle of the cave-dwelling cenobites who gathered around him, a rare view of early monastic life:

> Many also of the brethren had, in the same manner, fashioned retreats for themselves, but most of them had formed these out of the rock of the overhanging mountain, hollowed into caves. There were altogether eighty disciples, who were being disciplined after the example of the saintly master. No one there had anything which was called his own; all things were possessed in common. It was not allowed either to buy or to sell anything, as is the custom among most monks. No art was practiced there, except that of transcribers, and even this was assigned to the brethren of younger years, while the elders spent their time in prayer. Rarely did any one of them go beyond the cell, unless when they assembled at the place of prayer. They all took their food together, after the hour of fasting was past. No one used wine, except when illness compelled them to do so. Most of them were clothed in garments of camels' hair. Any dress approaching to softness was there deemed criminal, and this must be thought the more remarkable, because many among them were such as are deemed of noble rank. (Sulpitius Severus, *On the Life of St Martin*, X)

It is important to note that this monastic community was laid out as a colony of hermits rather than as a single integrated community. Monks living together intentionally as a community would come later, with Benedict of Nursia, who belongs to a later era.

Another figure of importance was John Cassian. John Cassian was born around 360, probably in modern-day Romania. He travelled to Palestine with an elderly companion Germanus, where they entered a hermitage near Bethlehem. After remaining in that community for about three years, they journeyed to the desert of Scete in Egypt, where Christians were divided over theological controversies, and they visited a number of monastic foundations which had been established through the influence of Anthony. After 15 years, they had to flee because of the theological division, and they went to Constantinople, where they appealed to the Patriarch of Constantinople, John Chrysostom, for protection, which they were granted. Cassian was ordained a deacon and started to work for the patriarch.

Meanwhile disagreement and division between Chrysostom and the emperor's family flared up, especially over Chrysostom's criticism of the ostentatious lifestyle of the emperor's wife Eudoxia. He was forced into exile from Constantinople in 404 and sent the Latin-speaking John Cassian to Rome to plead his cause with Pope Innocent I. While Cassian was in Rome, he accepted the invitation to found an Egyptian-style monastery in southern Gaul, near Marseille. He arrived in Marseille around 415. His foundation, the Abbey of St Victor, was a complex of monasteries for both men and women, one of the first such foundations in the West and served as a model for later monastic development, not least in the Celtic regions of the British Isles.

Cassian wrote two major spiritual works, the *Institutions* and the *Conferences*. In these, he codified and transmitted the wisdom of Anthony and other desert fathers of Egypt, the first volume dealing with the outward practices of a monk, illustrated with examples from Egypt and Palestine, and the second with 'the training of the inner man and the perfection of the heart'. Cassian saw the principal obstacles to perfection by monks as gluttony, impurity, covetousness, anger, dejection, listlessness, vanity, and pride. The *Conferences* contain important records of the conversations of Cassian and Germanus with the Egyptian hermits. He died in 435 in Marseille.

Cassian's story shows the influence of the Eastern Church on Western monasticism, for he was essentially relaying the Egyptian hermitic model of monasticism. But he was also aware of the needs and pressures when hermits lived in groups, and he bequeathed to Latin Christianity its first 'map of a pilgrim's progress' (Chadwick 2009, p. 162). It is this that provides a bridge to Benedict's cenobitic monasticism. Benedict would later use Cassian's writings as a basis for his own foundation in Italy. Cassian's story also demonstrates tensions and rifts with the imperial court and how the evolving monastic movement was travelling in a different direction from that of Constantine and Eusebius.

Self-understanding: Augustine's Two Cities

The fourth century therefore shows two very important but highly contrasting developments: the marriage of Church and state under Constantine and his successors, and the rise of a world-renouncing monastic movement with its roots in the Egyptian desert, a movement that would spread to the West and become key to the expansion of the Church in rural areas in the fourth and subsequent centuries. These might seem contradictory developments revealing the fundamental weakness of Christianity. Or can sense be made of this as a whole?

Augustine of Hippo (354–430) offers some sense. In his writings he brings to expression what would become a very influential ecclesiology. The story of his early life is told in his *Confessions*, which recounts his birth in 354 in Thagaste, a Roman town in Algeria. His mother Monica was a Christian. He spoke and wrote in Latin and never mastered Greek. He moved to Carthage, where as a young man he became a Manichee (a kind of Gnostic: see pp. 42–3). He had a partner for 15 years and with her a son. He was influenced by the writings of the Roman politician and writer Cicero, and sailed to Rome, then to Milan, to become a prestigious teacher of rhetoric. He was a seeker after truth and tried a number of different philosophies, including hedonism, stoicism and Platonism, the last of which proved to be a doorway into Christianity. It was in Milan that he encountered Bishop Ambrose (see p. 59), who encouraged his study of scripture. His mother Monica joined him and persuaded him to marry into society. He sent his partner away and then grieved for her for some time. While still in Milan and in some turmoil, he went into a garden where he heard a child's voice saying 'Take and read'. Remembering how Anthony had been called when he heard words of scripture, Augustine opened the scriptures at random and read Paul's words in Romans 13, 'put on the Lord Jesus Christ'. It was now that he was converted to Christianity and to a life of discipline. He was baptized by Ambrose at Easter 387.

Augustine returned to Africa and was soon made Bishop of Hippo by its Christian congregation. The rest of his life was spent defining and defending the Christian faith in his extensive writings, though he was also an untiring bishop and administrator. As well as the *Confessions*, he wrote *City of God* and *On the Trinity*, among many other works. He died in 430 at the age of 76, while Hippo was being besieged by the Vandals, a German tribe that was sweeping through North Africa.

His doctrine of the Church emerged out of the collapse of the Roman Empire. Pope Innocent I (401–7) had asserted the primacy of the see (bishop's jurisdiction) of Rome over all other sees, but then in 410 Rome was attacked by Alaric and the Goths, who overran and sacked the city. This event left Romans in a deep state of shock, and many saw it as punishment for abandoning traditional Roman religion for Catholic Christianity. It was in this atmosphere that Augustine set out to justify Christianity and encourage the Christian churches. He wrote the book in two parts. The first part, comprising Books I–X, was a critique of Roman cultures and pagan philosophy. In various ways, these describe the Earthly City, in contrast to the City of God discussed in the second part, which comprises the remaining 12 books. Here Augustine shifts from criticism to an account of the relationship between the two cities. He argues that despite Christianity's designation as the official religion of the Empire, its main concern is with the eternal reality of the mystical, heavenly city, the New Jerusalem, rather than with earthly politics. The City of God is made up of people who have renounced earthly pleasure and have dedicated themselves to the eternal truths of God, now revealed fully in the Christian faith. The City of Man, on the other hand, consists of people who have immersed themselves in the cares and pleasures of the present, passing world:

But the families which do not live by faith seek their peace in the earthly advantages of this life; while the families which live by faith look for those eternal blessings which are promised, and use as pilgrims such advantages of time and of earth as do not fascinate and divert them from God, but rather aid them to endure with greater ease, and to keep down the number of those burdens of the corruptible body which weigh upon the soul. Thus the things necessary for this mortal life are used by both kinds of men and families alike, but each has its own peculiar and widely different aim in using them. The earthly city, which does not live by faith, seeks an earthly peace, and the end it proposes, in the well-ordered concord of civic obedience and rule, is the combination of men's wills to attain the things which are helpful to this life. The heavenly city, or rather the part of it which sojourns on earth and lives by faith, makes use of this peace only because it must, until this mortal condition which necessitates it shall pass away. Consequently, so long as it lives like a captive and a stranger in the earthly city, though it has already received the promise of redemption, and the gift of the Spirit as the earnest of it, it makes no scruple to obey the laws of the earthly city, whereby the things necessary for the maintenance of this mortal life are administered; and thus, as this life is common to both cities, so there is a harmony between them in regard to what belongs to it. (Book XIX.17)

It is important to note that despite the Christian's primary concern for the heavenly city he or she will still have some concern for the earthly city as part of their duty to God. 'This is the discovery which lies between the early and final books of the City of God. Book XIX is in substance his exploration of the consequences of this discovery' (Markus 1970, p. 100). For example, Augustine writes of the calling to be a judge in the city courts:

Will a wise man sit as judge in this darkness of social life, or will he not dare? Of course he will sit. For the solidarity of human society, which he deems wicked to abandon, lays upon him this duty and draws him to its performance. (Book XIX.6)

Markus explains:

[For Augustine] the state originates in sin, and its purpose is both punitive and remedial. Political authority and its coercive agencies exist for the purpose of coping with the consequences of man's sin, with the disorganization and conflict endemic in the human condition. (ibid., p. 228)

There is, in other words, an important job to be done in keeping law and order in place so that disorganization and chaos will be kept at bay. It is not to do with the ultimate goal of salvation, so must be kept in perspective:

In the last resort man's destiny is not within his control. Not even in society can men work out their salvation. And this being so, as the functions, institutions and the quality of a society cannot be assessed in terms of the ultimates of human destiny, then the relevant language of politics must move in a more limited sphere, the sphere of the needs which social life exists to satisfy. Augustine's repudiation of the classical 'politics of perfection' prepared the ground for a political theory which he never in fact elaborated beyond the bare indications that its realm is that in which the two 'cities' overlap. But he saw the direction and indicated it clearly. The realities of the saeculum must be spoken of in historical or political, not in theological, terms. (ibid., pp. 103–4)

How, then, does Augustine make sense of the Church being involved in this world, through being 'married' to the state from Constantine onwards, and yet of being separated from the world, in 'the desert', as with the church of the hermits and the early monastic movement? He does this by showing that while its ultimate horizon and goal is the City of God, it still needs to play its part in upholding peace and order in the City of Man, so that the citizens of the latter are free to seek the former. The City of Man is not the place of salvation, it is too implicated in sin for that, but it does provide the setting in which people can seek the salvation of the City of God. Christians do not expect heaven on earth, but they do recognize that a peaceful and orderly earth is a gateway to heaven. In other words, the hermits were right to direct the attention of Christians to an eschatological horizon, but Constantine and his bishops were also right to work together to bring unity and good order to the Empire, because the former is strengthened by the latter. They are not contradictory but, paradoxically, complementary goals.

Finally, what does all this show about the evolving nature of the Church? How do the major developments of the fourth and fifth centuries add to or change its organizational form?

The Constantinian Church became wedded to the state in a significant way. But we have also seen that it maintained a distance from the state, especially through the witness of the hermits and the early monastic movement. And at certain points even the bishops stood up to the emperor and his family, as when John Chrysostom opposed the emperor and had to flee from Constantinople. The Church, then, was no simple arm of the state: it could not be described as a department of state or even a state church. It maintained its own independence while mostly being content to work under the emperor and his government. Furthermore, the Roman state continued to tolerate the presence of other religions in the Empire (at least to begin with): the Empire did not become uniformly Christian, even though Theodosius would try to make it so (and later in the east, as the Roman Empire became the Byzantine Empire, it would sometimes become so).

The Church, then, should still be described as an association, a structured and ordered body existing in its own right, one among other religions of the Empire, with its own eschatological horizon, a horizon that transcended the passing fortunes of emperors and their governments. It was an association, though, which was committed to working with the state under the emperor, as Augustine saw, for the peace and order of all people. To develop Cameron's second organizational form, it can therefore be described as an association-in-alliance-with-the state or, more simply, as an official association.

But what would be the impact of the break-up of the Roman Empire in the West? How could the Church survive when it no longer had the order and protection of a wider civil community? What would it become?

Discussion Questions

Is it wrong for the Church to become married to the state and for Christianity to become an official religion?

What can Anthony and Egyptian monasticism teach the churches today?

Can churches really combine seeking the City of God with serving the cities of the world?

Bibliography and Further Reading

Bettenson, Henry and Chris Maunder (eds) (2011), *Documents of the Christian Church*, 4th edn, Oxford: Oxford University Press.

Bosch, David J. (1991), *Transforming Mission: Paradigm Shifts in Theology of Mission*, Maryknoll, NY: Orbis.

Chadwick, Henry (1993), *The Early Church*, revised edn, Harmondsworth: Penguin.

Chadwick, Owen (2009), *John Cassian*, Ann Arbor: University of Michigan Press.

Frend, W. H. C. (1984), *The Rise of Christianity*, London: Darton, Longman and Todd.

MacCulloch, Diarmaid (2009), *A History of Christianity: The First Three Thousand Years*, Chs 6 and 9, Harmondsworth: Allen Lane.

Markus, R. A. (1970), *Saeculum: History and Society in the Theology of St Augustine*, Cambridge: Cambridge University Press.

Miles, Margaret (2004), *The Word Made Flesh: A History of Christian Thought*, Oxford: Wiley-Blackwell.

Pecknold, C. C. (2010), *Christianity and Politics: A Brief Guide to the History*, Ch. 3, Eugene, Oregon: Cascade Books.

Stevenson, J. and W. H. C. Frend (1987), *A New Eusebius: Documents Illustrating the History of the Church to AD 336*, London: SPCK.

Stevenson, J. and W. H. C. Frend,(1989), *Creeds, Councils and Controversies: Documents Illustrating the History of the Church AD337–461*, London: SPCK.

The writings of the church fathers quoted in this chapter are available in English translation in Alexander Roberts (ed.) et al., (1994), *Nicene and Post-Nicene Fathers: First and Second Series*, 28 vols, Peabody MA: Hendrickson Publishers. The translations quoted in this chapter are available online, for example at http://www.newadvent.org/fathers/.

5

The Rise of the Western Church: Tribal or Catholic?

From the Sixth to the Ninth Century: Germanic Tribes and the Rise of Islam

Spread of Germanic tribes

During the fifth century, the Western Roman Empire lost military strength and political cohesion. A number of Germanic tribal groups began migrating across its eastern and northern border and moved into Central, Western and Southern Europe. They were migrating under pressure from population growth and because of the invasion of their lands by Asian groups from further east. They came as far west as Great Britain, in the form of the Angles and the Saxons, and through continental Europe in the form of the Goths and Huns, to the Mediterranean and northern coast of Africa. This led to conflict and war over the dwindling amount of unoccupied territory. They then began staking out permanent homes as a way of ensuring their own protection. From these homes many of the tribes began again to expand outwards, often by assimilating surrounding groups. In Denmark, the Jutes merged with the Danes, and in Sweden, the Geats and Gutes merged with the Swedes. In England, the Angles merged with the Saxons and other groups (notably the Jutes), as well as absorbing some natives, to form the Anglo-Saxons.

Did these tribes defeat and overrun the Roman Empire in a frenzy of pillaging and looting? Recent archaeological and historical research suggests a more gradual process of transition between the Empire and what used to be called the 'dark ages'. It indicates that the Germanic peoples were co-opted into helping to defend territory that the central Roman government could no longer administer adequately. Individuals and small groups from Germanic tribes just outside the Roman Empire had long been recruited into it, and some of them had risen high in the command structure of the army. Then the authorities began to recruit entire tribal groups with their native leaders becoming officers. These groups assisted with administration and then, finally, took on outright rule. Roman government passed inexorably into the hands of Germanic leaders.

The presence of such successor states controlled by a Germanic nobility is evident in the sixth century. This was the case even in Italy, where Odoacer deposed Romulus Augustulus in 476, a date usually regarded as the formal end of the Roman Empire in the West. He was followed by Theodoric the Great, king of the Ostrogoths, who came to be regarded by Roman citizens and Gothic settlers as the legitimate successor of the rule of Rome. Germanic languages become dominant along the Roman borders, in modern-day Austria, Germany, Netherlands, Belgium and England. North European languages such as English, German, Dutch and the Scandinavian languages all have their roots in these languages. But in the rest of the western Roman provinces Germanic immigrants adopted Latin dialects, which became the 'Romance' languages of France, Spain, Portugal and Italy.

Timeline

410	Rome attacked by Alaric and the Goths
427	Augustine finishes *The City of God*
432	Beginning of Patrick's ministry in Ireland
451	Council of Chalcedon
455	The Vandals capture Rome
476	Odoacer deposes Romulus Augustulus, ending the Roman Empire in the West
c.480–c.550	Benedict of Nursia
496	Clovis king of the Franks converted to Christianity

527–65	Justinian Emperor of the Eastern Roman Empire (now the Byzantine Empire)
537	Dedication of Hagia Sophia in Constantinople
c.543–615	Columbanus
c.563	Columba leaves Ireland and establishes Iona
590–604	Pope Gregory I, the first monk to become pope
597	Augustine, sent by Gregory, arrives at Canterbury
622	Muhammad takes control of Medina
c.634–687	Cuthbert of Lindisfarne
636	Arab army defeats Byzantine army at Yarmouk
638–56	Arab armies conquer Palestine, Iraq, Syria and Egypt
664	Synod of Whitby
668–690	Theodore of Tarsus is Archbishop of Canterbury
c.673–735	Bede at Jarrow
711–16	Iberian peninsula conquered by Arab armies
715	Lindisfarne Gospels
716–754	Boniface in Frisia and Germany
726	Iconoclast controversy in the Byzantine Empire
732	Charles Martel halts the Arab advance at Poitiers
756	Rise of the Papal States
800	Charlemagne crowned Emperor of the West by Pope Leo III
848	Conversion of Sweden and Denmark
910	Founding of Cluny Abbey

continued through the centuries. The buildings survived until the Second World War, when they were bombed by the Allies.

Benedict's *Rule* describes a number of precepts for his cenobitic monks (monks who live together in the community of a monastery, as opposed to anchorites or hermits who live alone). It was heavily influenced by the writings of John Cassian (see pp. 63–4) and shows a strong affinity with the earlier *Rule* of the Master. But it also has a unique spirit of balance, moderation and reasonableness, and this persuaded many of the religious communities founded throughout the Middle Ages to adopt it.

In the Prologue Benedict describes what the *Rule* seeks to achieve, a description that sets the moderate tone of everything that follows:

> We propose, therefore to establish a school of the Lord's service, and in setting it up we hope we shall lay down nothing that is harsh or hard to bear. But if for adequate reason, for the correction of faults or the preservation of charity, some degree of restraint is laid down, do not then and there be overcome with terror, and run away from the way of salvation, for its beginning must needs be difficult. On the contrary, through the continual practice of monastic observance and the life of faith, our hearts are opened wide, and the way of God's commandments is run in a sweetness of love that is beyond words. (Benedict 1990: Prologue 45–9)

The *Rule* then describes how the monks are to take part in a course of seven prayers during the day, beginning before dawn with Matins and ending with Compline in the evening. It specified a diet that provided no meat except for the sick, but several different vegetables, bread and wine for the main meal. It emphasized work as a valuable act in itself: 'Idleness is the enemy of the soul. For this reason the brethren should be occupied at certain times in manual labour, and at other times in sacred reading' (XLVIII 1). This sacred reading required a library that was often extended to include a wide range of books on secular topics. It emphasized the idea of submission to the jurisdiction of monastic superiors as an essential step on the ladder of humility. But the reasonableness of the *Rule* is shown by the way it describes the place of the abbot:

> Yet the Abbot must not upset the flock entrusted to him, nor should he make any unjust arrangement as though he were free to give orders as he pleases,

for he must always bear in mind that he is going to have to render an account of all his decisions and actions. (LXIII 2–3)

Yet, all the younger monks were to show respect to the older: 'Whenever the brethren meet one another, the junior should seek a blessing of the elder. A younger monk should rise and offer the seat to an older one if he passes by, nor should he venture to sit down again, unless the older one tell him to' (LXIII 15–16).

Overall, the *Rule* has been described as

a practical guide to help men and women establish and maintain loving relationships with God, with others, with the material world, and also (perhaps surprisingly to those who associate Christianity, and in particular monasticism, with denial and asceticism) with one's own self. It is the whole person that is addressed in the *Rule of St Benedict*. The whole God-given human being made up of body, mind and spirit. The *Rule* is written for a life which recognizes that these three elements should be accepted and affirmed in a daily rhythm of prayer, study and work, alternating activities that make up that balanced life for which Benedictines are rightly renowned. (de Waal in Benedict 1990, p. xvii)

Others have gone even further than this, one writer describing the *Rule* as 'Christianity's paradigmatic framing and answering of the question of ethics' (Banner 2009 p. 10).

Celtic monasticism

Benedict's *Rule*, though, would not start to have widespread influence until the tenth century. In the meantime, another branch of monasticism would carry forward the life and mission of the Church between the sixth and ninth centuries. This was an extraordinary development from beyond the borders of the Roman Empire, in the remote and windswept Atlantic Isles. One of these, Ireland, had not experienced the same collapse and descent into disorder that much of the rest of the Empire experienced. Here the Church was able to continue to strengthen and then, in one of the great missionary endeavours of Christian history, to send missionaries across the seas to re-Christianize first the island of Britain and then the continent of Europe. It had been the first non-Roman area to adopt monasticism at the end of the fifth century, but in a unique form closely linked to traditional clan relationships. It was an approach that would now spread to other parts of Europe and especially France.

The first identifiable founder of a monastery (if she was a real historical figure) was Brigit (d. c.525), who is ranked with Patrick (390–c.461) as a major figure of the Irish Church. Her monastery at Kildare was a double monastery, for both men and women, ruled by an abbess, a pattern that spread to other places including Whitby in the seventh century.

Commonly, Irish monasteries were established by grants of land to an abbot or abbess, who came from a local noble family. It became the spiritual focus of the tribe or kin group. Successive abbots and abbesses were members of the founder's family, a policy that kept the monastic lands under the jurisdiction of the family. This is shown by an extraordinary story from the life of Columba, an Irish monk of Donegal born in 521, who would later travel to Scotland to establish the monastery on Iona.

> Tradition has it that after founding several monasteries, Columba copied St Finnian's psalter without the permission of Finnian, and thus devalued the book. When Finnian took the matter to High King Dermott for judgement, Dermott judged in favour of Finnian, stating "to every cow its calf; to every book its copy" … Columba refused to hand over the copy, and Dermott forced the issue militarily. Columba's family and clan defeated Dermott at the battle of Cooldrevny in 561. (Adamnan 1874, I)

The clan was sovereign! Even bishops were often under the clan's abbot or abbess and would reside in the monastery, having sacramental but not administrative functions. This is suggested by Bede's description of the monastic community on Lindisfarne. While this monastery was founded later than the Irish monasteries, it nevertheless came from and reflected Celtic monasticism:

> [N]o one should wonder that, though the island of Lindisfarne is small, we have above made mention of a bishop, and now of an abbot and monks; for the case is really so. For the same island, inhabited by servants of the Lord, contains both, and all are monks. For Aidan, who was the first bishop of that

place, was a monk, and with all his followers lived according to the monastic rule. (Bede 1910, Chapter XVI)

The contemplative life of the hermit was still seen as the highest form of monasticism: experienced monks (and abbots) would depart some distance from the monastery to live in isolation from the community. Irish monastic rules specified a stern life of prayer and discipline in which prayer, poverty and obedience were the central themes. Bede's account of Saint Cuthbert again gives us a vivid description of this:

WHEN he had remained some years in the monastery, he rejoiced to be able at length, with the blessing of the abbot and brethren accompanying him, to retire to the secrecy of solitude which he had so long coveted. He rejoiced that from the long conversation with the world he was now thought worthy to be promoted to retirement and Divine contemplation: he rejoiced that he now could reach to the condition of those of whom it is sung by the Psalmist: 'The holy shall walk from virtue to virtue; the God of Gods shall be seen in Zion.' At his first entrance upon the solitary life, he sought out the most retired spot in the outskirts of the monastery. But when he had for some time contended with the invisible adversary with prayer and fasting in this solitude, he then, aiming at higher things, sought out a more distant field for conflict, and more remote from the eyes of men. There is a certain island called Farne … lying off several miles to the East, and, consequently, surrounded on all sides by the deep and boundless ocean. No one, before God's servant Cuthbert, had ever dared to inhabit this island alone, on account of the evil spirits which reside there: but when this servant of Christ came, armed with the helmet of salvation, the shield of faith, and the sword of the Spirit, which is the word of God, all the fiery darts of the wicked were extinguished, and that wicked enemy, with all his followers, were put to flight. (ibid. Chapter XVII)

As with the Desert Fathers of Egypt, wild and lonely places were seen as the places where evil resided and therefore the location of spiritual battle. The highest calling of the monk was to go into such places alone and engage the enemy. The contrast with Benedict's *Rule* is striking: for Benedict the calling of the monk was to find perfection through living in a community of monks.

But Celtic monasticism also promoted scholarship and especially the reading, learning and copying of Latin texts, both spiritual and secular. The monks did this with an enthusiasm not found among their contemporaries in Europe, and by the end of the seventh century Irish monastic schools were attracting students from England and Europe. The distinctiveness of their approach to learning is shown by the incorporation of Celtic symbols and culture into their manuscripts. Evidence of this is provided by what is called Hiberno-Saxon or Insular art, a general term that refers to manuscripts produced in the British Isles between 500 and 900. These show an intricate and beautiful combining of Mediterranean, Anglo-Saxon and Celtic elements. The Lindisfarne Gospels, dating from around 715, and the Book of Kells, now thought to date from around 800, provide the finest example of these.

The Lindisfarne Gospels reveal a love of riddles and surprise, shown through the pattern and interlacing in their meticulously designed pages. The book was produced by the monk Eadfrith on Lindisfarne to commemorate Cuthbert. Interestingly many of its patterns date back beyond the Christian period:

> Prominent are curvilinear motifs ... The spiral, the trumpet and the pelta are all familiar in Celtic art of the Iron Age. There are many varieties of plait and knot work, woven from 'flat' bands of colour or from simple lines, sometimes used in alternating areas of contrasting colour. Step, fret and key patterns are also among the purely linear elements. Most characteristic of all is the zoomorphic interlace, adopted from Germanic art and distinguished in the Lindisfarne Gospels by the extensive introduction of interlaced birds in addition to the more usual interlaced quadrupeds. (Backhouse 1981, p. 47)

Celtic monasticism spread widely. Columba and his followers established monasteries not only at Bangor (NE Ireland), Iona and Lindisfarne, but on the continent of Europe. This is illustrated in the life of Columbanus (c.543–615), an abbot from an Irish noble family who travelled to Gaul with 12 companions in the late sixth century and established the Irish form of monasticism there, at Annegray and Luxeuil, sponsored by the Frankish King Childebert II. He encouraged private penance, which led to the compiling of penitential books where confessors were given lists of sins with a set of penances for each. In later centuries, this new reflective approach to the faith would develop into the widespread practice of confession across the Catholic Church. But Columbanus' monasticism was severe, and monks would be harshly punished if they failed to keep the rules and customs. He was critical of the laxity of the laity, criticizing the polygamy of the king, and as a result was expelled from Burgundy in 610. He travelled east to Metz, where Theudebert II allowed him to establish a new monastery among the semi-pagan Alemanni on the shores of Lake Constance. He was again forced to leave and travelled onward across the Alps to the kingdom of the Lombards in northern Italy. There the king granted him land where he established the monastery of Bobbio, which later became a great centre of learning. Here he wrote his *Monk's Rule* before his death in 615.

The *Monk's Rule* is a key text of Celtic monasticism. The tone is set by its opening words, on obedience:

> At the first word of a senior, all on hearing should rise to obey, since their obedience is shown to God, as our Lord Jesus Christ says: 'He who hears you hears Me.' … Yet if any murmurs, he too, as though not obeying heartily, must be considered disobedient. Therefore let his work be rejected, until his good-will be made known. But up to what measure is obedience laid down? 'Up to death' it is assuredly enjoined, since Christ obeyed the Father up to death for us. (Columbanus c.614, *Rule* 1)

The severity of the *Rule* is shown by a later rule in the section 'Of the Monk's Perfection':

> Thus him who has not kept grace at table and has not responded 'Amen', it is ordained to correct with six blows. Likewise him who has spoken while eating, not because of the wants of another brother, it is ordained to correct with six. If one has called anything his own, with six blows. And him who has not blessed the spoon with which he sups with six blows, and him who has spoken with a shout, that is, has talked in a louder tone than the usual, with six blows. (ibid.)

It is hardly surprising that as the more humane *Rule of Benedict* became known across Europe in the eighth and ninth centuries, it was preferred to Columbanus' rule. Nevertheless Columbanus is credited with reviving Christianity in many parts of Gaul where paganism was threatening to take hold once again.

Celtic monasticism also came into conflict with a different tradition of Roman Christianity, sponsored by Pope Gregory the Great and planted in Britain by the missionaries Augustine, Paulinus and later Wilfrid. They disagreed over the dating of Easter and over the kind of tonsure a monk should have. These disagreements represented a deeper divide between a tribally based church and a more centrally organized church. Which was to become dominant? The Synod of Whitby would help decide the outcome. Before looking at this the rise of Gregory's Roman Church must be explored.

Roman Christianity from Gregory to Charlemagne

As the Roman Empire gave way to the rule of local tribal leaders, the Church also became more locally and tribally focused. The bishops in Gaul were drawn from powerful territorial families, and identified with them. In Visigothic Spain, the bishops had little contact with Rome; in Italy the territories that nominally came under the papacy were stricken with famine and disease and had been invaded by the Lombard tribe from the north. The Emperor at Constantinople also wanted to take control through his provincial ruler, the exarch of Ravenna.

The importance of Pope Gregory is that he revived the temporal rule of the papacy over its lands and also began the process of re-asserting the primacy of the see of Rome over the Western Church in general. He was born around the year 540 and came from one of the ruling aristocratic families who had dominated the city before the end of the Empire. His father had been a senator, and Gregory became a prefect of the city. But he had a change of heart, selling his vast property and giving the proceeds to the establishing of six monasteries in Sicily and one in Rome, which he subsequently entered as a monk himself. After a few years of a very austere life, he was forced to start working for the pope and was sent to Constantinople as an ambassador. He later returned to Rome and became the abbot of his monastery of Saint Andrew. Finally, he was elected pope in 590, the first monk to be elected pope. He only took up the post after a severe internal struggle over whether to do so: he still felt drawn to the monastic life.

Gregory negotiated a peace treaty with the Lombards and pushed back the claims of the exarch of Ravenna. He reformed the civil administration of the papal state and built up its military defences. He also sponsored relief of the starving and poor, spending large sums of the Church's wealth on this. He resisted the claims of the Patriarch of Constantinople to be the 'Ecumenical Patriarch', i.e. the senior bishop in the Church. Gregory upheld the supremacy of the Roman see. He helped to strengthen the position of the Church in Spain, Gaul and northern Italy. He also, as we shall see later, sent one of the monks from his monastery, Augustine, on a mission to England and specifically to the kingdom of Kent.

Gregory was a prolific writer, and his book on the pastoral office of the bishop was influential. He argued that the primary responsibility of the bishop is to be a shepherd of souls. It would later be translated by King Alfred and come to be widely read in Britain. Gregory also energetically promoted monasticism and gave religious orders exemption from the rule of the local bishop, placing them under the direct authority of the papacy. In his understanding of the religious life he was influenced by John Cassian (see pp. 63–4) and believed the heart of the monastic life was the contemplation of God rather than good works or mission. He also reformed the liturgy and encouraged the singing of the text. Gregorian chant, which developed largely after his death, is named after him. All in all Gregory helped to raise the profile of the papacy and to see it established in the West as the primatial see. He called himself 'the servant of the servants of God', which shows his aspiration to humility, but also helped to increase his popularity and power. He was canonized a saint by popular acclaim immediately after his death in 604.

Pope Gregory's sending of Augustine and his companion monks to Kent was one of his most far reaching actions. It shows the strengthening and extending of Roman Christianity in the more remote areas of the old Roman Empire. Bede describes the mission in a very positive way in his church history of 731:

The powerful Ethelbert was at that time king of Kent; he had extended his dominions as far as the great river Humber, by which the Southern Saxons are divided from the Northern. On the east of Kent is the large Isle of Thanet containing, according to the English way of reckoning, 600 families, divided from the other land by the river Wantsum, which is about three furlongs over, and fordable only in two places, for both ends of it run into the sea. In this island landed the servant of our Lord, Augustine, and his companions, being, as is reported, nearly forty men. They had, by order of the blessed Pope Gregory, taken interpreters of the nation of the Franks, and sending to Ethelbert, signified that they were come from Rome, and brought a joyful message, which most undoubtedly assured to all that took advantage of it everlasting joys in heaven and a kingdom that would never end with the living and true God.

Accordingly he permitted them to reside in the city of Canterbury, which was the metropolis of all his dominions, and, pursuant to his promise, besides allowing them sustenance, did not refuse them liberty to preach.

As soon as they entered the dwelling space assigned them they began to imitate the course of life practiced in the primitive Church; applying themselves to frequent prayer, watching and fasting; preaching the word of life to as many as they could; despising all worldly things, as not belonging to them; receiving only their necessary food from those they taught.

There was on the east side of the city a church dedicated to the honour of St. Martin, built whilst the Romans were still in the island, wherein the queen, who, as has been said before, was a Christian, used to pray. In this they first began to meet, to sing, to pray, to say mass, to preach, and to baptize, till the king, being converted to the faith, allowed them to preach openly, and build or repair churches in all places.

When he, among the rest, induced by the unspotted life of these holy men, and their delightful promises, which, by many miracles, they proved to be most certain, believed and was baptized, greater numbers began daily to flock together to hear the word, and, forsaking their heathen rites, to associate themselves, by believing, to the unity of the church of Christ. Their conversion the king so far encouraged, as that he compelled none to embrace Christianity, but only showed more affection to the believers, as to his fellow-citizens in the heavenly kingdom. For he had learned from his instructors and leaders to salvation, that the service of Christ ought to be voluntary, not by compulsion. Nor was it long before he gave his preachers a settled residence in his metropolis of Canterbury, with such possessions of different kinds as were necessary for their subsistence. (Bede 1992, Book 1 Chapters XXV–XXVI)

Pope Gregory decided to send another monk to assist Augustine, and in 601 Paulinus arrived in Britain. He went to the north and converted King Edwin of Northumbria (who reigned between 616 and 632). Paulinus became the first Bishop of York, Justus the first Bishop of Rochester and Mellitus the first Bishop of London. At one point, they had to flee to the continent because of hostility from different Saxon kings but were invited to return by the king of Kent, whereupon Paulinus became Bishop of Rochester.

The tide was now flowing in favour of the new Church, especially after the Synod of Whitby in 664 brought a measure of uniformity to its worship and customs (see pp. 87–90). The key work in putting in place structures that would establish the Church across the country was undertaken by Theodore of Tarsus (602–90), who was consecrated Archbishop of Canterbury by the pope in 668. He travelled throughout England and reformed the government of the Church by dividing dioceses and extending the episcopate. In 672 or 673, he summoned and presided over the first major synod of the whole English Church at Hertford, and in 679, he held another synod at Hatfield, where a declaration of orthodoxy was drawn up and sent to the pope. In these ways, he also established the primacy of the see of Canterbury (though in Yorkshire he met some resistance from Wilfrid; the primacy of Canterbury would later be challenged by a number of archbishops of York). He also did much to prepare the way for the parochial system, supporting the subdivision of dioceses into different areas under the care of monastic churches. (In the tenth century, these 'minster churches' would be supplemented by churches built by local lords of the manor, which became known as manorial churches. By the time of the Doomsday Book in 1086, there were many thousands of these, and they have formed the basis of the parish system that is still in place today.)

Boniface

Missionary and pastoral activity was not confined to the British Isles. Between the sixth and ninth centuries, the Germanic peoples were gradually Christianized: Franks, Saxons, Vandals, Angles, Lombards, Burgundians, Goths, slowly turning the pagan lands of the old Roman Empire into Medieval Europe. Boniface provides an important example of the missionary initiative that came from the British Isles. He was born as Wynfrith in Wessex around 675, was educated at Exeter and became a monk and a scholar at Southampton. After an unsuccessful missionary journey to Frisia, he went to Rome, was commissioned by Gregory II to convert the heathen and was given the name Boniface. He returned to Frisia and then to Hesse, where in front of a hostile crowd he felled the oak of Thor. When he was not struck dead by the god, many then converted to Christianity. It was a turning point. He was able to establish a number of monasteries and set up an episcopal system under the papacy east of the Rhine. He also helped to reform the Frankish Church and was made Archbishop of Mainz around 746. He later returned to missionary work in Frisia and was martyred by brigands in 754. This great Anglo-Saxon missionary became known as the Apostle of Germany.

Charlemagne

Charles the Great (c.742–814) was the King of the Franks from 768. The Franks were the most powerful of the Germanic tribes and had taken control of much of Gaul as Roman power crumbled away. They had converted to Nicene Christianity in about 500, unlike many of the other Germanic tribes which were Arian in their theology (see pp. 71–2). Clovis their king had accepted Christianity through the influence of his mother Clotilde. The Franks retained certain aspects of Roman culture such as Roman roads, buildings, chariot races and the use of Latin. They halted the advance of the Moors at the battle of Poitiers in 732, led by Charles Martel (c.690–741). This was a turning point as now the Frankish kingdom would begin to push the Moors back into the Iberian Peninsula.

Charlemagne expanded the Frankish kingdom into an empire that incorporated much of Western and Central Europe. During his reign he conquered Italy and defeated the Lombards in 774. He came to Rome in 800, and Pope Leo III crowned him 'Emperor of the Romans' (*Imperator Romanorum*). This took place on 25 December 800 and for a time made him a rival of the Byzantine Emperor in Constantinople. After his death, though, his domains would be broken up, and Vikings would make destructive incursions from the north. His was not a new Roman Empire, though he set in place a vision of what Western Europe might become, a vision that was pursued by the papacy in the later Middle Ages. He is also regarded as the founder of the Holy Roman Empire, a loose collection of German states.

Charlemagne's rule is also associated with the Carolingian Renaissance, a revival of art, religion and culture throughout the Catholic Church. He gathered to his court Italian historians and grammarians, Spanish poets and Irish theologians. He created centres of learning in the monasteries at Tours and Fulda. He was influenced by the Roman philosopher Boethius (c.480–524), who in his book *The Consolation of Philosophy* had outlined a systematic approach to all learning. Charlemagne's schools taught the seven liberal arts of arithmetic, astronomy, geometry, grammar, logic, music and rhetoric. It was the high point in the cultural history of the early Middle Ages.

Self-understanding: Bede on the Synod of Whitby

How did these developments affect the institution of the Church? Up to the beginning of this period, as we have seen, the Church was an association within a wider and mostly stable Roman society. It was supported by the Roman state, through Constantine and his successors, and so had a civic status. But it also enjoyed some autonomy and would on occasion criticize the emperor. So it should not be described as a state church but more as an official association. Now, however, that wider social framework had gone, through the Germanic invasions of the Empire from the north and then Islamic encroachments from the south and east. For Western Christians, the question therefore becomes this: how does the corporate life of the Church evolve in the new relationship with tribal princes and kingdoms? Has it, at heart, become a tribal church, with each part under the rule and whim of whichever tribal lord is dominant in that area? Or was the Church through Pope Gregory and his missions rising above the fractures and fissures of tribal struggles and becoming some kind of trans-continental society of people and clergy under the authority of the papacy?

The Synod of Whitby of 664 was a key moment for the identity of the Church and might provide an answer to this question. Bede again gives a graphic account, though it is important to recognize he has a particular point of view on what took place:

And a greater controversy arose about the observance of Easter, and the rules of ecclesiastical life … This reached the ears of King Oswy [or Oswiu, of Northumbria] and his son Alfrid [or Ahlfrith]; for Oswy, having been instructed and baptized by the Scots, and being very perfectly skilled in their language, thought nothing better than what they taught. But Alfrid, having been instructed in Christianity by Wilfrid, a most learned man, who had first gone to Rome to learn the ecclesiastical doctrine, and spent much time at Lyons with Dalfin, Archbishop of France, from whom also he had received the ecclesiastical tonsure, rightly thought this man's doctrine ought to be preferred before all the traditions of the Scots. (Bede 1992, Book 3, Chapter XXV)

Bede, then, begins to show his preference for Wilfrid and the Roman customs. He continues that it was resolved

> that a synod should be held in the monastery of Streaneshaich, which signifies the Bay of the Lighthouse [Whitby], where the Abbess Hilda, a woman devoted to God, then presided; and that there this controversy should be decided. The kings, both father and son, came thither, Bishop Colman with his Scottish clerks, and Agilbert with the priests Agatho and Wilfrid, James and Romanus who were on their side; but the Abbess Hilda and her followers were for the Scots, as was also the venerable Bishop Cedd.

Cedd became 'a most careful interpreter for both parties'. The king opened the Synod with a revealing statement about the importance of uniformity:

> King Oswy first observed, that it behoved those who served one God to observe the same rule of life; and as they all expected the same kingdom in heaven, so they ought not to differ in the celebration of the Divine mysteries; but rather to inquire which was the truest tradition, that the same might be followed by all.

Colman then spoke for the Celtic Church, linking their customs with John the beloved disciple. Wilfrid spoke for the Roman customs and was forthright and harsh against his opponents:

> The Easter which we observe, we saw celebrated by all at Rome, where the blessed apostles, Peter and Paul, lived, taught, suffered, and were buried; we saw the same done in Italy and in France, when we travelled through those countries for pilgrimage and prayer. We found the same practiced in Africa, Asia, Egypt, Greece, and all the world, wherever the church of Christ is spread abroad, through several nations and tongues, at one and the same time; except only these and their accomplices in obstinacy, I mean the Picts and the Britons, who foolishly, in these two remote islands of the world, and only in part even of them, oppose all the rest of the universe.

The debate then moved into technical arguments about which form of calculation had more authority. The hectoring Wilfrid again sought to demean and undermine his opponents:

> But as for you … though your fathers were holy, do you think that their small number, in a corner of the remotest island, is to be preferred before the universal church of Christ throughout the world? And if that Columba of yours (and, I may say, ours also, if he was Christ's servant), was a holy man and powerful in miracles, yet could he be preferred before the most blessed prince of the apostles, to whom our Lord said, 'Thou art Peter, and upon this rock I will build my church.'

Despite this invective, however, it was not Wilfrid who was able to decide the matter. It was the tribal chief, King Oswy, who pronounced judgement, after asking whether Columba had as much power as Peter. When he was told the answer was no, he threw in his lot with Peter: 'And I also say unto you, that he is the door-keeper, whom I will not contradict, but will, as far as I know and am able, in all things obey his decrees, lest, when I come to the gates of the kingdom of heaven, there should be none to open them, he being my adversary who is proved to have the keys.' Everyone else then gave their consent and the Roman customs were triumphant (Bede 1992, Book 3 Chapter XXV).

Not everyone was happy. Bishop Colman was replaced and many of the Celtic monks withdrew to Iona and later to Ireland. The monastery at Iona would not accept the Roman customs for another century. But the Synod brought the Anglo-Saxon Church into line with Roman Christianity on the continent and paved the way for the reforming work of Theodore of Tarsus as Archbishop of Canterbury. Nevertheless, despite this increasing uniformity in the practices of the Church, it is hard to deny that ultimately the British Church and its identity were under the control of the tribal kings rather than the pope in Rome. It was they who decided to adopt Christianity and 'convert' their kingdoms to its practice. It was they who led whole villages, towns and districts to the local river to be baptized and incorporated into the Church. Correspondingly, while the papacy re-asserted and strengthened its authority over the Western Church, this was only because it had been granted authority by different kings to do so, and not the other way round: many kings wanted the status of their churches being linked to Rome. Furthermore a different movement, independent of the papacy, was the real engine of growth for the Church, namely monasticism. This, again, was usually sponsored and encouraged by local kings, who usually appointed one of their own family as the local abbot or abbess. It began in Ireland and then moved across the continent at large. It showed that the Church had become something very different from its former self and was now a tribal entity incorporating everyone within the respective tribe and under the direction of its king.

Returning to Cameron's organizational forms we are in the realms of the first form, that of the Church as a kind of public utility, providing an essential religious service, covering the country, with no membership but 'legal' officers. We have seen that in the early Middle Ages in Western Europe the Church became a kind of tribal utility, intimately connected with the king and his family, who supplied the chief 'officers', and which provided religious authorization and extension of his rule. While it must be acknowledged that the Church still retained a sense of Catholic identity transcending local lords and kingdoms, an aspiration expressed in its use of the Latin language and by the existence and strengthening of the pope in Rome, this aspiration existed because it suited many of kings that it should do so.

But in the next period the aspiration to Catholicity would steadily strengthen the hand of the papacy and create one of the great power struggles in church history. What happened to the nature of the Church itself within this turbulent period?

Discussion Questions

Why did cenobitic monasticism gradually replace hermitic monasticism?

Should Pope Leo III have crowned Charlemagne as 'Emperor of the Romans'?

Was the Celtic Church right to oppose the Romanizers and protect its own customs?

Bibliography and Further Reading

Adamnan (1874), *Life of Saint Columba, Founder of Hy. Written by Adamnan, Ninth Abbot of that Monastery*, ed. William Reeves, Edinburgh: Edmonston and Douglas.

Backhouse, Janet (1981), *The Lindisfarne Gospels*, Oxford: Phaidon.

Banner, Michael (2009), *Christian Ethics: A Brief History*, Oxford: Wiley-Blackwell.

Bede (1992), *Bede the Venerable, Saint, 673–735: Bede's Ecclesiastical History of the English people*, eds, Bertram Colgrave and R. A. B. Mynors, Oxford: Clarendon Press.

Bede (1910), 'Life and Miracles of St. Cuthbert', in *Ecclesiastical History of the English Nation*, trans. J. A. Giles, Everyman's Library 479, London: J. M. Dent.

Benedict (1990), *The Rule of Saint Benedict*, trans. Abbot Parry OSB with commentary by Esther de Waal, Leominster: Gracewing.

Bettenson, Henry and Chris Maunder (eds) (2011), *Documents of the Christian Church*, 4th edn, Oxford: Oxford University Press.

Bosch, David (1991), *Transforming Mission: Paradigms Shifts in Theology of Mission*, Maryknoll, NY: Orbis.

Clark, James G. (2011), *The Benedictines in the Middle Ages*, Woodbridge: The Boydell Press.

Columbanus, (c.614), *The Monk's Rule*, trans. G. S. M. Walker, at http://www.ucc.ie/celt/published/T201052/index.html.

MacCulloch, Diarmaid (2009), *A History of Christianity: The First Three Thousand Years*, Chs 8 and 10, Harmondsworth: Allen Lane.

Miles, Margaret (2004), *The Word Made Flesh: A History of Christian Thought*, Oxford: Wiley-Blackwell.

6

Medieval Catholicism: Papal or Monastic?

The tenth century saw the end of the Viking raids and an opportunity for the new nation states of northern Europe to consolidate their national life. Improvements in agriculture over the next two centuries saw rising populations and greater prosperity. Towns and cities began to grow. The parish system became more and more widespread, with churches being built and re-built by local lords of the manor and becoming parish churches within wider dioceses and increasingly under the authority of an urban bishop as opposed to a remote abbey. All this resulted in the biggest programme of church building in Europe's history between 1100 and 1300. The Romanesque style, which had grown out of classical architecture, evolved into the Gothic style and to the building of some of the finest cathedrals and churches of any era of Christian history.

This was a period with a rich culture and an abundance of cultural and ecclesiological developments, so all we can do in this chapter is look at a selection of developments that throw light on our underlying theme, the evolution of the corporate life of the Church. There are many developments that could be described but four especially demand attention.

Timeline	
910	Founding of Cluny Abbey
988	Baptism of Vladimir, prince of Kiev: 'the conversion of Russia'

1049–54	Pope Leo IX begins reforming the Western Church
1054	East–West Schism: mutual excommunications
1073–85	Pope Gregory VII (Hildebrand)
1090–1153	Bernard of Clairvaux (preaches to the Second Crusade 1146)
1093–1109	Anselm Archbishop of Canterbury
1095	Pope Urban II calls for the first Crusade
1098	Citeaux Abbey founded (the Cistercians)
1098–1179	Hildegard of Bingen
1099	First Crusade captures Jerusalem
1123	First Lateran Council
1131	Rievaulx Abbey founded
1140	Start of the rise of the Cathars, in Germany then southern France
1170	Martyrdom of Archbishop Thomas Becket
c.1184–1226	Francis of Assisi
1187	Loss of Jerusalem and 1189 beginning of Third Crusade
1198–1216	Pope Innocent III: the height of papal power
1204	Sack of Constantinople by Crusaders
1209	Beginning of the Franciscans
1215	Fourth Lateran Council (annual confession made obligatory)
1220	Dominicans founded, to oppose the Cathars
c.1225–74	Thomas Aquinas
1232	Papal Inquisition established
1291	Loss of the Holy Land
1302	Boniface VIII issues *Unam Sanctam*

Papal Power Struggles Between the Tenth and Thirteenth Centuries

Between pope and king

In Western Europe the next four centuries witnessed some bitter power struggles between rising kingdoms and the papacy. At some points the papacy was dominant and, at others, certain kings (usually German) held sway. The origin of these struggles lay in the tenth century, when the papacy was weakened through a succession of corrupt and sometimes incompetent popes. Rival Italian aristocratic families competed with each other to get their own family member onto the throne of Saint Peter. One of these popes, John XII, sought the help of the German King Otto I against a rival king, Berengar, and in return he crowned Otto as Roman Emperor. Otto then gained control over the papal states and over the papacy itself. When John fell out with Otto on other matters, he was deposed by the king, who then installed a succession of different popes from his own dynasty.

The eleventh century, on the other hand, witnessed a resurgence of the papacy under a succession of reforming popes who came from Germany: Clement II (1046–7), who began to enforce clerical celibacy and stopped simony (the buying and selling of ecclesiastical offices); Leo IX (1049–54), who continued this programme through travelling across Europe to enforce it; and Gregory VII, who at the Lateran Synod of 1059 (before he became pope) helped to establish the practice of cardinals electing a new pope. When he became pope himself (1073–85), he turned the papacy into a structured and disciplined institution. He further enforced clerical celibacy and sought to end lay investiture, which was the practice of kings and other secular rulers appointing bishops in their own territories. This was clearly going to strengthen the papacy and weaken the kings because bishops would have a stronger loyalty to the pope than to their local king.

Unsurprisingly this last measure was resisted by rulers including William I of England, Philip I of France and especially Henry IV of Germany. At first, Gregory had the upper hand because Henry was in a weakened position owing to the presence of rival Normans in southern Italy. Gregory capitalized on this by issuing his 'Dictates', which contain the following trenchant assertions:

Only the Bishop of Rome is legitimately called universal bishop.

He alone can depose or reinstate bishops.

He alone is permitted, if the age requires it, to decree new laws, establish new bishoprics, transform chapters of canons into monasteries and vice versa, divide rich sees and combine poor ones.

He alone may use imperial insignia.

All rulers have to kiss only the Pope's feet.

He is permitted to depose emperors.

Henry called two synods, at Worms and Piacenza, at which Gregory's papacy was declared invalid. However, Gregory had support from others including the Normans and could respond by excommunicating the king. German nobles were thereby released from their oaths of allegiance to Henry. The king realized he had gone too far and travelled to the Alpine castle of Canossa, where Gregory was residing, to try to find reconciliation. On 25 January 1077, bare-footed and in penitential garb, he appeared before the castle gate asking for Gregory's pardon. This was a highly symbolic moment in European history: a king was showing to the other rulers of Europe that the pope had superior authority. It showed that the clergy had the right to oversee and guide aspects of civil government in Europe and that Rome had a degree of political as well as ecclesiastical supremacy.

Gregory reinstated Henry but resentment continued, and three years later Henry set up a rival papacy. In 1084, he marched against and took Rome. Gregory had to flee from the city when the population turned against him and he died at Salerno. But the whole dispute destabilized Henry's rule and created an environment in Western Europe in which prince-fiefdoms would rise to power in the twelfth century. Struggles between monarchies and churches would also continue, for example the struggles between Anselm the Archbishop of Canterbury and Henry I of England in 1100, and then again between Thomas Beckett and Henry II, leading to Beckett's famous martyrdom in 1170. Popes and German kings came into conflict as well, such as that between Pope Callistus and Henry V and Pope Hadrian (the only English pope) and Frederick Barbarossa in the 1150s.

The papacy finally gained the upper hand at the start of the thirteenth century under Pope Innocent III (1198–1216). He was the first pope to make regular use of the title 'Vicar of Christ', which elevated his status above everyone else. He reformed church administration and the hierarchy; he supported Francis of Assisi and Dominic (see pp. 103–6); and convened the Fourth Lateran Council in 1215. This confirmed the official doctrine of the mass, employing the term 'transubstantiation' for the first time. Certain heresies were rebutted, such as those of the Albigensians, Cathars and Waldensians. Various clerical abuses were forbidden. Innocent also intervened in the elections of new emperors of Germany; he forced the English King John to accept his choice of Stephen Langton as Archbishop of Canterbury and intervened in a number of other countries, showing a level of political power over the kings of Europe that no other pope enjoyed. But part of the reason for his power was the weakness of the current occupants of the thrones of Europe. King John, for example, was unable to stand up to his nobles and needed the support of the pope to secure his own position. In reality, Innocent was just one among a number of other players in European politics.

Between East and West

As the Western Church gained in strength through its alliances and competition with feudal kings and lords, so tensions with the Byzantine Christianity of Constantinople deepened. These tensions erupted with the East–West Schism of 1054, which divided Christendom into Eastern (Greek speaking) and Western (Latin speaking) branches, becoming Eastern Orthodoxy and Roman Catholicism respectively.

Division was focused on the *Filioque* clause in the Nicene Creed. This term is the Latin for 'and from the Son', a phrase that had been officially sanctioned at the Council of Toledo in 589. However, by the ninth century, it had become a bone of contention for the Eastern Church, and when Patriarch Photius attacked the Church of Rome in 864, he cited the *Filoque* clause as one of the main reasons for his attack. The Eastern Church could not accept the 'double procession' of the Holy Spirit 'from the Son' as well as from the Father: for them it was an insertion that had not been approved by an ecumenical council and it also undermined the Father being the 'origin' of the other two persons. There was also disagreement on whether Constantinople or Rome was the primary see of the whole Church, and also on the relationship between Constantinople and the pentarchy of the most senior patriarchs (i.e. of Jerusalem, Alexandria, Antioch, Rome and Constantinople itself). Behind all this lay fundamental differences between Greek and Western Latin ways of speaking and thinking.

Pope Leo IX (1049–54) and Patriarch of Constantinople Michael Cerularius heightened the conflict by suppressing Greek or Latin in their respective domains. In 1054, Roman legates travelled to Constantinople to deny Cerularius the title of Ecumenical Patriarch and insist that he recognize the Church of Rome's claim to be the head and mother of the churches. Naturally, Cerularius refused. The leader of the Latin contingent, Cardinal Humbert, then excommunicated Cerularius. Cerularius in return excommunicated Humbert and the other Latin legates. Unbeknown to them, Pope Leo had died in Rome so Humbert's action was of doubtful validity, while Cerularius's excommunication applied only to the legates personally and not to the Western Church as a whole. Nevertheless, the outcome of this unhappy meeting was the formalizing of a tragic split along doctrinal, linguistic, political and geographical lines.

It would be deepened and embittered by the massacre of Latin traders in Constantinople in 1182 and then, in 1204, by the shocking sack of Constantinople (including the destruction of its library) by the Crusaders. To this day, the breach has never been healed. But it left the pope as undisputed head of the Western Church.

Between Christian and Muslim

Muslim control over Asia Minor and Syria tightened during the eleventh century and the Byzantine Empire felt increasingly vulnerable. In the early 1090s, Emperor Alexius Comnenus appealed to the West for help, and Pope Urban II answered the appeal. In 1095, he called for Christian soldiers to liberate Jerusalem and protect Christendom against the Muslim invaders. The first to respond were Frankish armies from France and southern Italy who sailed to Syria and captured territory there, and then marched on Palestine and took the city of Jerusalem. This was accompanied by a shameful slaughter of the Jews and Muslims living there. Latin states were created at Antioch, Tripoli, Edessa and Jerusalem, and Duke Godfrey of Bouillon became its first ruler in 1099.

However, the Muslim armies re-grouped and fought back, re-capturing Edessa in 1144. Fear that Jerusalem would also soon fall led the pope to proclaim a second crusade in 1147. This time it was French and German armies that marched through Syria but they were defeated by Seljuk Turks and had to withdraw from Damascus. Then in 1187 Jerusalem was captured by Saladin, and many of the crusaders were forced out of their fortified cities and killed.

Crusades were also launched against pagan tribes in Scandinavia and Russia: the Saxons and Danes against the Wends in 1147, and against Finns in the 1150s, and the Danes against the Slavs in 1184. Latvia, Lithuania and Estonia were subjected to forced conversions and military conquest by Pope Celestine's crusade in 1193. Furthermore, in 1147, a crusade was launched against the Moors in the Iberian Peninsula. Catalonia was reconquered by 1148.

After Saladin's victory it was only a matter of time before a third crusade to the Holy Land would be launched. This took place between 1189 and 1192 and was led by Germans, French and the English army of Richard I. It was the largest military endeavour of the medieval period but it was only able to recapture Palestinian coastal territory.

Pope Innocent III then called a fourth crusade in 1202, which assembled a smaller force than before. Venetian ships were needed to transport the army to the Holy Land, but while en route the crusaders were unable to pay for their passage, and so they agreed to join forces with the Venetians and attack Constantinople! In 1204, against the wishes of the pope, the combined armies of the Christian West therefore attacked and sacked the principal city of the Orthodox East. The Greek Patriarch was replaced by a Latin patriarch from Venice. The onward crusade to the Holy Land was abandoned.

This episode, as already noted, showed the complete disunity of Christian West and East. It also made it very unlikely that the Holy Land would be recovered. The Muslim armies would continue to threaten and encroach on Europe, though Jerusalem was briefly re-captured between 1229 and 1244. In 1291, the last Latin possessions on the Syrian mainland fell to Mamluk. Constantinople itself would fall, finally, in 1453.

But, despite these failures, one side effect of the crusades was to stop the European barons fighting each other and to become united against a common non-Christian enemy. Ultimately they failed to hold Jerusalem for Christendom, but they united their emerging nation states in a common 'Christian' endeavour (and united the Muslim states against them). Ironically the crusades allowed the papacy to draw together the fractious tribal peoples of Europe under its own leadership.

Monasticism: From Cluny to the Cistercians

But is the medieval Catholic Church to be defined ultimately by the rising power of the papacy? There is a different, multi-faceted development that suggests otherwise. This is the evolution of monasticism, which in wave after wave of renouncing worldly power paradoxically exercised a greater and greater power over the hearts and minds of the general population of Europe and also over its Church.

Cluny

At the beginning of the tenth century, most monastic houses were owned by local lords and the appointment of their abbots and abbesses was up to the families that owned them. This led to the appointment of untrained and some-times unordained men and women and a loss of the vision of what the houses were meant to be about. It was in this setting that William of Aquitaine, want-ing something better, decided to found a monastery that would be independent of local rulers and would report to the pope. He founded Cluny Abbey in the Burgundy region of France in 910. He nominated Berno as the first Abbot of Cluny, to be subject only to Pope Sergius III. The Abbey was to follow the Rule of Benedict, which was becoming well known across Europe. The second abbot, Odo, brought about a strict adherence to Benedict's Rule, cementing the con-nection between it and Cluny and creating what would become known as the Benedictine order. Quite soon, other abbeys in the region were being put under his supervision, showing that his approach was popular with benefactors and brethren.

Under subsequent abbots the net widened, taking in abbeys in northern France, Italy and the Iberian Peninsula. 'In the first quarter century of the foun-dation, there were seventeen houses bound together by Cluny; by the time of its first centenary, there were several hundred' (Clark 2011, p. 41).

What was the secret of this growth? Every house had to recognize the abbot of Cluny as its abbot. The abbot made regular visits to priories and the priors met at Cluny once a year. The abbot also accrued the patronage of a large number of parish churches. 'By 1050 the churches of southern Burgundy bore the imprint of Cluny in their architecture, their patrons and pastors, and presumably, their patterns of worship' (ibid.). Their influence would extend throughout Western Europe by 1130.

What was at the heart of their life? 'There can be no doubt its mode of life was founded on an *ad literam* adherence to the Rule of Benedict. Berno and his successors embraced the liturgical regime of the rule ... The special character of Cluny's opus strengthened the attachment of her patrons and caused her to embellish, and lengthen, the founder's offices' (ibid.). The monks of Cluny, then, came to embrace a commitment to offer perpetual prayer, emphasizing liturgy and spiritual pursuits over labour and other monastic activities. At Cluny, the liturgy became extensive and beautifully presented in increasingly inspiring architectural surroundings, reflecting a new personally felt wave of piety in the eleventh century. Monastic intercession came to be seen as indispensable for a believer to achieve a state of grace, and rulers competed to be remembered in Cluny's endless prayers, giving endowments in land as well as cash. Cluniac estates, in turn, became very productive and wealthy. Cluny's monasteries attracted many of the most able people in society and became the central store-houses and producers of knowledge in eleventh-century Europe.

On 30 September 1088, construction began on the third abbey church at Cluny ('Cluny III'), financed by kings and nobility. In 1098, Pope Urban II (him-self a Cluniac) declared that Cluny was the 'light of the world'. In 1130, the abbey was dedicated by Pope Innocent II. Construction continued until 1190. It was now the largest church in Christendom and would remain so until the re-building of Saint Peter's in Rome in the sixteenth century. (It would survive until the French Revolution, when it was demolished for its stone.)

At the start of the twelfth century, Cluny was at the height of its influence: it was head of a monastic 'empire' of 10,000 monks; abbots of Cluny were almost as powerful as popes (four of them actually became popes); and the general monk was now raised to the level of the nobility. It shows, significantly, that the medieval Catholic Church was not centred on Rome: the engine of revival and growth was elsewhere.

Cistercians

But in the same year that the pope had declared Cluny to be the 'light of the world', one of its abbots, Robert of Molesme, decided that the Cluniac communities had abandoned the rigours and simplicity of Benedict's Rule. A new and simpler start must be made, and this became the second great wave of monastic renewal and growth in the medieval period. In 1098, Robert acquired a plot of marshland just south of Dijon called Citeaux (Latin: Cistercium, Cisteaux means 'reeds' in old French) and left his Cluniac monastery with around 20 supporters to settle there. The monastery was established, and then, in 1108, Stephen Harding was elected as abbot. He framed the original version of the Cistercian 'constitution' or rule, called the *Carta Caritatis* (Charter of Charity). This emphasized a simple life of work, love, prayer and self-denial. The monks were to wear white habits rather than the black habits of Cluny. They were not to admit children, unlike the Cluniac monasteries, so ensuring that monks chose their religious vocation for themselves at a suitable age. Harding also acquired farming land for the abbey to ensure its survival, but he would accept only un-developed land, so that the monks would have to work the land by their own labour. He accepted illiterate peasants as lay brothers, who were bound by vows of chastity and obedience to their abbot, but were otherwise permitted to fol-low a less demanding form of Cistercian life. Their incorporation into the order represented a new outreach to the peasantry.

One of the most influential Cistercians was Bernard of Clairvaux (1090–1153). He was sent by Harding to found a new abbey, and he did this at Clair-vaux in 1115. It soon became one of the chief centres of the Cistercian Order. Bernard taught a personal faith with great devotion to Mary. His monastery had a rigorous discipline that attracted large numbers of recruits. He also came to exercise immense influence in ecclesiastical and political affairs across Europe. He supported Innocent II in a disputed election for the papacy, and when Inno-cent was successfully elected he showered privileges upon the Cistercian order. Bernard wrote about the Church being the bridegroom of Christ. He was an opponent of the theologian Abelard and helped to arrange his condemnation at the Council of Sens in 1140. Unusually for this time, he opposed the persecu-tion of Jewish people across Europe. Less attractively, Bernard also rallied kings and barons to support the second crusade. But he was above all a monk, who embodied the humility and devotion of the religious life. As his fame grew, so did the Cistercian order, with houses being established across Europe.

In 1128, the order reached the British Isles at Waverly Abbey, Surrey. It often sought out solitude in the mountains and moorlands. In Wales, for example, 13 Cistercian monasteries, all in remote sites, were founded between 1131 and

1226. The first, Tintern Abbey, depended largely on its agricultural and pastoral activities for survival. The austere discipline of the Cistercian monks seemed to echo the ideals of the Celtic saints, and an emphasis on sheep farming fitted well into the Welsh stock-rearing economy. Cistercians brought the Welsh to faith more successfully than the Benedictines had done.

In Yorkshire, the Cistercians from Clairvaux founded Rievaulx Abbey in 1131, on a small property 'in a place of horror and dreary solitude'. By 1143, 300 monks had entered Rievaulx, including the famous Aelred, who became known as the 'Bernard of England'. Fountains Abbey was founded in 1132 by Benedictine monks from St Mary's Abbey, York, who desired a return to the austere Rule of Benedict. But after experiencing many struggles and hardships, they appealed to Bernard for help, and he agreed to send a monk from Clairvaux to instruct them, and in the end they prospered. Fountains had many offshoots, of which Newminster Abbey (1137) and Meaux Abbey (1151) are the most famous. Other Cistercian Abbeys in Yorkshire were founded at Byland, Roche and Kirkstall. It is recognized that these abbeys and others across Europe made an extensive impact on the lives of ordinary people, not least through the example of their sheep farming and care of their estates.

By the time of Bernard's death, there were 345 houses, in almost every part of Europe and the Latin East. By the end of the thirteenth century, the order reached its maximum of 740 houses, and there were still 700 on the eve of the Reformation. The abbeys stayed in contact with each other through annual visits by their abbots to the houses from which they were founded, or to Citeaux, where an annual general chapter was held. This chapter had authority over the whole order.

Once again, then, an extensive and highly influential order had developed independently of the see of Rome and its power, functioning as an ordered network to support the work of intercessory prayer by monks.

Hildegard of Bingen

Benedictine monasteries could still be found across Europe and some of them continued to be centres of renewal and growth. One of these, at Disibodenberg near Mainz, had a remarkable abbess, Hildegard (1098–1179). She had had a series of intense mystical experiences of God and wrote about them. She gained the support of her bishop and, with Bernard's support, of the pope as well. Between 1147 and 1151, she moved her community to Rupertsberg near Bingen, where a large convent was built. She travelled widely and became an adviser to the Emperor Frederick Barbarossa and other kings. She not only governed her nuns but became a famous herbalist. She wrote treatises about the natural history and medicinal uses of plants, animals, trees and gemstones. Her writings include the earliest known reference to using hops in beer: 'when put in beer, stops putrification and lends longer durability'. She used the curative powers of natural objects for healing. She was also a musician, composing chant to accompany her verse. Her haunting chants are sung to this day.

Renouncing Wealth: the Franciscan and Dominican Friars

But monastic renewal had not yet run its course. A third wave of renewal and growth transformed it into something very different from its former self. This wave originated with Francis of Assisi, one of the most venerated religious figures in history, and with the Order of Friars Minor, which he founded in 1209.

Francis was born as Giovanni Francesco di Bernardone around 1181. He was the son of a wealthy cloth merchant in Assisi and lived a high-spirited life typical of a wealthy young man, including fighting as a soldier for Assisi. He was held captive for a year and when he returned home he also experienced a long illness. When going off to war again in 1204, he had a vision that directed him back to Assisi, where he lost his taste for his former life. On a pilgrimage to Rome, he joined the beggars outside St Peter's and, exchanging his clothes with one of them, began begging with them. Returning home, he broke with his old life and was renounced by his father. He overcame his fear of leprosy when he embraced a leper, and then experienced a call from the Lord to rebuild the Church. At first he took this literally, physically rebuilding a derelict church at San Damiano outside Assisi. But then he saw that the call was to spiritually rebuild the whole Church. This, as we have seen, was at a point when the papacy was at the height of its worldly power, yet Francis was being shown that all was not well with the Roman Church.

One morning in about 1208, while attending mass in the church of the

Portiuncula in the plain below Assisi, he heard Jesus' words from scripture calling on his disciples to leave everything and follow him, and Francis took this personally. He discarded his staff and shoes, put on a sackcloth garment with a rope as a belt, and began a preaching ministry among the ordinary people, depending on their alms to live. His simple and unaffected faith was combined with a passionate devotion to God and a love of nature. His profound humility won over those who came across him. Soon a number of other young men joined him in this life, and Francis drew up a short and simple rule of life (*Regula Primitiva*, now lost) to guide their common life. On a visit to Rome, he was able to get verbal approval for this from Innocent III, a remarkable achievement given the oddness of what Francis was advocating. Francis sent his brethren out to preach in pairs, calling them 'friars minor', the first of what would be the first mendicant (begging) order. The number of friars began to increase dramatically, and in 1212 a noble lady from Assisi, Clare, secured his agreement to found a parallel contemplative community for women, the Poor Clares, who would be based at San Damiano.

Francis probably attended the Fourth Lateran Council in Rome in 1215, one of the great reforming synods of church history. At the Council, his order was not obliged to adopt an existing rule but was allowed to continue to live in the world in poverty and simplicity. By 1217, the order had grown so much that it was divided into provinces, each with its own minister to supervise its life.

In 1219, with a mixture of courage and foolishness, Francis travelled to Egypt to try to convert the Sultan. The crusades were still taking place, and Francis was present at the siege and capture of Damietta. At great risk, he walked across the enemy lines and asked to meet the Sultan. He was granted an audience with Ayyubid sultan al-Kamil, but did not convert him!

On his return to Italy, he found division within the order and mounting opposition from bishops who found the order's way of life disturbing. Francis re-wrote the rule but only sought and obtained approval for it from the pope in 1223. This rule is known as the *Regula Bullata*: 'The rule and life of the lesser brothers is this: To observe the holy gospel of our Lord Jesus Christ, living in obedience without anything of our own, and in chastity' (Francis of Assisi 1223, Chapter I).

The rule insisted on complete poverty not only for the friars but for the order as a whole:

The brothers should appropriate neither house, nor place, nor anything for themselves; and they should go confidently after alms, serving God in poverty and humility, as pilgrims and strangers in this world. Nor should they feel ashamed, for God made himself poor in this world for us. This is that peak of the highest poverty which has made you, my dearest brothers, heirs and kings of the kingdom of heaven, poor in things but rich in virtues. Let this be your portion. It leads into the land of the living and, adhering totally to it, for the sake of our Lord Jesus Christ, wish never to have anything else in this world, beloved brothers. And wherever brothers meet one another, let them act like members of a common family. (ibid., Chapter VI)

The contrast with the Cluniacs and Cistercians could not be greater: there was to be no accumulation of vast estates and construction of huge buildings. There is also implicit criticism of the central structures of the Church, which were working hard to acquire wealth and influence. This is one of the reasons Francis was criticized by many of the bishops. Yet, he pledged loyalty to the papacy: 'Brother Francis promises obedience and reverence to the Lord Pope Honorius and his canonically elected successors, and to the Roman Church' (Chapter I). This was a key reason why his rule was approved and why the order was allowed to grow.

Francis handed over the day-to-day leadership to others but remained as spiritual leader. Lay people started joining the friars, and they were formed into the Third Order. In 1223, Francis also arranged for the first Christmas crib to be made. In September 1224, while on retreat on Mount St Verna, he somehow received the marks of the crucifixion in his hands and side, the stigmata. He died on 16 July 1228, and only two years later, because of his popularity, was pronounced a saint by the pope. By now Franciscan friars were to be found across Europe.

After his death it was inevitable that the order would begin to acquire property, and as it did two schools of thought developed within the order: the 'Spirituals', who did not want this to happen, and the 'Conventuals', who believed some property was necessary. After 1245, there was sharp division in the order, but Bonaventura, Francis' successor as Minister General, was able to restore some unity. But the disagreement would continue into the thirteenth and fourteenth centuries, showing the ultimate impossibility of fulfilling what Francis required. Nevertheless, the existence and popularity of the order kept before the wider Church the need to renounce rather than accumulate power and wealth. It is a tribute to the papacy that it was willing to give approval to the Franciscans, even though it embodied a very different vision of the Church.

It is important to add that the Friars Minor sent missionaries to the farthest corners of the known world. Franciscan friars followed Marco Polo to China and worked in North Africa among the Muslims. They accompanied Christopher Columbus to the New World, building their famous missions throughout Latin America and California. Friars accompanied La Perouse to Australia, and after his death one of them was buried in Sydney, which became Australia's oldest European grave.

The Franciscans were not the only new order of mendicant friars to be established at this time. The Dominicans, or Order of Preachers, was founded by Dominic in 1220 in Bologna. They were founded to rebuff heretics such as the Cathars, a popular sect in Lombardy and southern France, not least in Albi, who were dualists and believed Christians should live lives of austere purity (the name Cathar comes from the Greek word for 'pure'). Dominican friars travelled around the affected areas, preaching against the Cathars and being supported by alms. They quickly became closely associated with study, education and the new universities. They also became officers of the Inquisition, when it became active from around 1230. Thomas Aquinas, the subject of the next section, is their most famous representative.

The story of monasticism, from Cluny to the mendicants, is also a story of the Church itself being transformed. Now there were not only national churches, acting as the religious arm of the ruler and linked to his family, and a papacy wielding power within the shifting politics of the day, but also a series of dynamic monastic networks serving the work of prayer and evangelization across the continent. It is clear that the orders won over broad swathes of the ordinary people, who welcomed and supported them as they created houses or walked through their villages preaching and depending on begging. They allowed the Church to grow from the grass roots upwards as well as from the top down.

Self-understanding: Aquinas on Princely Government

This chapter has charted some very contrasting developments in the life of the medieval Catholic Church. On the one hand, the papacy has been seen to engage in various struggles for power and to have increased its sway over the life of Western Europe, not least through bringing together the barons and kings of Western Europe to fight the crusades. The reign of Pope Innocent III represents the high water mark of this power. Yet, on the other hand, popular initiatives for renewal and growth have come from elsewhere and, in particular, from the monastic movement. Two successive orders sought to recapture a simple and authentic form of monastic life away from the centres of power, and both quickly gained great support and growth. Ironically, in doing so, they acquired a level of influence and power that rivalled and sometimes outshone that of the papacy. This was true of the Benedictine order that grew out of Cluny and of the Cistercian order that grew from Citeaux. It was also true of the Franciscans, who explicitly renounced wealth and embraced a lifestyle dependent on the charity of others but who then became more popular and more influential than any other order within the Church. While all three orders sought out and received the support of the papacy and needed the papacy to provide some form of validation, there is no hiding the fact that their energy and inspiration came from elsewhere, from the rural hinterlands and emerging townships of Europe, rather than from its papal centre.

How, then, can the nature of the Church in this period be characterized? Has it become a centrally organized institution transcending the tribal and national identities of its people, a community or society over and above the different societies of the continent, as theologians of a later era would argue? Or is it something else, a series of interlocking networks of people whose primary identity still comes from their geographical location in different clans and nations but whose spiritual and religious life is directed by the example and teaching of a succession of monastic orders, orders that bring wave after wave of renewal and growth to the Church?

It is a complex picture and cannot easily be summed up. With so many centres of power and growth the organizational form of the Church cannot be described as a single community or society but might best be described as a polycentric network, with links to Cameron's fifth form of 'network resource', an organizational form 'to support a group of people who already have a shared and stated aim' (see p. 4). In this case, the shared and stated aim was the work of monastic intercession to assist the souls of the living and departed on their journey from earth to the state of grace of heaven. It is possible to see that the Church had now grown into an impressive web of routes and centres of communication – monastic, mendicant, national and papal – facilitating this key work.

As in previous chapters this question can be further explored through looking at the ways the Church understood its own life and, in particular, through exploring the views of the period's greatest theologian, Thomas Aquinas (c.1225–74).

Aquinas is an especially appropriate figure to examine because even though he was a Dominican friar his education and intellectual life was rooted outside the confines of the Church, in the new universities. This gave him something of an independent vantage point. The universities had been founded out of monastic schools in response to the influx of learning from the Islamic world. This learning had come from Spain, particularly Toledo, which had been conquered by Spanish Christians in 1085 and where Gerard of Cremone (1114–87) had translated many Arabic texts. Secondly, it came through Sicily, which had been conquered by Muslims in 965 but reconquered by the Normans in 1091. Here, an intense Arab-Norman culture developed, exemplified by Roger II, who had Islamic soldiers, poets and scientists at his court. The Moroccan Muhammad al-Idrisi wrote for Roger 'The Book of Pleasant Journeys into Faraway Lands' or *Tabula Rogeriana*, one of the greatest geographical treatises of the Middle Ages.

The Crusades also intensified exchanges between Europe and the Middle East; Italian maritime republics took a big role in these exchanges. In Antioch, Arab and Latin cultures intermixed intensively. Burgundio of Pisa (d.1193) discovered lost texts of Aristotle and translated these into Latin. They would come to have a profound influence on Aquinas.

As prosperity increased and towns grew in size in the twelfth century so the need for an educated class of citizen grew. University halls were founded by those who wanted to become students: in Bologna (1088), Paris (c.1150), Salerno (1173), Oxford (c.1190), Vicenza (1204), Palencia (1208), Cambridge (1209) and then a large number of other cities.

Aquinas had joined the Dominicans at an early age and they were now a dominant force at the new University of Paris. Thomas moved to Paris to study theology after initial philosophical training at Cologne under Albert Magnus.

His great project became the integration of Aristotle's philosophical method with theology and especially with the theology of Augustine of Hippo.

Aquinas produced commentaries on scripture and on Aristotle's works. He wrote two major treatises: the *Summa contra Gentiles*, which gave an account of the Christian faith based upon reason and nature rather than upon revelation in scripture; secondly, *Summa Theologica*, a vast and unfinished theological treatise. Among other things it famously shows how God's existence can be 'proved' in 'five ways'; it shows how ethics can be derived from the natural functions and goals of things (natural law); and it combines the virtues from Aristotle, such as courage, temperance and magnanimity, with the Christian virtues of faith, hope and love.

Aquinas presents an unsurpassed synthesis of reason and revelation, Greek philosophy and scripture, ancient learning and medieval Catholicism. But towards the end of his life he had an intense mystical experience of God, which led him to put down his pen for his remaining days.

What light, then, does Aquinas shine on the nature of the Church? A suitable point of entry to his vast thought is his teaching on natural law. He is convinced that natural law is ubiquitous in humans. Following Aristotle, he believes that humans have a natural tendency towards happiness or well-being (*eudaimonia*), leading ultimately, for the Christian, to a beatific vision of God. This is the 'end' of humans (in both senses) and is the main spur for morality in all people. While sin has impaired the capacity of humans to achieve this, God provides help through his grace, and especially through instilling the theological virtues.

Politics shares in this: it can and should be all about helping human communities move toward their end, and so is a high calling. It can and should be based on natural law deriving from creation and can lead communities along the road to salvation. In his epistle to a king, *De Regimine Principium* (on princely government), Aquinas writes that

[a] king ... should realise that he has assumed the duty of being to his kingdom what the soul is to the body and what God is to the universe. If he thinks attentively upon this point he will, on the one hand, be fired with zeal for justice, seeing himself appointed to administer justice throughout his realm in the name of God, and, on the other hand, he will grow in mildness and clemency, looking upon the persons subject to his government, as the members of his own body. (Aquinas, p. 125)

Aquinas then provides a memorable metaphor for the point he is making:

> We must first have in mind that to govern is to guide what is governed to its
> appointed end. So we say that a ship is under control when it is sailed on its
> right course to port by the skill of a sailor. Now when something is ordered
> to an end which lies outside itself, as a ship to its harbour, it is the ruler's duty
> not only to preserve its integrity, but also to see that it reaches its appointed
> destination. (ibid., p. 126)

This presents the role of kingship in very exalted terms: it is a high view of the
role of the ruler in the emerging nation states of Europe. What of the Church
and the role of its clergy and papacy? Where is this to be located?

> The enjoyment of God cannot be attained by human virtue alone, but only
> through divine grace … Only a divine rule, then, and not human government,
> can lead us to this end … The ministry of this kingdom is entrusted not to the
> rulers of this earth but to priests, so that temporal affairs may remain distinct
> from those spiritual: and, in particular, it is delegated to the High Priest, the
> successor of Peter and Vicar of Christ, the Roman Pontiff, to whom all kings
> in Christendom should be subjects, as to the Lord Jesus Christ Himself. (ibid.,
> pp. 127–8)

Aquinas is here retrieving and re-presenting the separation of the temporal and
spiritual realms that we saw in Augustine of Hippo, which that theologian described as the distinction between the City of God and City of Man (see pp. 65–
9). The clergy and the pope have a role in relation to the first but not the second.
The pope, then, should not seek to govern the temporal affairs of European
kings and princes, as Innocent III tried to do, but keep to his own realm of
jurisdiction, the ministry of the kingdom of heaven. The Roman pontiff cer-
tainly has an exalted role in this ministry, but it is clearly a role limited to being
the servant of something that comes from elsewhere, the grace of God.

In temporal terms, then, the Church is not being presented as an institution
with the same kind of power as the monarchies and nations of Europe. It is a
different kind of body. Aquinas' description therefore is consistent with our
earlier description of the Church as interlocking 'networks' of people, whose
primary community is located in their different clans and nations. It is a net-

work of spiritual and religious life that exists to resource the work of prayer and intercessions to assist the people on their journey towards the grace of heaven. It is given life and growth by a succession of monastic orders and by the papacy, as well as by local benefactors such as kings and barons. However, Aquinas is here emphasizing that the Roman pontiff has a primacy within this ministry, and in contrast to the story told in this chapter he might not want to accept that the Church is a *polycentric* network. Nevertheless, his rootedness in the new university world does suggest that his Church was indeed polycentric in its sources of inspiration and growth.

Should the primacy of the Roman pontiff always include the right to appoint local bishops and to rule on matters of marriage and divorce? In the next period of church history, the Western Church would divide down the middle on these questions.

Discussion Questions

Did Innocent III assist or hinder the mission of the Church?

Is there still a role for monks and nuns to pray for the souls of Christian people?

Can good government lead people towards heaven?

Bibliography and Further Reading

Aquinas, Thomas, *De Regimine Principium*, extracts in Robin Gill (2006), *Textbook of Christian Ethics*, London: Continuum Publishing.

Benedict (1990), *The Rule of Saint Benedict*, trans. Abbot Parry OSB with commentary by Esther de Waal, Leominster: Gracewing.

Bettenson, Henry and Chris Maunder (eds) (2011), *Documents of the Christian Church*, 4th edn, Oxford: Oxford University Press.

Burton, Janet (2011), *The Cistercians in the Middle Ages*, Woodbridge: The Boydell Press.

Clark, James G. (2011), *The Benedictines in the Middle Ages*, Woodbridge: The Boydell Press.

Francis of Assisi (1223), *Regula bullata*, http://www.francis-bible.org/writings/witings_francis_later_rule_2.html.

MacCulloch, Diarmaid (2009), *A History of Christianity: The First Three Thousand Years*, Chs 11 and 12, Harmondsworth: Allen Lane.

Miles, Margaret (2004), *The Word Made Flesh: A History of Christian Thought*, Oxford: Wiley-Blackwell.

Pecknold, C. C. (2010), *Christianity and Politics: A Brief Guide to the History*, Ch. 4, Eugene, Oregon: Cascade Books.

Robson, Michael (2006), *The Franciscans in the Middle Ages*, Woodbridge: The Boydell Press.

7

Reformation Churches: Monarchical or Congregational?

The Weakening of the Papacy after 1300

At the start of the fourteenth century, parish churches and their priests were to be found in every community across Western Europe, many of the buildings recently built or re-built and providing the central hub of those communities. Hierarchies of bishops and archbishops were in place providing governance of this vast network in conjunction with the crown and nobility. A number of powerful religious orders were also present, in a variety of networks criss-crossing the continent, providing centres of worship, learning, charity and business. Over all this the pope presided, in an unprecedented position of influence and sometimes political and military power. The question, then, is this: in which direction would the Western Church now travel: towards further centralization of administration and uniformity of practice in all these churches and abbeys, or in some other direction?

The reign of Pope Boniface VIII (1294–1303) was a turning point. First, it witnessed the greatest claim to authority by any pope, in Boniface's bull *Unam Sanctam* of 1302:

> We are compelled in virtue of our faith to believe and maintain that there is only one holy Catholic Church, and that one is apostolic. This we firmly

believe and profess without qualification. Outside this Church there is no salvation and no remission of sins … [She is] the one mystical body whose head is Christ, of Christ indeed, as God. And in this, 'one Lord, one faith, one baptism' (Ephesians 4:5) … We declare, say, define, and pronounce that it is absolutely necessary for the salvation of every human creature to be subject to the Roman Pontiff. (Boniface 1302)

Boniface has recalled Cyprian's teaching that there is no salvation outside the Church (see pp. 46–7), but in a breathtaking way has now attached it to the office of the papacy, making one coterminous with the other. Would he get away with this?

In the shifting sands of European politics it was not a wise claim. The nation states of Europe, not least the Holy Roman Empire of the German states and the kingdoms of France and England were now more unified and stronger than ever before. Boniface's claim enraged King Philip IV of France, who was already controlling large parts of the Italian peninsula and had overwhelming military superiority over Boniface. He sent a force into the city of Rome and captured and imprisoned Boniface. The pope died in prison a few weeks later, a profound humiliation for the papacy showing that from now on the Church would be under the European monarchies rather than over them. But would the kings of Europe continue to uphold the vision of the Crusading era and its popes from Gregory VII to Innocent III that the Church was to have jurisdiction over all their people as a single institution?

The cardinals were divided in their reaction to Philip, who maintained his pressure on the papacy. Pope Clement V was crowned at Lyons in the watchful presence of Philip and then in 1309 moved the papal seat to Avignon, adjoining the French kingdom, showing his subservience to the French king. It remained in Avignon for 70 years. (A by-product of this was that Avignon became a centre of learning and culture and at the Council of Vienne (1311–12), among other decrees, the bishops promoted the study of Arabic, Chaldean, Hebrew and Greek at the universities of Paris, Oxford, Salamanca, Bologna and the papal court, all of which helped to sow the seeds of the Renaissance.)

The move to Avignon was only the first of a series of crises to hit the Church. Philip went on to appropriate the wealth of the Knights Templar, a military order that had been founded in the early twelfth century to protect crusaders and pilgrims on their journeys to the Holy Land. Then, the Franciscans became deeply divided between the Spirituals, who believed in absolute poverty for the order, and the Conventuals, who took a more pragmatic view of the need for the order to have some property. In 1317, Pope John dissolved the Spirituals but could not end the argument. In 1324, the German King Louis IV invaded Rome, crowned himself Holy Roman Emperor and installed a Spiritual Franciscan as an alternative pope!

Unsurprisingly, struggles over the primacy of the papacy versus that of the state became more intense. Marsiglio of Padua (though he was actually from Bavaria) in *Defender of the Peace* of 1324 argued that it was the state and not the Church that unifies a society. The pope only has spiritual power, and any earthly power he happens to have is given by the secular ruler. Naturally the pope condemned the book but King Louis approved of it and installed Marsiglio as a vicar in Rome, when he had control of the city. His book would be influential with the sixteenth-century Reformers.

Then calamity struck Europe in the form of the bubonic plague or 'Black Death' of 1347–51. This was a blow to the Church as well as to society, with a large number of priests as well as laity being killed by the disease. In some places, 40 per cent of the population was wiped out, wrecking local economies as well as personal lives. The life of the Church as well as society was painfully diminished.

Timeline

1302	Pope Boniface VIII issues *Unam Sanctam*
1309–77	Popes at Avignon
c.1329–84	John Wycliffe
c.1342–c.1416	Julian of Norwich
1347–51	Black Death
1414–18	Council of Constance (conciliarism supported)
1415	Jan Hus burned
1453	Constantinople taken by the Ottoman Turks
1455	Bible printed by Gutenberg at Mainz

c.1466–1536	Erasmus
1475–1564	Michelangelo
1483–1546	Martin Luther
1484–1531	Ulrich Zwingli
1491–1556	Ignatius Loyola
1492	Muslims expelled from Spain; Columbus lands in America
1493	Pope Alexander divides newly discovered lands between Spain and Portugal
1506	Pope Julius II begins rebuilding St Peter's in Rome
1516	Erasmus' new edition of the Greek New Testament
1517	Luther's 95 theses: start of the Reformation
1521	Luther's excommunication. Diet of Worms
1525	Defeat of the peasants and Anabaptists
1526	William Tyndale's English New Testament
1527	Reformation in Sweden and Denmark
1534	Henry VIII 'Supreme Governor' of the Church of England
1509–64	John Calvin
1536	Calvin's *Institutes of the Christian Religion*
1540	Founding of the Society of Jesus (the Jesuits)
1545–1563	Council of Trent

Wycliffe and Hus

Out of the trauma came voices calling for reform of Church and society, with one of the most influential being John Wycliffe (1329–84), priest, scholar and master of Balliol College, Oxford. He developed Augustine's doctrine of the two cities and applied it to the Church. In *On Civil Dominion* in 1375, he argued that the true eternal Church is 'invisible'. This is distinct from the 'material' Church which is constituted by the worship and regular life of its members, and this can sometimes be wayward and corrupt. This material Church should be under the state, and the state should sometimes punish recalcitrant priests. Wycliffe's de-centralizing ideas were condemned by the pope. His response was to become more radical. He argued that the Bible and not the pope was the primary author-ity in Christian life and doctrine, and that it could be read and understood by anyone without always needing the Church's interpretation. This was a radical departure from the view that had held sway since Irenaeus and Tertullian that the Bible came from the Church and was to be interpreted by the Church. But Wycliffe had more to say. In 1379, he denied the doctrine of transubstantiation, that the bread and wine actually become the body and blood of Christ in the Eucharist. His writing therefore called for reform of the Church in a remarkable pre-figuring of the sixteenth-century Reformation.

The pope condemned his teaching in a papal bull, and Oxford University, which had protected him up to this point, expelled him. But, remarkably, he escaped any further persecution. His followers, who became known as the Lollards (initially a term of abuse meaning 'mumblers'), would not be protected and many were imprisoned and put to death, especially after they were believed to have encouraged the Peasants Revolt of 1381 and the beheading on Tower Hill of Simon Sudbury, the Archbishop of Canterbury, by a group of labourers. Even so, the Lollards translated the Bible into English (from the Latin Vulgate), the first time this had been done, and so anticipated Tyndale and Coverdale's English Bible of 1534. But unlike the sixteenth-century Reformers, the Lollards did not have the backing of princes and kings, nor the use of the printing press, which was yet to be invented, so their attempts at reform were quickly extinguished.

However, this repression did not strengthen the papacy. Division deepened between the French cardinals and the other cardinals, and when the time came for the election of a new pope in 1378, Urban VI was elected in Rome, recog-nized by the Germans, English, Italians and Scandinavians, and Clement VII was elected in Avignon, recognized by France, Naples and Sicily, Scotland and Spain. Then at the start of the fifteenth century, in 1409, a third line of popes was created at Pisa. All of this was only resolved in 1417 at the Council of Constance, under pressure from the German Emperor, with the unanimous election of Martin V. The Council of Constance was important, because it gave expression to 'conciliar' theology, the outlook that argued that a general council of bishops has authority over the papacy, rather than the other way round. This, again, would influence the sixteenth-century Reformers.

Wycliffe's writings influenced Jan Hus, a Czech priest of the University of Prague in Bohemia, who also led a movement for the reform of the Church. Hus criticized the pope for his power and ostentation, called for more rigorous obedience to scripture and also resistance to German domination in his country. Hus was called to defend his views at the Council of Constance, but when he arrived he was immediately arrested and later tried for heresy and burnt. His followers, however, were not deterred, and Hus became a national hero in Bohemia. Their *Four Articles of Prague* of 1420 anticipated later Protestant demands. They called for a more disciplined clergy, communion in both kinds (up to now the laity in medieval Europe had only received bread), the liturgy in the local language, and closer co-operation between national churches and states. The Emperor Sigismund tried to repress the Hussites in a number of 'Crusades' against them between 1420 and 1434. However, others in the Church were sympathetic to some of their demands and the Council of Basle of 1431 declared that general councils were superior to the pope, another example of conciliarism supported by the German theologian Nicholas of Cusa. The council placed limitations on the role of the pope and enhanced the authority of bishops and lower clergy. In 1437, it granted some independence to the Bohemian Church, as the Hussites had demanded.

Social and political developments

The fifteenth century saw a number of social and economic changes in northern Europe that would further weaken the power of the pope. These included the increasing size and economic power of the merchant class in the trading cities of northern Europe. Between the beginning of the fourteenth and the end of the fifteenth century, the economy in Europe had been transformed, from what was essentially the local exchange of goods to a currency economy where goods were moved across regions and national boundaries. Money became not just a means of exchange but a commodity in itself, and new professions arose to deal with it, such as bankers and accountants. All of these comprised the new merchant class, and in some places, they took control of the political life of cities, as in Venice and Florence. The crusades had opened new routes to the east, and these now brought goods in for further trading and the accumulation of wealth. This new powerful class also became great sponsors of the arts, such as the Medici's in Florence (a banking family), leading to the Renaissance.

In the German states, the rise of the merchant class resulted in the weakening of not only the papacy but the emperor as well. The position of the emperor was an elected one and therefore its occupant did not necessarily have their own lands and populations to draw upon. Fourteenth-century emperors were increasingly preoccupied with the threat of the Ottoman Empire, which in 1453 finally captured and took control of Constantinople. Ottoman forces also penetrated far into Eastern Europe, and in the following century would even lay siege to Vienna (in 1529). This would result in the over-extension of rule of Emperor Charles V (1516–56), who through marriage became king of Burgundy, Spain, Flanders and the Spanish colonies as well as being Holy Roman Emperor. As well as resisting the Ottoman Empire, he engaged in expensive wars with France, which meant that he could not keep a cap on change within the German states. When the merchants decided they were no longer going to send taxes over the Alps to Rome and were sometimes supported in this by their local rulers, there was now little the emperor, let alone the pope, could do about it.

Erasmus

The late fifteenth century also witnessed a renewed enthusiasm for ancient Greek and Roman literature, sculpture and architecture. Scholars and artists wanted to get behind what now came to be known as the 'Middle Ages' and return to the excellence and elegance of Greek and Roman culture. Their encounter with this classical inheritance would, they believed, bring about a re-birth or 'renaissance' of their own cultural life. A watchword became the Latin phrase *ad fontes*, meaning to go 'back to the sources', and this was applied to many areas of artistic and scholarly creativity.

Desiderius Erasmus of Rotterdam (c.1466–1536), priest, scholar and reformer, was caught up in this movement. In 1509, he was the first person in print to attack widespread corruption in the Church. But his main work was study of the earliest manuscripts of the Greek New Testament. He embodied the aspiration of Renaissance scholarship to get back to the original version of ancient texts. For him, *ad fontes* meant retrieving the most accurate version of the writings of the New Testament through comparison of the earliest copies of the books and producing an original version of the Greek text.

Erasmus' new edition of the Greek New Testament was published in 1516. It went behind the official Latin Vulgate version of the Bible and began to undermine some of the assumptions that had held Catholic devotion in place. It revealed a number of discrepancies between the words used in the worship of the Church and the original text. For example it showed that when the angel addresses Mary at the annunciation (Luke 1.28), the angel does not say that Mary is 'full of grace' but 'anointed'. This subtlety undermined the very popular Marian devotion called the Angelus, which used the Vulgate wording. Secondly, in the Vulgate when John the Baptist calls the people to be baptized (Matt. 3.1, 17), he calls them to 'do penance', which associated his call with the penitential system of the medieval Church. But Erasmus revealed that a more accurate term is to 'repent', something to do with the inward life of the believer. Once again, then, the authority of the medieval Roman Church, with its sacramental and penitential system built upon the Vulgate, was subtlety undermined. Erasmus did not ultimately break with Rome but his Greek New Testament became one of the main reasons that others felt able to do so.

Luther's Reformation

It was not until the sixteenth century that major changes to the organization of the Church took place, but when they did so they were decisive. This was through the Reformation, a protracted and complex movement of ideas, people and political and military power. It is not for this chapter to describe all that happened but what can be attempted here, in line with the underlying investigation of this Studyguide, is to identify and describe key ways that Luther and those who followed him made an impact on the life of the Church.

Martin Luther (1483–1546) began his adult life as an Augustinian monk highly committed to the religious life. He was very serious about securing his eternal salvation through living a holy and righteous life, but he experienced an increasing sense of anguish and despair, as he realized he was not succeeding in this. Meanwhile, he was lecturing at the newly founded university at Wittenberg on the epistles of Paul, with Erasmus' Greek text of the New Testament to hand. He believed the Epistle to the Romans was 'the most important document in the New Testament, the Gospel in its purest expression' (Miles 2004, p. 252). In later life, he recounted how he had studied and meditated on Romans 1.17 and 'the righteousness of God', sometime between 1516 and 1519, comparing his own sinfulness with God's commandments:

> For my case was this: however irreproachable my life as a monk, I felt myself in the presence of God to be a sinner with a most unquiet conscience, nor could I believe him to be appeased by the satisfaction I could offer … I raged with a savage and confounded conscience … At last, as I meditated day and night, God showed mercy and I turned my attention to the connection of the words, namely – 'The righteousness of God is revealed, as it is written: the righteous shall live by faith' – and there I began to understand that the right-eousness of God is the righteousness in which a just man lives by the gift of God, in other words by faith, and that what Paul means is this: the righteous-ness of God, revealed in the Gospel, is passive, in other words that by which the merciful God justifies us through faith, as it is written, 'The righteous shall live by faith.' At this I felt myself straightway born afresh and to have entered through the open gates into paradise itself. There and then the whole face of scripture was changed … (from 'Autobiographical Fragment', March 1545, in McGrath 1999, pp. 106–10)

These words show that Luther's starting point was the hopelessness and futil-ity of the human situation: he accepted fundamentally Augustine's doctrine of original sin and the dependence of humanity on God. Secondly they show that he understood righteousness to be given to the believer as an undeserved gift, which is the grace of God. Thirdly, that the response of the believer can only be passive, to simply accept the grace that God gives, rather than in any sense to actively seek it or earn it. Fourthly, they show the sense of liberation and joy that this realization gave Luther: he now knew that the securing of salvation did not depend in any way on his own futile attempts to win it: it was already secured, by the death of Christ on the cross, and all he needed to do was trustingly receive it. This is the doctrine of justification by grace through faith: 'that the believer can be justified (declared righteous and therefore saved) only through faith (*per solam fidem*), by the merits of Christ imputed to him or her, with works or religious observance as irrelevant to this'. For Luther, this doctrine became the centrepiece of his teaching (Migliore 2005, p. 236).

There were a number of profound implications of this doctrine for the life of the Church, and Luther became more and more determined to put them into practice. From a seemingly small theological insight came a whole new way of viewing the corporate life of the Church and its relationship with the nations of Europe.

Downgrading the Church

Luther followed Augustine in recognizing a subjective dimension of salvation: that the crucial arena for receiving it was within the soul of the believer and that what took place there was known only to God. This was a turn to what is *within*, as it were, and it downgraded the outward life of the Church: that life ceased to have a direct role in the securing of salvation. But whereas Augustine had also reiterated Cyprian's view of the necessity of the Church to salvation, Luther did no such thing. He had already witnessed the corruption of the institutional Church, especially on his visit to Rome, and was outraged by the commercialization of religion taking place through the selling of indulgences, and so had other reasons for downgrading the authority of the Church. The doctrine of justification by grace through faith gave a profound theological rationale for sidelining the institutional Church. The key relationship was between the individual believer and their God, a direct and one-to-one engagement: everything else was secondary to this.

A second implication was the elevation of scripture over the institutional Church as the authoritative guide in the life of the Christian. Luther quickly saw that it was his meditation on the letter to the Romans that had opened his eyes to the true nature of God's righteousness. The teachings of the papacy and other ecclesiastical authorities had clouded these truths and so must be downgraded. It was scripture that taught all things necessary for salvation and it was scripture that should be recognized as the primary authority in the life of the Christian. The phrase *sola scriptura* became a slogan for the Lutheran Reformation.

This, in turn, meant that the Bible should be accessible to the Christian and therefore should be translated into the vernacular tongue of the people. Up to now, it had only been available in Latin and had only been encountered by ordinary people within the liturgy of the mass. Luther saw the importance of translating the Bible into the German tongue and, through the new printing presses (invented by Gutenberg in the mid-fifteenth century), making copies widely available to the German people. So when he was imprisoned in the Wartburg castle in 1521 (after being condemned by Charles V at the Diet of Worms), he began the work of translation and produced what became the definitive version of the German Bible (the New Testament published 1522 and the complete Bible in 1534). His translation used the variant of German spoken in Saxony, intelligible to both northern and southern Germans. It used a vigorous, direct language to make the Bible accessible to everyday Germans, 'for we are removing impediments and difficulties so that other people may read it without hindrance'. The printed edition was furnished with notes and prefaces by Luther, and with woodcuts by Lucas Cranach that contained anti-papal imagery. It quickly became a popular and influential Bible translation, making a major contribution to the evolution of German language and literature. William Tyndale would shortly begin to do the same for the English people, producing the first printed English New Testament in 1526 (printed, ironically, in Worms).

A third implication of Luther's affirmation of justification by grace was the dissolving of the hierarchical culture of the medieval Church. In 1520, in ringing tones, Luther wrote that

[i]t is an invention that the Pope, bishop, priests and monks are called 'the spiritual estate', while princes, lords, craftsmen and farmers are called 'the secular estate'. This is a spurious idea, and nobody should fear it for the following reason. All Christians truly belong to the spiritual estate, and there is no difference among them apart from their office ... We all have one baptism, gospel and faith which alone make us spiritual and a Christian people ... We are all consecrated priests through baptism ... Therefore someone who bears the status of a priest is nothing other than an officeholder. He takes priority for as long as he holds this office; when he is deposed, he becomes a peasant or citizen like all the others ... It follows from this that there is no

basic difference between lay people, priests, princes and bishops, between the spiritual and the secular, except for their office and work and not on the basis of their status. (From 'The Appeal to the German Nobility', 1520, in McGrath 1999, pp. 203–4)

This has become known as the doctrine of the priesthood of all believers, and it became a central feature of Reformation thinking. Furthermore, with the abolition of the spiritual distinction between clergy and laity, it became possible for clergy to marry and raise families. This Luther did, marrying a former nun, Katharina von Bora, in 1525. They had six children and, with an energy to match his, she also bred and sold cattle and ran a brewery.

Luther also developed a common or popular culture in his churches, not least through his hymns, which combined high art and folk music. They were sung in German in church, school, home and the public arena. They drew together all classes, clergy and laity, men, women and children. The most famous became 'A Mighty Fortress Is Our God' (German: *'Ein feste Burg ist unser Gott'*) written and composed between 1527 and 1529. This became known as the 'Battle Hymn of the Reformation' because of the effect it had in increasing the support for the Reformers' cause.

Magisterial Protestantism

The downgrading of the institutional Church, with the dissolving of any sense of a spiritual hierarchy, meant that the way was now clear for Luther to recognize that the civil authorities were free to govern the day-to-day life of the churches in their own lands. There was no theological reason to recognize the ultimate authority of the pope: that position was now occupied by scripture.

Furthermore, the invisibility of justification by grace, and with it the invisibility of those who could be called members of the true spiritual Church, led him to articulate the doctrine of the two kingdoms (recalling Wycliffe and behind him Augustine): one is spiritual and invisible and one secular and visible. On matters of salvation the spiritual kingdom holds sway, while on matters of daily living the earthly kingdom, and especially the secular government of magistrates, princes and kings, holds sway. Each are assigned to their own domain and have jurisdiction within that domain. God wills both to exist side by side:

For Luther, secular government includes much more than political authorities and governments; it includes everything that contributes to the preservation of this earthly life, especially marriage and family, the entire household, as well as property, business, and all the stations and vocations which God has instituted. Luther distinguishes all this from the spiritual reality of grace, of the word of God, and of faith and describes it as an 'external matter', that is, related to our bodies, and also as the 'secular sword'.

This secular or temporal government is necessary alongside the kingdom of Christ. 'For without it this life could not endure.' (Althaus 1972, p. 47)

The view that monarchs were in charge of the visible Church is called Magisterial Protestantism and is a defining feature of Luther's Reformation. When, then, the peasants rose up in revolt against their lords in 1524 and appealed to Luther for support, he was quick and harsh in his response. In his tract 'Against the Robbing and Murdering Hordes of Peasants', he called on the princes to use violent and coercive means to re-establish social order. He was no radical egalitarian, as the Anabaptists in Mühlhausen, led by Thomas Müntzer had become.

The creation of local independent churches in states with Protestant rulers began in Luther's Saxony and quickly moved to other parts of Germany and Switzerland. Ulrich Zwingli (1484–1531) led the city of Zurich to break with Rome and embrace the Reformation: for him the Christian religion was about 'only what Scripture demands'. Martin Bucer (1491–1551) did the same in Strasbourg and John Calvin (1509–64) in Geneva. In England, King Henry VIII would become 'Supreme Head' of the Church of England in 1534 and would be excommunicated by the pope at the same time (for more on the English Reformation, which was more gradual in its implementation, see Spencer 2010).

This proliferation of independent monarchical churches meant that differences of opinion would inevitably arise, and this happened most seriously over the nature of the Eucharist. When in 1529 Philip I, Landgrave of Hesse, called an assembly of German and Swiss theologians at the Marburg Colloquy, to establish doctrinal unity in the emerging Protestant states, agreement could not be reached on the nature of the Eucharist. Luther insisted on the real presence of the body and blood of Christ in the consecrated bread and wine, which he called the sacramental union. The 'Reformed' theologians, led by Zwingli and including Bucer, believed God to be only spiritually or symbolically present. Zwingli denied Jesus' ability to be in more than one place at a time: for him the Eucharist was 'only a memorial'. According to transcripts, the debate sometimes became confrontational, with Zwingli citing Jesus' words: 'The flesh profiteth nothing' (John 6.63) and saying to Luther 'This passage breaks your neck.' Luther replied, 'Don't be too proud, German necks don't break that easily. This is Hesse, not Switzerland.' On his table, Luther wrote in chalk the words '*Hoc est corpus meum*', 'This is my body', indicating that he would not give way.

Despite the disagreement, Luther and his colleague Philipp Melanchthon (1497–1560) were able to draw up a definitive Protestant confession of faith. This arose because Emperor Charles V had been shaken by the Ottoman siege of Vienna and had convened an Imperial Diet at Augsburg in 1530, aiming to unite the German states against the Turks. To achieve this, he needed first to resolve the religious controversies in his lands. He asked for a statement of the Reformers' case, and Melanchthon produced the 'Augsburg Confession', one of the major confessional writings of the Reformation churches. However, despite its avoidance of strident language or abuse of the pope, Charles and the Diet rejected it and ordered the Reformers to renounce heresy and submit to the control of the church authorities or face the imperial army. This prompted the German princes who supported Luther to rally behind the Augsburg Confession and the whole Lutheran Reformation. They formed a military alliance, the Schmalkaldic League, which Luther in his *Warning to His Dear German People* of 1531 cautiously supported on grounds of self-defence. Magisterial Protestantism, with its recognition that the Western Church was to be governed locally rather than centrally, was now a political and military reality.

Loyola and Tridentine Catholicism

The initiative for reform and renewal in the sixteenth century did not only lie with the Protestant Reformers. A wave of reform swept through churches still in communion with Rome. In the past, historians have described this as the Counter-Reformation because they have seen it as a reaction to what the Reformers were doing. But now there is recognition that many of the new movements and ideas within its constituent churches occurred without reference or connection to events in northern Europe or even, in some cases, to Rome. Furthermore, as we shall see, in important ways they took the Roman churches in a direction similar to that of the Protestant churches.

Ignatius Loyola and the Jesuits

Reform began with the founding of religious orders. The Theatines were founded in Rome in 1524 to try to stop the abuses and scandals common in the hierarchy of the Church. The Capuchins were established in 1529 to return Franciscanism to the absolute poverty and austerity of Francis himself, a vision very far from the grandeur of papal aspirations. Then the Society of Jesus was founded in 1540, the inspiration for which came not from the hierarchy but from the hospital bed of an injured soldier.

The story of the Society of Jesus begins with the devout and committed Ignatius of Loyola (c.1491–1556), a nobleman brought up by a member of the Castile court who pursued a military career in his early life. An injury from a cannon ball, which somehow shot between his legs without killing him, followed by a lengthy convalescence (the hospital bed), made him think and wonder about God's will for his life. He could not get hold of books to read except for some theology and the lives of the saints. This reading began to make a deep impression and, like Francis before him, he resolved to put aside his soldiering and embrace poverty. He hung his sword at an altar, confessed his sins and exchanged his clothes with the rags of a beggar. A year of profound spiritual experiences followed, and from this he began to write down notes and instructions that would become his *Spiritual Exercises*. It would later be published and become very popular. The first annotation from the work reveals its tone and purpose:

> by this name of Spiritual Exercises is meant every way of examining one's conscience, of meditating, of contemplating, of praying vocally and mentally, and of performing other spiritual actions, as will be said later. For as strolling, walking and running are bodily exercises, so every way of preparing and disposing the soul to rid itself of all the disordered tendencies, and, after it is rid, to seek and find the Divine Will as to the management of one's life for the salvation of the soul, is called a Spiritual Exercise. (Ignatius of Loyola 1556)

The work provides a four-week course for the penitent, assisted by a spiritual director. Its discipline and insight, with its sharp focus on the interior life and conscience of the soul, made it immediately influential, and it has remained so ever since.

Ignatius travelled to Rome and lived off alms for a time. He then became a university student for 11 years in different cities in Spain and then Paris. By the end of this period, he had acquired a group of companions which included Francis Xavier. They made a vow of life-long poverty and service to others, and to do this in the Holy Land or wherever the pope should send them. They were ordained priests but were unable to sail for the Holy Land so the group went to Italy, and Ignatius felt directed to travel to Rome. There he entered into negotiations with the pope about the group, which was now expanding, to see if they might become a religious order. In 1540, they were formally constituted as the Society of Jesus, with Ignatius becoming its first General (his experience as a soldier made him impose a military form of discipline on the order). He then spent the final years of his life organizing what was a rapidly expanding society, soon to be known as the Jesuits. His aim, springing from his own intense spiritual experiences earlier in life, was to rekindle a religious fervour within the Church at large and for this to happen through a renewed and organized minis-try. He also wanted to see the Church extend its reach around the world through mission, something that Xavier was able to pioneer in India, Malaya and Japan. Ignatius also gave attention to the education of young people, setting up schools first in Messina in 1548 and then across the world, schools that would become academically outstanding and educate generation after generation of leaders wherever they were established.

The Society of Jesus flourished, especially in Italy and the Iberian Peninsula. But unlike other orders its members did not wear a distinctive habit, nor were they obliged to sing the offices together, so they did not build great abbey church-es for their common life. Their vocation was in the world rather than in the mon-astery. Nor were they allowed to accept positions within the church hierarchies, for example as bishops: they were to be a separate society, though Ignatius was careful and clever enough to get the backing of the papacy and to put the order under the ultimate direction of the pope. If the pope wanted Jesuits to go and serve the Church in a far off place, they would go. Nevertheless, the founding and rise of the Jesuits demonstrates not the power of the papacy but the capacity of the Western Church to create yet another network of relationships and loyal-ties alongside the diocesan hierarchies, monastic orders and mendicant orders of friars. In many ways, the Roman Church was not so very different from the increasingly diverse network of Protestant churches in northern Europe, except that the pope rather than the Bible was still seen as the supreme authority.

The Jesuits encouraged renewal on a broad front. They did this in education through their schools, in spiritual direction through promoting Loyola's spiritual exercises and regular confessions and through 'missions' to remote parts of Europe and the world beyond, which at this time was rapidly opening up through exploration and trade. (They were responsible for introducing the word 'mission' into general Church discourse through talk of their 'missions'.) They also founded orphanages and houses for reformed prostitutes. When Ignatius died there were about 1,000 members of the society, and by 1600, it numbered over 8,500 members in 23 provinces. Only in the latter part of the seventeenth century would they encounter serious opposition from within their own Church.

The Council of Trent

But what did all of this imply about the nature of this increasingly polycentric Roman communion of churches? It had been clear for some time, as we have already seen, that the papacy did not have the power to impose its will on the kingdoms of Western Europe, north or south. As the Council of Constance had shown, reconciliation and uniformity could only come through those kingdoms coming together and agreeing on a way forward.

This had become blatantly obvious through the rise of Protestantism in the 1520s, but successive popes resisted calling a council, because they knew it would further limit their own power. Finally, the German Emperor Ferdinand I, Charles IX of France and Pope Paul III agreed to call a council, and, after further delays, a council of archbishops, bishops and generals of orders met at Trent (Trento) in northern Italy in December 1545. The Council addressed issues of doctrine and church discipline in a series of sessions between 1545 and 1563. In many ways it was a continuation of the conciliar process seen at Constance and also at councils at Basle (1431–49) and Florence (1439). But now the Protestants needed rebutting, and Trent took a hard line against Protestant teaching, insisting on the Vulgate as the only legitimate edition of the Bible, and that scripture was held and interpreted by the Church and especially by the papacy, not the other way round. The Council reaffirmed the seven sacraments, the doctrine of purgatory, the use of relics, the veneration of the Blessed Virgin Mary and the doctrine of transubstantiation. It also sought to strengthen the authority of the papacy by saying that this and other councils had authority only inasmuch as the pope ratified its decisions. It also set in place practical reforms to strengthen the institutions of the Church, such as bishops being restricted to only one diocese, the setting up of seminaries in every diocese for the proper training of priests, and the enforcing of clerical celibacy.

There is no doubt that all of this amounted to a turning point in those churches still loyal to the papacy. A new discipline in their administration, worship and pastoral practice became apparent. This led to a new uniformity in their general life, controlled by the pope and his administrative curia. But this was not a return to the past. A new self-consciousness in the culture and ritual of the church became apparent, deliberately different from that of Protestant churches, with a renewed focus on the Blessed Virgin Mary and widespread adoption of Marian devotions such as the 'Hail Mary' and 'Ave Maria'. It was as if Tridentine Catholicism accepted that the Western Church was not going to be re-united and that it must amplify its own distinct identity within a range of competing denominations. While the Council and its implementation made it possible to start talking of a single Roman Catholic Church across much of Europe and across those parts of the wider world where its missionaries were active, paradoxically within this development was an implicit recognition of Western ecclesial diversity.

There was also a significant point of agreement with the Protestants in the decree on justification, from the sixth session of the Council. While as a whole the decree was opposing the Protestant view of good works as 'irrelevant' to justification (asserting that they do play a part), there was the following statement on the primary requirement for salvation:

And whereas the Apostle saith, that man is justified by faith and freely, those words are to be understood in that sense which the perpetual consent of the Catholic Church hath held and expressed; to wit, that we are therefore said to be justified by faith, because faith is the beginning of human salvation, the foundation, and the root of all Justification; without which it is impossible to please God, and to come unto the fellowship of His sons: but we are therefore said to be justified freely, because that none of those things which precede justification – whether faith or works – merit the grace itself of justification. For, if it be a grace, it is not now by works, otherwise, as the same Apostle says, grace is no more grace. (Trent, Chapter VIII)

This meant that membership of the Church, reception of the sacraments, veneration of the Blessed Virgin Mary, and so on, is not sufficient to be justified: a hidden trust within the heart of the individual believer is required. So even though the Council was primarily concerned to criticize the Protestants, it was here acknowledging some crucial common ground.

This was an important marker showing the untenability of the popular medieval mindset which saw the obtaining of salvation as a kind of transaction in which the individual somehow earned or paid their way to heaven, whether through reception of sacraments or doing a penance or going on pilgrimage. Indeed, the Council deliberately curtailed the trade in indulgences (a practice of buying and selling a kind of certificate to speed progress of the soul through purgatory), and it abolished the position of indulgence-seller. Something quite different was needed in the believer, the gift of faith, which depended on the grace of God. Clearly not everyone possessed this trust or faith, which meant that society was divided between those who had it and those who did not, nor could those without it be coerced into receiving it. The use of force in conversion was being ruled out, whether by missionaries or crusaders or kings or emperors. The Council was implicitly recognizing that the domain of the Church, the realm in which it truly operated, was not that of centralized control, but of the inner life of the conscience of individual believers living in countless local communities across the world. Ignatius of Loyola had pointed to this in his *Spiritual Exercises*, and now the bishops at Trent were agreeing. The old days of compulsion and control by those with power were over. Some of the Roman Catholic monarchies, however, would take a long time to recognize this.

Self-understanding: Church as 'Congregation'

The Reformers drew out this emerging understanding of the Church in yet another way. It is seen in the word they used to translate the New Testament term *ekklesia* (see pp. 27–9). William Tyndale is typical. When he came to translate this word from the Greek into a vernacular English, he used the word 'congregation'. This describes the action of congregating or collecting in one body or mass. It appears in his translation of 1526, for example of 1 Corinthians 16.19:

'The congregacions of Asia salute you. Aquila and Priscilla salute you … and so doeth the congregacion that is in their house'; and also for Matthew 16.18: 'Apon this roocke I wyll bylde my congregacion.'

Martin Luther's close collaborator Philip Melanchthon in Wittenberg would use the equivalent German word in Article VII of the definitive Augsburg Confession of 1530: 'The Church is the congregation of saints, in which the Gospel is rightly taught and the Sacraments are rightly administered.'

This use was taken up by Thomas Cranmer, when he drew up and published the Articles of Religion in 1553, later printed in the Book of Common Prayer published in 1662. It is seen in Article XIX, 'Of the Church', which has a defining importance for Anglicans (see further Spencer 2010, pp. 37–8):

> The visible Church of Christ is a congregation of faithful men, in which the pure Word of God is preached, and the Sacraments be duly ministered according to Christ's ordinance, in all those things that of necessity are requisite to the same.

Luther affirmed that this congregating might be of only a few souls but that it would still be enough to truly constitute the Church:

> Now, anywhere you hear or see [the Word of God] preached, believed, confessed, and acted upon, do not doubt that the true ecclesia sancta catholica, a 'holy Christian people' must be there, even though there are very few of them. ('On the Councils and the Church', 1539, in McGrath 1999, p. 202)

The Church, then, is not like a modern multinational corporation, with a head office and multiple branches across the world. It is more like a federation, where each member, dispersed around the world, however big or small, fully constitutes the activity that the federation as a whole represents. This implies that the ownership and governance of such churches is localized rather than centralized. It is worth adding, however, that the Reformers believed consultation and agreement among members was desirable (following conciliarism) and tried very hard to facilitate this.

Furthermore, the use of the word 'congregation' in all these statements shows that they saw the Church as a dynamic reality, a deliberate action of people 'of faith' congregating and coming into face-to-face interaction with each other and with Christ and, in particular, of the action of gathering to hear the word of

God preached and to receive the sacraments. This means it must be deliberately undertaken, which also means there are others who do not choose to congregate and interact in this way. The important implication here is that Church life is associational rather than communal: it is the association of those who actively associate themselves with each other, rather than being an activity that encompasses everyone within a community or nation. A definite shift has therefore taken place, from medieval notions of the Church as a kind of public utility, to Cameron's second organizational form, that of the Church as a voluntary association.

This emerging ecclesiology is found in the writings of probably the greatest of Reformation theologians, the Frenchman John Calvin (1509–64). He became the leading teacher in the Reformed city of Geneva, especially after 1541. His ecclesiology is found in his *Institutes of the Christian Religion*, most notably in the final edition of 1559, and has been described as one of the major contributions to Reformation theology. But his thought took two decades to mature and was already taking shape in the 1536 edition. In words that show the influence of the Augsburg confession, he wrote: 'Wherever we see the Word of God purely preached and heard, where we see the sacraments administered according to Christ's institution, there, it is not to be doubted, the Church of God exists' (in Methuen 2011, p. 161). This implies that the Church is not present when the word is not purely preached and the sacraments not properly celebrated, so it cannot be simply equated with the general religious practice of a village, town or nation as a whole.

In the 1559 edition, Calvin also introduces the distinction between the visible and invisible Church. Up to this point, he has been describing the Church in the civil community, the one that congregates each Sunday and is under the laws of the state. Now, though, he acknowledges that the true Church is invisible, because its membership is made up of those who have true faith in God, and only God can know who these are because only he can read the secrets of our hearts. The visible Church, on the other hand, will be made up of these people of faith and others: 'in this church are mingled many hypocrites who have nothing of Christ but the name and outward appearance', who are tolerated either because the Church's discipline was not strong enough, or because no one was able to pass judgement over them. The visible Church, for this reason, was always going to be imperfectly holy, 'mingled of good men and bad', and it was necessary to bear with these imperfections (Methuen 2011, p. 162).

These statements show an increasing use of the distinction between those who belong to the true Church, and others within a community. It is a distinction applied to local communities and even within families. Church life at heart is about faith, which some have and others do not have, and therefore the true Church is selective (or in Calvin's language 'elective') rather than communal.

This insight would not find very much practical expression in the sixteenth century, because kings and princes would still insist on uniformity in their own domains, but from the seventeenth century onwards, as the next chapter will show, it came increasingly to form and mould Protestant church life.

Discussion Questions

Did Luther weaken or strengthen the Church?
How far was Loyola pursuing the same aims as Luther and Calvin?
Were the Protestant churches of the Reformation era monarchical or congregational?

Bibliography and Further Reading

Althaus, Paul (1972), *The Ethics of Martin Luther*, Philadelphia: Fortress.

Boniface VIII, Pope (1302), *Unam sanctam*, http://www.fordham.edu/halsall/source/B8-unam.asp.

Book of Common Prayer, The, (1968), Cambridge: Cambridge University Press.

Cameron, Euan (2012), *The European Reformation*, 2nd edn, Oxford: Oxford University Press.

Francis of Assisi (1223), *Regula bullata*, http://www.francis-bible.org/writings/witings_francis_later_rule_2.html.

Janz, Dennis R. (2002), *A Reformation Reader: Primary Texts with Introductions*, new edn, Philadelphia: Augsburg Fortress Press

Loyola, Ignatius (1556), *The Spiritual Exercises of St. Ignatius of Loyola*, trans. Fr E. Mullan SJ, New York: P. J. Kenedy & Sons, 1914.

MacCulloch, Diarmaid (2003), *Reformation: Europe's House Divided 1490–1700*, Harmondsworth: Allan Lane.

McGrath, Alistair (1999), *Reformation Thought: An Introduction*, 3rd edn, Oxford: Blackwell.

Methuen, Charlotte (2011), *Luther and Calvin: Religious Revolutionaries*, Oxford: Lion Hudson.

Migliore, Daniel (2005), *Faith Seeking Understanding: An Introduction to Christian Theology*, 2nd edn, Grand Rapids: Eerdmans.

Miles, Margaret (2004), *The Word Made Flesh: A History of Christian Thought*, Oxford: Wiley-Blackwell.

Spencer, Stephen (2010), *SCM Studyguide Anglicansim*, London: SCM Press.

Trent (1848), *The Council of Trent: The canons and decrees of the sacred and oecumenical Council of Trent*, ed. and trans. J. Waterworth, London: Dolman.

8

Churches of the Enlightenment: Communal or Voluntary?

The Reformers began to suggest that church life is associational rather than communal, the gathering of those who elect (or are elected) to do so, rather than being something that naturally encompasses everyone within a community or nation. This suggestion was not taken up by the monarchs of the time: for them uniformity remained not only what they wanted but what they enforced (the phrase '*cuius regio eius religio*', meaning the religion of the king will be the religion of the realm, had generally been accepted at the Peace of Augsburg in 1555). This is seen above all in the Thirty-Years War on the continent of Europe (1618–48), in which the Hapsburgs sought to re-impose Catholicism on Bohemia and on territories in central Germany such as the Palatinate and southern Germany such as Bavaria. The Protestant powers of north Germany, Denmark and Sweden were equally determined to maintain Lutheranism and Calvinism within their territories. The Treaties of Westphalia, which ended the war, formally recognized that each monarch was free to impose his or her own religion on their own state and therefore to seize large tracts of church land as part of the deal (though some protection was given to minorities). The idea of a united Christendom under one Church was dead, but the principle of an established or communal religion within each state was not. The question now was whether this settlement would hold or whether the different denominations would gradually become separated from the state, acquiring their own independent life and a voluntary membership. The next period of Western Church history would not be dominated by war but by the Enlightenment: what became of the Church in this new setting?

Timeline	
c.1513–72	John Knox
1536	Calvin's *Institutes of the Christian Religion*
1555	Peace of Augsburg: *'cuius regio eius religio'* ('whose realm, his religion')
1560	Scotland adopts Calvinist confession
1596–1650	Rene Descartes
1607	Colony of Virginia established in North America
1611	Authorised ('King James') version of the Bible
1618–1648	Thirty Years War in Europe, ending with the Peace of Westphalia
1620	Pilgrim Fathers sail to America
1624–91	George Fox
1628–88	John Bunyan
1635–1705	Philip Jakob Spener
1642–45	Civil War in England
1648	The Westminster Confession
1660	Restoration of the monarchy in Britain
1682	William Penn founds Pennsylvania
1703–91	John Wesley
1712–78	Jean-Jacques Rousseau
1714–70	George Whitfield
1722	Count Zinzendorf founds the Pietist Herrnhut community in Saxony
1724–1804	Immanuel Kant
1726	Start of the 'Great Awakening' in America

1738	John Wesley's 'awakening'
1773	Suppression of the Jesuits by the pope
1776	Independence of the United States of America
1768–1834	Friedrich Schleiermacher
1789	French Revolution begins
1801	Concordat between Napoleon and the pope
1833	Antoinette Brown's ordination

Reformed Protestantism and 'the Elect'

At the start of the seventeenth century, the fastest growing branch of the Church in Europe were the Reformed Protestant churches, which took their inspiration from the teaching of John Calvin and his *Institutes of the Christian Religion*. They could be found in many cantons of Switzerland, the south west of France, the Netherlands and in a patchwork of towns and churches across Germany, Bohemia and Hungary and were dominant in England and Scotland.

The struggles of the Reformed Protestants in Scotland provide a good example of how this tradition became implanted in European life. They were led by John Knox (1513–72), a fearless and outspoken preacher who had spent time in London assisting Cranmer with the production of the second Book of Common Prayer in 1552. When Mary Tudor came to the English throne, Knox fled to the continent and visited Calvin in Geneva, returning there later to minister to the English congregation in that city. In 1558, he published his famous tirade against Mary Tudor and Mary of Guise (who was regent of Scotland in 1554–60), *The First Blast of the Trumpet against the Monstrous Regiment of Women*. He asserted that government by a woman is contrary to the laws of nature and God, which did not endear him to the future Queen Elizabeth. He returned to Scotland, secured military support and preached and organized opposition to Rome. After the death of Mary of Guise in 1560, he was largely responsible for the Scottish Confession, a Calvinist statement of faith, and for the commission that abolished the authority of the pope and the mass in the Scottish Church. Mary Stuart returned to Scotland as queen in 1561, and Knox clashed with her on many occasions. He was the primary author of the *Book of Common Order* (1556–64), the Scottish service book. When the young James became king of Scotland in 1567, Knox was closely associated with his regent, the Earl of Mory and had much influence, but Mory was later murdered and when Knox himself died the place of Presbyterianism in the Scottish 'kirk' was not secure.

Presbyterianism was an adaptation of Calvin's church polity in Geneva, in which the presbytery (made up of the pastors and elders of a church) were responsible for governing its life. Calvin and his followers abolished the threefold order of bishops, priests and deacons and instead, using terms taken directly from the New Testament, instituted four kinds of minister: pastors, teachers, elders and deacons (*Institutes of the Christian Religion*, Book 4, Chapters 3.4–9). In Scotland, following this pattern, the parish church came to be governed by the local presbytery, and when disputes arose, appeals could be made to a regional synod. The national church as a whole would send representatives to an annual General Assembly, which only had control of mission. In this assembly, lay elders and ordained ministers were equally represented. The principle that lay people have a share in the government of the Church was very important, though it was a role that only operated within a clearly defined constitution written by Knox. A new minister of a church would be chosen by its presbytery and then ordained by it. Ministers were required to have achieved a university degree as part of their training, so were highly educated.

Clearly the principle of local self-government was crucial for this tradition, which also made the establishment of the Church of Scotland puzzling. It has been the only Presbyterian Church to have been a state church with the monarch as its head. The politics of the time required this establishment for the survival of Presbyterianism in Scotland, but it is still an anomaly in the Reformed tradition. James VI (and I of England) tried to re-introduce episcopacy, and succeeded for a while, but when his son Charles I sent Archbishop Laud, a high-church Anglican, to impose a more Catholic liturgy, there was uproar and a General Assembly of the Church in Glasgow in 1638 swept episcopacy away again. Then, when the Civil War broke out across the country, the Westminster parliament legislated for Presbyterian uniformity throughout the British Isles. A national assembly was convened at Westminster in 1643 which passed a number of Calvinist measures abolishing episcopacy and the Book of Common Prayer in England and drawing up the Westminster Confession, which was ratified in Edinburgh in 1647 and approved by the Westminster parliament in

1648. This has become a classical statement of Calvinist theology and church polity, influencing Presbyterians and Baptists in many parts of the world. But after the restoration of the monarchy in 1660 it was thrown out in England, while episcopacy and the Book of Common Prayer were reinstated. In Scotland, though, Presbyterianism remained in place and it has held sway in the Church of Scotland ever since.

The Westminster Confession illustrates the widening gap between Church and nation state in Protestantism. This is seen in the heavy emphasis it places on the doctrine of election, in which only some are elected to salvation by God:

> All those whom God hath predestinated unto life, and those only, He is pleased, in His appointed time, effectually to call … Others, not elected, although they may be called by the ministry of the Word, and may have some common operations of the Spirit, yet they never truly come unto Christ, and therefore cannot be saved: much less can men, not professing the Christian religion, be saved in any other way whatsoever, be they never so diligent to frame their lives according to the light of nature, and the laws of that religion they do profess. ('Of Effectual Calling', Chapter X)

This hard and sharp distinction is reflected in the way the Confession stipulates that it is only the elect who are members of the true catholic Church:

> The catholic or universal Church, which is invisible, consists of the whole number of the elect, that have been, are, or shall be gathered into one, under Christ the Head thereof; and is the spouse, the body, the fullness of Him that fills all in all. ('Of the Church', Chapter XXV)

The confession recognizes the existence of a visible Church, which is also catholic, which 'consists of all those throughout the world that profess the true religion'. But particular churches 'are subject both to mixture and error; and some have so degenerated, as to become no Churches of Christ, but synagogues of Satan' (ibid.). Belonging to this visible catholic Church, then, is no guarantee of salvation. It all depends on whether you are one of the elect.

The Confession also shows a distancing of the Church from the king (the 'magistrate') in certain circumstances:

As magistrates may lawfully call a synod of ministers, and other fit persons, to consult and advise with, about matters of religion; so, if magistrates be open enemies to the Church, the ministers of Christ, of themselves, by virtue of their office, or they, with other fit persons upon delegation from their Churches, may meet together in such assemblies ('Of Synods and Councils', Chapter XXXI)

The Presbyterians had clearly learnt a lesson in their bitter experience with Charles I and his Archbishop William Laud. Not all kings should be obeyed. The key point is that the Church has authority to govern its own life if need be. Cranmer's *Articles of Religion* did not go this far.

Arminianism

But not all Reformed Christians were happy to follow the logic of predestination and election, especially when Calvin's followers started talking of double predestination as well. This came from the theologian Theodore Beza (1519–1605), who pointed out that if God had predestined some to be saved he must have predestined the rest to be damned. Furthermore, Christ's atonement on the cross could not have been for all people but must have been only for the elect. This was rejected by one of Beza's students, the Dutch theologian Jacobus Arminius (1560–1609), who become a professor at Leiden and argued his case with increasing support from others at The Hague. He argued that Christ died for all people and therefore it was possible for any and for all to be saved if they freely chose to believe. He did not succeed in getting the Dutch Reformed Church to change its official beliefs and after his death his opponents convened the Synod of Dort (1618–19) with delegates from across Europe. In a politically tense setting in which Spain was threatening the Netherlands, and its Church was dangerously split down the middle, the synod decided that Arminius was unorthodox and ejected 200 of its clergy from the country. But others were not persuaded, including Archbishop Laud in England, who is sometimes called an Arminian.

In the eighteenth century, John Wesley adopted the views of Arminius. He was deeply attracted to the view that Jesus died for all and that all should therefore hear the gospel message. This was one of the main reasons that he set off on his marathon preaching tour, covering thousands of miles in a horse drawn cart, so that the whole population might hear the invitation to repent and believe. But this Arminianism resulted in his falling out with his close colleague in the Evangelical revival George Whitfield and their going separate ways. There has been continuing division between these two schools of thought, even within Methodism between Wesleyan and Calvinistic Methodists. However, the main source of inspiration for Wesley and the Methodist movement came from a different source examined later in this chapter.

Nonconformity

In late sixteenth century and early seventeenth century England, those Calvinists who wanted the reforming of the Church of England to continue were called Puritans. Their demands were resisted by Elizabeth I and James I, and they began to meet for worship away from their local parish churches. These 'dissenters' formed themselves into a number of denominations such as the Congregationalists, who took their lead from Robert Browne (c.1550–1633), who in 1582 argued that 'the Kingdom of God was not to be begun by whole parishes, but rather of the worthiest, were they never so few'. He insisted that these 'gathered churches', bound under God by covenant, should be independent of the state and have the right to govern themselves. Such separatist principles became the 'congregationalism' of those who followed him. The Pilgrim Fathers set off for America in 1620 with members of a congregational church in Plymouth, Devon (as well as Puritans from Holland) to found Plymouth, Massachusetts, where they were glad to escape the constraints of the Anglican establishment.

Another nonconformist group were the Baptists, founded by John Smythe (c.1560–1612), who in 1609 persuaded his congregation to accept the practice of believer's baptism. Their church was to be just for freely converted adults, with infant baptism regarded as null and void. By 1660, having gained strength through the years of civil war and Oliver Cromwell's commonwealth, there were around 300 Baptist churches in England and Wales. In 1639, they would also establish a church in Providence, Rhode Island, which became the first of many influential Baptist churches in North America. They would later become energetic missionaries and have been very influential in the spread of Christianity around the world. The cobbler William Carey (1761–1834), who became a brilliant linguist and translator in India, was the most famous of these.

A third Puritan group were the Quakers (called that because they would sometimes quake or tremble in worship), also called the Society of Friends. The Society was founded in 1647 by the preacher George Fox (1624–91) who called people to look within themselves rather than to clergy or church buildings for Christ's word in their lives. Quakers should sit in expectant silence during worship for the Holy Spirit to make them aware of Christ speaking to them. By 1655, they had spread throughout Britain and Ireland. But they refused to take oaths, pay tithes or be conscripted into the army, so were persecuted by the authorities, both under Cromwell (himself a Puritan) and Charles II. Over 20,000 were fined or imprisoned and shockingly 450 died in prison. Only in 1688, with the Act of Toleration, did persecution end. Meanwhile in 1682 William Penn led 2,000 Welsh Quakers over the Atlantic to found Pennsylvania as a 'Holy Experiment' on Quaker principles. This shows that while the nonconformists would remain a minority in England and not bring about whole-scale separation of Church and state, in America it was another matter. The nonconformist churches there would create a culture in which, when in 1791 the time came to adopt an American Constitution, the principle of separation between Church and state was enshrined in the law of what would become the most powerful nation on earth.

Pietism and the Rise of Feeling in Religion

Reformed Protestantism was not the only major Protestant tradition in seventeenth-century Europe. There were still many churches that remained committed to the teaching of Martin Luther and these were well established in much of Germany, Denmark, Sweden, Norway, Finland, Hungary, Latvia and Poland. Their worship took a variety of forms, ranging from the more sacramentally focused and 'high church' traditions of Scandinavia to the plainer word-centred worship of the German Lutheran churches. Their doctrine was defined by the Augsburg Confession as well as by the 'Small' and 'Large' catechisms that Luther had written in 1529. These were all collected together with the Schmalkaldic Articles (which Luther had written in 1537, and which are vigorous in their opposition to the mass, purgatory, the pope, the invocation of saints and monasticism) in the definitive *Book of Concord* of 1580. The churches subscribing to this book became known as the Lutheran churches. At the centre of these formulae was the doctrine of justification by faith alone as the 'first and chief article' on which rests 'all that we teach and practice' (Schmalkaldic Articles). There were differences between the churches on certain points of doctrine, such as original sin, free will, predestination and what should be *adiaphora* (indifferent to salvation). But as other Protestant traditions gained in strength the need arose for the Lutherans to develop an 'orthodoxy', and this took place through an ever increasing body of academic studies and formulae. By the mid-seventeenth century, this had come to resemble the complexity of medieval scholasticism. This approach dominated the self-definition and self-identity of Lutheran churches throughout the seventeenth century.

It is not surprising that there was a reaction against this. In 1675, Philip Jakob Spener (1635–1705), a pastor and academic in Leipzig, published *Pia Desideria* ('*Pious Longings*'), which emphasized the need for Christians to engage in devotional reading of the Bible and the avoidance of religious arguments. It emphasized the role of feeling in strengthening the Christian life, in order to lead the believer to a stronger expression of love. It argued that students and professors of theology should not only gain a clear understanding of doctrine but embody and express Christian charity in their lives. In their sermons, pastors should not just teach doctrine but strive to renew the devotion of their congregations. *Pia Desideria* became popular, and Spener was able to set up devotional circles for prayer and Bible reading. These groups, spontaneous and unstructured, can be described as 'friendship groups', to use one of Cameron's organizational forms (see p. 4), because they were voluntary and informal, with the aim of fellowship with each other and the Lord.

The Leipzig theological faculty were not happy, however, and Spener had to leave and move to Berlin. But others embraced his teaching and went further than he wanted, beginning to emphasize the work of the Holy Spirit in believers' hearts, which undermined Luther's teaching on the sufficiency of scripture and the sacraments for receiving grace. These radical Pietists also developed anti-establishment tendencies and a strong expectation in the imminent end of the age and return of Christ: 'millenarianism'. Others, though, followed Spener's teaching and Paul Gerhardt put his ideas into hymns that would become widely sung, such as 'O sacred head now wounded', a translation of an ancient mystical hymn that struck the right personal note for this new Pietism:

O sacred Head, now wounded,
with grief and shame weighed down,
now scornfully surrounded
with thorns, thine only crown:
how pale thou art with anguish,
with sore abuse and scorn!
How does that visage languish
which once was bright as morn!

What thou, my Lord, has suffered
was all for sinners' gain;
mine, mine was the transgression,
but thine the deadly pain.
Lo, here I fall, my Saviour!
'Tis I deserve thy place;
look on me with thy favour,
vouchsafe to me thy grace …

(English translation, James P. Alexander)

The combination of attention to the physical and mental anguish of Christ with intense expressions of individual personal devotion to him is typical of Pietism and shows why it became popular in comparison to the dry academic debates of the theological faculties.

Other centres of Pietism developed in Germany at Halle under August Hermann Francke and then on the Saxony estates of the strong-willed Count von Zinzendorf (1700–60) who was Spener's godson. Zinzendorf gave sanctuary to the Moravian Brethren, who were a remnant of the Hussite or Bohemian brethren (see p. 118). They named their settlement Herrnhut, 'the Lord's Watch'. Here the emphasis on personal devotion to the Redeemer, expressed especially through meditation on the blood and wounds of Christ on the cross, became a central feature of their worship in church and at home. The breakthrough for the community came in 1727, when it decided it was time to stop arguing about points of doctrine and spend time together in prayer. The Count poured out his soul in a prayer accompanied with a flood of tears. This prayer produced an extraordinary effect. The whole community began praying as never before, and one of the pastors 'was overwhelmed by the power of the Lord about noon. He sank down into the dust before God. So did the whole congregation.

They continued till midnight in prayer and singing, weeping and praying.' A few days later 'the Holy Spirit was poured out on them all. Their prayers were answered in ways far beyond anyone's expectations' (Greenfield 1930). Many of them decided to set aside certain times for continued earnest prayer, a practice that continued for many years to come. This prayer also led to action, especially evangelism. More than 100 missionaries left that village community in the next 25 years, all constantly supported in prayer. These Moravians would go on to establish churches in the West Indies, Greenland and Labrador, South Africa and elsewhere.

Their resolve and devotion was witnessed by John and Charles Wesley. In 1736, they sailed to America as Anglican missionaries. A company of Moravian immigrants were also on the vessel. During a terrible storm they all faced the danger of shipwreck. John Wesley wrote in his journal:

> At seven I went to the Germans. I had long before observed the great serious-ness of their behaviour. Of their humility they had given a continual proof by performing those servile offices for the other passengers which none of the English would undertake; for which they desired and would receive no pay, saying, 'It was good for their proud hearts', and 'their loving Saviour had done more for them', And every day had given them occasion of showing a meekness, which no injury could move. If they were pushed, struck or thrown down, they rose again and went away; but no complaint was found in their mouth. Here was now an opportunity of trying whether they were delivered from the spirit of fear, as well as from that of pride, anger and revenge. In the midst of the Psalm wherewith their service began, the sea broke over, split the mainsail in pieces, covered the ship and poured in between the decks, as if the great deep had already swallowed us up. A terrible screaming began among the English. The Germans calmly sung on. I asked one of them afterwards: 'Were you not afraid?' He answered, 'I thank God, no.' I asked: 'But were not your women and children afraid?' He replied mildly: 'No, our women and children are not afraid to die'. (Wesley 1974)

When he returned to England Wesley sought out the company of the Moravian pastor Peter Boehler, who had a formative influence on Wesley's own famous 'awakening' at Aldersgate Street in London in May 1738.

At the start of the following year there was a meeting at Fetter Lane, also in London, of about 60 Moravians and John and Charles Wesley, George Whitefield and several other Anglicans. It illustrates very well what the Moravians were channelling into the wider church. John Wesley records that

> [a]bout three in the morning, as we were continuing instant in prayer, the power of God came mightily upon us, insomuch that many cried for exceeding joy, and many fell to the ground. As soon as we were recovered a little from that awe and amazement at the presence of His Majesty, we broke out with one voice 'We praise Thee, O God; we acknowledge Thee to be the Lord!' (ibid.)

John Wesley's preaching ministry and his organization of Methodist meetings would allow this revival to spread up and down the length of the country. It is seen in his commitment to travel the country 'to promote as far as I am able vital practical religion and by the grace of God to beget, preserve, and increase the life of God in the souls of men'. He did this first through preaching in churches and then, when denied access by hostile incumbents, in fields and market squares, up and down the country, covering over 200,000 miles on horseback or in a carriage over the course of his life. He regularly rose at four in the morning, preached at five, and spent his days in a full round of preaching, counselling, and organizing. He travelled around England annually, paid twenty visits to Scotland, and the same number to Ireland. He was sometimes attacked by hostile mobs but was not deflected. He was influenced by Arminianism (see pp. 141–2) and so believed that everyone on the planet could be justified and therefore needed to be given the opportunity to hear the gospel and respond with faith. He disregarded the parochial boundaries of the Church of England, ranging widely and freely, famously declaring that 'I look upon all the world as my parish' (Journal 3, July 1759).

Wesley did not see evangelism taking place just through preaching, however. His genius was to recognize that the support and fellowship that believers receive from each other after their conversion was just as important as the preaching itself. He therefore established a system of 'class meetings' for the teaching and support of converts, some 60 per cent of whom were women. Each convert was put into a class of twelve or so members who met under a leader, normally another lay person, for fellowship and instruction. The small group was crucial in allowing members to learn the faith in an interactive way, for unlike in a large meeting there was opportunity for questions and discussion. Wesley organized the Methodist movement so that this interactive form of evangelism would be embodied in its structures. After his death it cut its links with the Church of England and became the Methodist Church, but his approach influenced many beyond the movement, such as Charles Simeon, the leader of Anglican Evangelicalism in the next generation, who adapted these principles for home groups in his parish in Cambridge.

Charles Wesley, the brother of John, was also caught up in the revival and poured out his thoughts and feelings in hymns. He wrote around 6,000, and many are still in use. It is said that Peter Boehler had told him: 'If I had a thousand tongues I would praise Jesus with every one of them.' This prompted Wesley to write the immortal lines

Oh for a thousand tongues to sing
My dear Redeemer's praise
The glories of my God and King
The triumphs of His grace.
He breaks the power of cancelled sin,
He sets the prisoner free;
His blood can make the foulest clean,
His blood availed for me.

Enlightenment and Revolution!

In various ways, the Protestant Reformation was creating an awareness of separation between the elect and everyone else. European rulers tried very hard to keep the churches of their domains under their own control and within their own chosen denomination, but church members themselves were increasingly making distinctions between those who were 'in' and 'out'. This was the case with the doctrinal statements of the Presbyterian churches of Scotland, and even the case with the new Puritan denominations of England, who physically removed themselves from parish churches to form Congregationalist, Baptist and Quaker churches, among others. They also spread to other parts of the world, not least North America where their influence would be immense. Then the rise of Pietism made many Christians aware of the role of feeling and devotion in faith, showing that it was an essential requirement. This created yet another division between those who had such feelings and the rest who did not. In the eighteenth century, John Wesley, George Whitfield and others would generate a revival movement in Britain and America that would fan the flames of these feelings and lead yet more of the population into an awareness of how they were different from the rest.

But what of the old established churches, in Roman Catholic as well as Protestant Europe? They still held the loyalty and obedience of a majority of the populations. Could they resist these pressures and remain churches of the nation?

After the Peace of Westphalia of 1648, it may have seemed that their position was secure once again. The Hapsburgs had regained control of large parts of central Europe and the Bourbons under Louis XIV (1643–1715) would rise to a position of unrivalled power and influence that the Roman Catholic Church could share. Yet, in the eighteenth century, a movement that was initially intellectual would become dangerously political for the churches and would rock their boats in a most dramatic way.

From cosmology to politics

The roots of this movement lie in scientific exploration across the European continent, with early pioneers like Leonardo da Vinci (1452–1519), Copernicus (1473–1543), Galileo (1564–1642) and Kepler (1571–1630), opening up new fields for exploration. Copernicus is especially representative of this movement because his cosmology removed the earth from the centre of the universe: it showed that humanity was living on a globe rotating around something else, the sun. The only security now lay in the power of human reason to try and solve some of its mysteries. This Copernican revolution in Western thought simultaneously removed humanity from the centre of a hierarchical universe and made humanity's power of reason the measure of all things.

The work of Sir Isaac Newton (1642–1726) represents both the climax of this enquiry and its elevation to a whole new plane of understanding. He demonstrated the success of scientific reasoning in understanding and regulating the world around us, and the need for that reasoning to reach into all other aspects of human life. The Enlightenment as a wider philosophical and cultural movement was born out of this success.

Philosophical developments began with the empiricism of Francis Bacon (1561–1626), who argued that the only kind of knowledge that science can rely upon is gained through sensory observation. This led to the elimination of the notion of purpose from nature: explanations were to be in terms of mechanistic causes and effects rather than divine goals and intentions. There was to be no reference to supernatural revelation.

The dualism of René Descartes (1596–1650) was another key philosophical development: he decided to rely solely on human reason and doubt everything else. This led him to formulate his famous maxim *cogito ergo sum*, 'I think therefore I am.' It is important to note the individualism of this statement: it is not the community's thinking that becomes the basis of knowledge but the reasoning of the individual mind. This led him to formulate a philosophy that became known as Cartesianism, in which a sharp distinction is drawn between the subject who looks out on the world, and the object that he or she looks at. In his philosophy, the observing *subject* makes sense of the objective world 'out there' through the use of reason. The collective thinking of institutions like the Church therefore becomes subservient to this kind of observing individual.

Immanuel Kant (1724–1804) provided the most sophisticated and powerful description of the scope of reason of any modern philosopher in his *Critique of Pure Reason* (1781). In this work, he sought to map the limits of what reason can do, but paradoxically he also strengthened its authority within those limits. Crucially, he showed how the truths of religion lay beyond this domain. Kant did not deny those truths, but he removed them from the main arena of human thought and intellectual endeavour. It was no longer possible to prove the truths of Christianity using reason alone. This implicitly paved the way for the marginalization of Christianity in society.

The Enlightenment also saw the rise of historical consciousness, developing out of the critical study of history, including of the Bible. Thinkers became aware of the developing nature of human society, stretching back through many ages. If this age was different from and better than the preceding one, this showed that something called history existed and that it could be studied in a critical way. Edward Gibbon (1737–94) author of the great *The History of the Decline and Fall of the Roman Empire* (first part published in 1776) is the most famous example: he gave materialistic rather than spiritual explanations for the decline of Rome and the rise of Christianity.

These waves of new and different kinds of thinking were famously summed up by Kant in his 1784 essay 'What is Enlightenment?'

Enlightenment is man's emergence from his self-incurred immaturity. Immaturity is the inability to use one's own understanding without the guidance of another. This immaturity is self-incurred if its cause is not lack of understanding, but lack of resolution and courage to use it without the guidance of another. The motto of enlightenment is therefore: Sapere aude! Have courage to use your own understanding! (Kant 1784)

It would not take long for this sea change of thinking to have dramatic political consequences. The rise of individualism implied the rise of democratic ideals and the overthrow of the medieval monarchies. In France the philosopher Jean-Jacques Rousseau began his treatise *The Social Contract* (1762) with the rallying call 'Man was born free but is everywhere in chains.' He set out a vision for a different kind of society, free of the medieval shackles of monarchy, Church and stifling tradition, which would be based on the general will of all the people. The actions of the state would reflect people's desire to live together in peace and order, and so the state and not the Church would be the ultimate object of their allegiance. The citizen would control the government of the nation. Tom Paine's *The Rights of Man* (1791–92) helped to translate this outlook into a concrete political manifesto which inspired the revolutionaries of Paris.

The French Revolution of 1789–95 had many causes, not least the financial ruin of France under Louis XVI and the onset of famine after several years of crop failure. But the rise and popularity of Enlightenment thinking prepared the ground for revolution in that it allowed the populace to imagine a nation without the 'old regime' of monarchy and Church controlling their lives. Events began with the commoners in the States General (parliament) declaring that they were now the National Assembly and passing the 'Declaration of the Rights of Man'. This put the Church as well as monarchy and aristocracy under the authority of the National Assembly, and in 1791 all the clergy were required to swear an oath of obedience to the civil constitution. The pope condemned the oath and half of the clergy with many of their parishioners refused to swear, resulting in the country being split down the middle. Division became open rebellion in some regions. Republican troops occupied the papal territories of Avignon and Venaissin and in the following year the leaders of the revolution, in a desperate attempt to secure their position, unleashed the 'reign of terror'. This led to the rounding up and guillotining of large numbers of clergy as well as aristocracy. They also declared war on the Holy Roman Empire and the Roman

Catholic Church. In 1793, the king and queen were executed. A campaign to de-Christianize France was then launched, which saw the drowning of more priests, nuns and monks, the destruction of churches and the closing of all Christian institutions. It was now that the great abbey church at Cluny (see pp. 99–100) was dismantled for its stone. Secular pageantry and ceremonies were instituted, with a large church in Paris converted into a 'pantheon' in honour of humanistic heroes, and an opera singer was installed in Notre Dame to represent the Goddess of Reason and to sing the praises of the revolution.

Over the next few years, one of the revolutionary generals, Napoleon, rose to power through his military successes with the republican army. His troops had ranged widely across Europe and at one point had captured the Papal States. His supporters had later staged a coup in Rome, captured Pope Pius VI and shipped him across the Alps as a prisoner, resulting in his death in 1799. But Napoleon now saw that the persecution of the Catholic Church had turned much of Europe against France and had disillusioned the poorer members of French society, who previously had benefitted from its educational and charitable work. In 1801, he signed a Concordat with the new pope, Pius VII, which restored its presence in France. However, in 1802 he took back to the state control of public worship and religious education, and in 1804 made Pius attend his crowning as emperor in Notre Dame, an action of great symbolism. In 1808, Napoleon's troops were back in Rome, and after gaining control of Spain and Italy, he abolished the inquisition. In 1813, he took control of the bishops of France and Italy and while he would be out of power two years later, after the battle of Waterloo, all these actions illustrate how the Catholic Church was now in a severely weakened position and that it had a place in European society only with the permission of the civil powers. While the revolutionaries had gone further in trying to extinguish the Catholic Church than the general population would allow, the events of 1789–1815 as a whole illustrate how the people of France, and in the subsequent century many of the other nations of Europe, could and did curtail the power of the Church whenever they chose to do so. The once mighty Roman Catholic Church, the partner and sometimes rival of monarchies across the continent, a partnership and rivalry that had existed for a thousand years under the name of Christendom, was now a shadow of itself, a mere servant at the beck and call of the state and the representatives of the popular will.

Self-understanding: Schleiermacher's Writings

How was the Church as a whole to make sense of these bewildering events? The proliferation of Protestant denominations after the Reformation was confusing enough, with some of them cutting themselves off entirely from their national churches and ploughing their own furrows. Then the wave of revivals and awakenings brought about by the Pietists and their English and American followers showed that Protestantism had a dynamic and growing future, but where was it leading? Finally, the devastating blows to the Roman Catholic Church of the revolutionary years in France and then across Europe showed that the era of Christendom was well and truly over.

Protestantism had begun to find an alternative future for the Church, that of being a voluntary association of those who chose to become its members. But what was there to stop the Church generally becoming a sect, a self-serving group that had no involvement with wider society apart from occasional forays into its public spaces to recruit new members? Some of the Congregationalist, Baptist and Quaker groups were apparently taking the Church in this direction. Then in 1791, the American Congress adopted Article 1 of the *Bill of Rights* that 'Congress shall make no law respecting an establishment of religion': this expressed a complete separation of Church and state and pointed in a similar direction. But was that the only future for the Church? Could it not still have a ministry to society as a whole? Could it not still retain a communal dimension to its life even though it was now bereft of its worldly power?

Friedrich Schleiermacher (1768–1834) was the son of a Reformed army chaplain. Both his parents became Moravians, and so their son was educated at a Moravian school and then a Moravian seminary for the ministry. But he read widely and found this pathway too narrow. He entered the University of Halle, where he read the newly published works of Kant, which made a great impression. Kant's argument that God is beyond the scope and reach of human reason provided Schleiermacher with a question that he became determined to answer: could God be found in ways that would convince his increasingly sceptical friends and colleagues in the university world? He became a tutor to a Prussian family and then found his way to Berlin, where he was appointed Reformed minister to the Charity Hospital. He mixed in the literary and artistic circles of those caught up in Romanticism, a movement that was reasserting passion and imagination in reaction to the rationalism of the Enlightenment. It was a mood or tendency rather than a system of thought and appeared first in the writings of Goethe. Its influence spread to England, in the work of Blake, Wordsworth, Coleridge, Shelley and Keats and to France in the work of Chateaubriand and Hugo. Schleiermacher was inspired, because he recognized a connection between the feelings and consciousness of this movement and the Pietism with which he had grown up. He decided to compose some addresses to his sophisticated friends and a wider public on the necessity of the Christian religion. In 1799, they were published anonymously as *On Religion: Speeches to its Cultured Despisers*.

The *Speeches* were a brilliantly argued piece of rhetoric, in which in high flown prose typical of the Romantics he showed how those 'cultured' souls who dismissed religion as superstitious or irrational were missing something crucial: 'I maintain that in all better souls piety springs necessarily by itself; that a province of its own in the mind belongs to it, in which it has unlimited sway; that it is worthy to animate most profoundly the noblest and best and to be fully accepted and known by them' (Schleiermacher 1958, p. 21). What is this province? It is contemplation of all that is.

> The contemplation of the pious is the immediate consciousness of the universal existence of all finite things, in and through the Infinite, and of all temporal things in and through the Eternal. Religion is to seek this and find it in all that lives and moves, in all growth and change, in all doing and suffering. It is to have life and to know life in immediate feeling, only as such an existence in the Infinite and Eternal. (ibid., p. 36)

Later in the Second Speech this contemplation is linked with intuition and feeling, as opposed to rational thinking or of doing some kind of activity. It is the kind of feeling that 'issues from your heart and overspreads your whole being' (p. 44). And it is not intuition and feeling about a certain person or object of anything in particular, but of existence as such: 'Your feeling is piety, in so far as it expresses ... the being and life common to you and to the All. Your feeling is piety in so far as it is the result of the operation of God in you by means of the operation of the world upon you' (p. 45). Thus, 'the true nature of religion is ... immediate consciousness of the Deity as He is found in ourselves and in the world' (p. 101).

Later in life he would provide a more precise definition of religion as the 'self-consciousness (*Gefühl*) of absolute dependence on God', a pre-cognitive consciousness that is distinct from the knowledge of science and of the morality of right action. It is necessary to both and so is part and parcel of a full human life, developing the contemplative dimension of our natures just as philosophy and science develop the rational side. It is a dimension with deep roots in the Christian tradition going back through the mystics to the Christian Platonism of the Gospel of John and to Paul (Sykes 1971, pp. 49–50). Schleiermacher also recognized other religions as participating in this consciousness, so in a pioneering way opened the door to dialogue between religions; but he still regarded Christ as the perfect expression of this *Gefühl*.

The *Speeches* were widely read and discussed in German intellectual circles and began to change the way Christianity and the churches were viewed by sections of the cultural elite. He followed them up with other writings and soon found employment as an academic and preacher and finally as Rector of the newly founded University of Berlin. He helped to secure the place of theology and ministerial training within that university, creating a model of Christian academic life that would be replicated in countless European and American universities in the next two centuries. His next major contribution was his book *The Christian Faith* published in 1821–2. This is a comprehensive statement of how the point of view outlined in the *Speeches* can be more fully expressed in the doctrinal categories of Reformed Protestantism. It does this by using the kind of systematic methodology that had come to prominence through Enlightenment philosophy and so represents a landmark integration of the insights of Romanticism with Reformation theology and Enlightenment philosophical methodology. It is the first example of what has become termed systematic theology, the attempt to state and interpret a full range of Christian doctrines in an internally consistent and coherent way. As such it would institute a whole new discipline within theology and is one of the reasons Schleiermacher has been called 'the father of modern theology'.

The Christian Faith draws out a number of key implications of his position. It presents Christ as the perfect expression of self-consciousness of absolute dependence on God. As such, Christ offers redemption to any who draw close and take on his teaching and example: 'The Redeemer assumes believers into the power of his God-consciousness, and this is his redemptive activity' (Schleiermacher 1999, p. 425). Christ demonstrates a 'constant potency of

God-consciousness'. Correspondingly, Schleiermacher argued that sin was the antithesis of this, the pride of thinking that we can live independently of God. Such pride can lead to the distortions and abuses of human life.

There is therefore an important social dimension to his view, which is where the Church comes into the picture: 'All that comes to exist in the world through redemption is embraced in the fellowship of believers, within which all regenerate people are always found.' Schleiermacher asserts that the two expressions 'the fellowship of believers' and the 'Christian Church' are equivalent, and then writes, 'the truth is that the new life of each individual springs from that of the community, while the life of the community springs from no other individual life than that of the Redeemer'. He is not going to pre-judge what form this fellowship must take:

> no particular form of fellowship is here asserted or excluded; every form, perfect and imperfect, that has ever been or that may yet appear, is included … wherever regenerate persons are within reach of each other, some kind of fellowship between them is bound to arise. For if they are in contact, their witness to the faith must in part overlap, and must necessarily involve mutual recognition and a common understanding as to their operation within the common area. (ibid., p. 525)

This view of the Church, within his wider scheme, was important because it integrated the insight and energy of the Protestant Pietist movement, which had been spreading out across Europe and the New World and soon would be planted within Africa, within an Enlightenment framework of understanding. Schleiermacher was showing that these two great movements do not have to live in opposition to each other, because they do not necessarily contradict each other. Rather, they complement each other.

For the churches, the importance of this cannot be overstated. Schleiermacher and his followers (who included Coleridge in England) showed how some parts of the Protestant tradition came to recognize that they had an essential role within a modern and cultured society, which was that of addressing and cultivating a dimension of life that would otherwise remain neglected. In other words, these churches were not going to separate themselves and become self-serving sects, as might otherwise happen, but were going to see their place and ministry at the heart of society as a whole. While they were broadly developing into voluntary associations in the wake of the Reformation, as we have already seen, they were now also beginning to embrace a communal mission. This would not be imposed or even assisted by the state, and therefore the Church could no longer be seen as a public utility, but would grow out of the voluntary commitment and passion of those who chose to enter its fellowship. In the modern period, this communal mission would be developed in some unexpected and radical ways.

Discussion Questions

Does the Doctrine of Election have a place in the modern Church?
Was Pietism right to emphasize the role of feeling in religious faith?
Can a voluntary association have a mission to society as a whole?

Bibliography and Further Reading

Bettenson, Henry and Chris Maunder (eds) (2011), *Documents of the Christian Church*, 4th edn, Oxford: Oxford University Press.

Grass, Tim (2008), *SCM Core Text Modern Church History*, London: SCM Press.

Greenfield, John (1930), *Power from on High, or, the Two Hundredth Anniversary of the Great Moravian Revival, 1727–1927*, Atlantic City: The World Wide Revival Prayer Movement.

Hempton, David (2011), *The Church in the Long Eighteenth Century*, London: I. B. Tauris.

Kant, Immanuel (1784), 'What is Enlightenment?' http://philosophy.eserver.org/kant/what-is-enlightenment.txt.

MacCulloch, Diarmaid (2003), *Reformation: Europe's House Divided 1490–1700*, Harmondsworth: Allan Lane.

MacCulloch, Diarmaid (2009), *A History of Christianity: The First Three Thousand Years*, Chs 20 and 21, Harmondsworth: Allen Lane.

McGrath, Alistair (1999), *Reformation Thought: An Introduction*, 3rd edn, Oxford: Blackwell.

Miles, Margaret (2004), *The Word Made Flesh: A History of Christian Thought*, Oxford: Wiley-Blackwell.

Schleiermacher, Friedrich (1958), *On Religion: Speeches to its Cultured Despisers*, English trans. John Oman, New York: Harper Torchbooks.

Schleiermacher, Friedrich (1999), *The Christian Faith*, trans. Hugh Ross Mackintosh and J. S. Stewart, Edinburgh: T & T Clark.

Sykes, Stephen (1971), *Friedrich Schleiermacher*, London: Lutterworth.

Wesley, John (1974), *Journal of John Wesley*, Chicago: Moody Publishers.

Westminster Confession of Faith, The (1647, 1648).

9

Churches in the Modern Era: Communities or Cells?

In the previous chapter, the Western Church was seen to be evolving into a collection of voluntary associations, with some sectarian tendencies, but also sometimes with a sense of needing to serve the wider society, a communal mission. How did this play out over the next two centuries, the nineteenth and the twentieth, the era of history that is often called the modern period? Did the sectarian tendencies lead to greater separation of the churches from society, with their becoming communities in their own right? In other words, did voluntarism become communitarianism? Or did they go in the opposite direction, becoming more enmeshed within and identified with their societies and states, which were becoming more and more nationalist as the nineteenth century gave way to the twentieth? In other words, did 'voluntarism-with-community-service' become 'nationalist religion'? The marriage of two partners, Church and state, who had been more-or-less equal partners, was over: was their future to be one of separation or amalgamation?

The next two centuries would witness acute trauma for the peoples of Europe and the wider world, with the gradual escalation of nationalism leading to imperialism and then to two world wars and the unprecedented horrors of twentieth-century warfare. The broad outlines of these events are well known and do not need to be rehearsed. The question to be faced in this chapter is how the body of the Church fared through all this and, in particular, how its corporate life was affected.

Timeline

1759–1833	William Wilberforce
1807	Slave trade made illegal in British territories
1814	Abdication of Napoleon; reinstatement of Pius VII; reconstitution of Jesuits
1835	D. F. Strauss' *Life of Jesus*
1846–78	Pope Pius IX
1858	Appearances at Lourdes
1859	Darwin's *Origin of Species*
1860	Unification of Italy
1869–70	First Vatican Council, with declaration of papal infallibility
1870	Franco-Prussian war; end of papal states
1886–1968	Karl Barth
1905–7	Separation of Church and state in France
1906–45	Dietrich Bonhoeffer
1907	Papal condemnation of modernism
1907	Azusa Street revival, Los Angeles, and spread of Pentecostalism
1910	Edinburgh Missionary Conference
1914–18	First World War with Russian Revolution (1917)
1929–68	Martin Luther King Jr
1933	Hitler becomes German Chancellor
1934	Barmen Declaration by the German Confessing Church
1939–45	Second World War

1948	World Council of Churches founded
1949	Billy Graham begins evangelistic work
1962–65	Second Vatican Council
1968	Pope Paul VI condemns artificial birth control;
	Medellín Conference supports liberation theology
1978	Year of three popes: Paul VI; John Paul I; John Paul II
1988	First woman bishop in the USA (Barbara Harris)
1989–90	Collapse of Communism in Eastern Europe

Ultramontanist Roman Catholicism

The nineteenth century witnessed an extraordinary paradox in the life of the Roman Catholic Church in Europe. On the one hand, the power of the different national churches and hierarchies was dramatically weakened. In France, the Concordat that Napoleon signed with Pius VII in 1801 weakened the influence of Gallicanism, an eighteenth-century movement within the French clergy, which had emphasized the relative independence of the French Church from Rome and had sought greater control over its life. Then the end of the Napoleonic Wars saw the end of clerical rule in some of the smaller German states: in most cases Protestant monarchies gained the advantage over archbishops and prelates. In many parts of the continent, liberalism was on the ascendency, a movement championing the rights of ordinary citizens against the Church as well as the aristocracy and monarchy. But, paradoxically, the Concordat strengthened the hand of the papacy, because it was the pope that Napoleon negotiated with and who was given rights over the French Church. After the defeat of Napoleon, the pope then became the rallying point for all those who had hated the 1789 revolution and its liberal ideology. A movement known as 'Ultramontanism' (literally meaning 'over the mountains', shorthand for 'we support the pope who resides over the Alps in Rome') gained strength in France, Germany and among the growing Roman Catholic population of England. It was encouraged by the revival of the Jesuit Order in 1814, an order always committed to serving the pope over the local hierarchies in the Church. It was encouraged by Pope Gregory XVI (1831–46), who issued a number of encyclicals condemning modern liberal ideas such as liberty, equality and the separation of Church and state, and those within the Church who wanted to accommodate such ideas. His successor Pius IX (1846–78) was initially sympathetic to liberalism, but when revolution came to Rome in 1848 he had to temporarily flee the city. When he returned, his liberalism had turned into a strong conservatism. In 1849, he condemned socialism and communism, in 1864 he condemned religious toleration and unrestricted press freedom, and in 1866 he condemned attempts at reunion between Anglicans and the Roman Catholic Church. Meanwhile, devotion to the Blessed Virgin Mary saw a strong upsurge in many places, and in 1854, Pius IX declared that the popular belief in her immaculate conception (her conception in her mother's womb without original sin) was now official church dogma. He also declared that the popular devotion to the sacred heart of Jesus, which had become popular in France, was now official and therefore available to everyone in the Church. In 1858, a peasant girl from Lourdes, Bernadette Soubirous, reported that she had had several visions of the Virgin Mary. Within a short time, the site of her visions became a place of pilgrimage with many people reporting miraculous healings taking place. It received official recognition in 1862.

This mixture of centralization, political conservatism and traditional medieval piety centred on the papacy reached its apotheosis in 1870 with the first Vatican Council. This had been called to reform and renew the Church, but as the bishops gathered in Rome the armies of the Italian nationalists under Victor Emmanuel marched on the Papal States to take control of them and end the last vestige of papal temporal power. The Council had to be cut short, but before the bishops left the city they acceded to one of Ultramontanism's strongest demands, that the pope be declared infallible when he makes, by virtue of his office, a solemn pronouncement on faith or morals: in other words, that he need not wait for consent from cardinals, bishops or anyone else when pronouncing on these matters. But he was not declared to be infallible on administrative matters, which the Ultramontanists had also wanted, so his domination of his Church would not be total.

What kind of Church was implied by all this? The preparatory documents shed light on the official teaching:

We teach and declare: The Church has all the marks of a true Society. Christ did not leave this society undefined and without a set form. Rather, he himself gave its existence, and his will determined the form of its existence and gave it its constitution. The Church is not part nor member of any other society and is not mingled in any way with any other society. It is so perfect in itself that it is distinct from all human societies and stands far above them. (in Dulles 1988, pp. 36–7)

Avery Dulles points out that some of these themes were taken into the decrees on the papacy adopted by the council, and also used later by subsequent popes such as Leo XIII, Pius XI and Pius XII in their encyclicals. In this outlook spiritual grace is seen as almost a kind of substance inherent in the Church. The pope and bishops, assisted by priests and deacons, are described by some writers in this tradition as if they are engineers opening and shutting the valves of grace. Furthermore, government of the body is placed in the hands of the hierarchy. They govern the flock with pastoral authority and as Christ's vice-regents impose new laws and precepts which all must obey. The Church is not conceived as a democratic or representative society, but as one in which the fullness of power is concentrated in the hands of a ruling class that perpetuates itself by co-option. A preparatory document for Vatican I describes this in the following terms:

But the Church of Christ is not a community of equals in which all the faithful have the same rights. It is a society of unequals, not only because among the faithful some are clerics and some are laymen, but particularly because there is in the Church the power from God whereby to some it is given to sanctify, teach, and govern, and to others not. (ibid., p. 38)

This hierarchical Church exists for the benefit of those who belong to it. It is a shelter where the faithful are protected against the assaults of the enemy of their souls. The Church is compared to a loving mother who nourishes her infants at the breast, or, more impersonally, to the boat of Peter, which carries the faithful to the farther shore of heaven, provided they remain on board. They have only to be docile and obedient, and to rely on the ministrations of the Church. According to the Vatican I documents, 'It is an article of faith that outside the Church no one can be saved … Who is not in this ark will perish in the flood' (ibid., p. 41).

Dulles points out, however, that this outlook is not indifferent to the eternal destiny of the rest of humankind: it gives strong support to the missionary effort by which the Church goes out to non-members. But it seeks to save their souls precisely by bringing them into the ark of the institution. Success in this can be measured precisely, by the number of baptisms performed, by the number of regular worshippers and by the number of those who regularly receive the sacraments (ibid., pp. 41–2).

These are remarkable statements because while they appear to uphold traditional Catholic doctrine they in fact do precisely the opposite, overturning medieval notions of Christendom, which saw Church and society as one and indivisible with pope and prince working in harmony to bring society to perfection (see pp. 107–11), and instead present the Church as a separate and perfect society or community, like Noah's ark riding above the storms and corruption of the world. The transition from a communal to a communitarian view is striking: the Church is not part of a wider community, but forms its own community, with its clergy becoming rulers and chaplains of that community. Pius IX and the documents of Vatican I would not use the word 'voluntary' to describe this body, for that word was too reminiscent of liberal ideas of freedom of choice, and nor would they describe the Church as a sect, because that contradicts its aspiration to be catholic, but there is a clear sense of separation between Church and society which has sectarian tendencies and shows a surprising convergence with some Protestant traditions.

Did this basic outlook change very much within the twentieth century? There is little evidence that it did in the first 60 years, but with the Second Vatican Council in Rome between 1962 and 1965 a different and surprising outlook began to emerge. Before examining this we must see what happened within the other major tradition of the Western Church in this period.

Protestantism's Growing Diversity

In the wake of the French Revolution and its all-conquering liberal ideology, it may have seemed as if the days of Protestantism were numbered. Was not the revolution the natural successor of the Reformation, with its advocacy of the individual's political rights a consequence of the Reformation's advocacy of the individual's spiritual rights? Karl Marx, who described religion as the opium of the people, went one step further in his *Communist Manifesto* in 1848 and called for the sweeping away of the entire structure of European life. Furthermore the Enlightenment produced a wave of historical and scientific scholarship that seemed to undermine Protestantism's main source of authority, the Bible. David Friedrich Strauss' *Life of Jesus*, a critical deconstruction of the historical reliability of the gospels, was published in Germany in 1835 and generated great controversy. Charles Darwin's *Origin of Species*, apparently undermining the account of creation in the book of Genesis, was published in 1859. Many of the educated began to lose their faith after encountering this scholarship.

But Protestantism did not collapse. It had already erupted into a multitude of noisy and colourful expressions which gained strength over the nineteenth century. The roots of this lay in the Evangelical revival of the eighteenth century (see pp. 146–8), which continued to exert its influence at the start of the nineteenth and emphasized the place of feelings and emotions within Christian discipleship. In North America, a second 'Great Awakening' took place at the start of the nineteenth century, beginning among students within the Congregational churches in New England and spreading to Presbyterians in the northern and eastern states and Methodists and Baptists in the West and South, increasing their size, so that they became the largest Protestant denominations in North America. The revival very quickly became highly emotional, with weeping, fainting, fits and babbling. The leaders tried to restrain this and emphasized the need to engage in charitable works. Many social agencies and voluntary organizations came out of this, as well as Christian colleges and Sunday schools. (One by-product of all this was the ordaining of the first woman to be a minister, Antoinette Brown, who was ordained into the ministry of a Congregational Church in 1853.) A third 'Great Awakening' took place between 1875 and 1914.

Other independent churches also sprang into being, especially in the United States. In 1827, Joseph Smith received a 'revelation', which he published as *The Book of Mormon*. This led to the founding of the Church of Jesus Christ of Latter-Day Saints, which from 1847 was based in Salt Lake City, Utah. In 1844, the Seventh Day Adventists were formed, a group who expected the second coming of Christ to take place that year. When Christ failed to appear, they decided to keep meeting and worshipping together, expecting him to return soon, and opting to do this on Saturdays in recognition of Old Testament law to keep the sabbath day. The name 'Seventh Day Adventist' was adopted in 1861, and in 1878 they planted a church in Southampton in Britain. They required strict abstinence from alcohol and tobacco by their members and avoidance of tea, coffee and meat. They paid tithes on their income and practised adult baptism. They have since spread all around the world and are now very well established in Africa.

The Evangelical revival and Great Awakenings also encouraged the founding of black-led churches in the United States. In 1816, Richard Allen became the first bishop of the newly founded African Methodist Episcopal Bethel Church in Philadelphia. Another episcopal Methodist Church was founded in New York in 1821 by James Varick. After the Civil War (1861–65), black missionaries from the northern states travelled to the southern states to help the emancipated slaves create their own independent churches, many of them Baptist in tradition. African–American Christianity would now grow and strengthen, especially through the influence of the Pentecostal movement. This arose out of an outpouring of the kind of spiritual gifts mentioned in 1 Corinthians 12.8–11. It began to emerge in Topeka, Kansas under the leadership of Bible college teacher Charles Parham and his student Agnes Ozman. It then manifested itself in a church congregation in Los Angeles in 1906, at the Azusa Street church under the minister J. Seymour. There were connections between this and the Holiness tradition in North American Methodism, which itself had originally drawn inspiration from John Wesley's own heart being 'strangely warmed' (see p. 146). While Afro-American in ethos and often in leadership, this kind of Pentecostalism attracted all races. It included an expectation of the imminent return of Christ at the end of the age, with an imperative on its members to go out and preach the gospel throughout the world. By 1908, the Azusa Street church had sent missionaries to China. Then Pentecostalism spread rapidly through South America, from Brazil to most parts of the continent, drawing adherents away from the Roman Catholic Church into new independent churches that would, among other things, reform the lifestyles of their members. In 1914, in the USA the Assemblies of God were founded, an affiliation of independent churches. Since then the growth of Pentecostalism in every part of the world has been remarkable. Today it accounts for a quarter of all Christians in the world, half of whom are in Latin America.

In the 1960s and 1970s, the gifts of the Spirit also started to manifest themselves within the Roman Catholic and Anglican communions. This became known as the Charismatic movement and was encouraged by John Wimber and his Vineyard Church movement in the USA. The manifestation of these gifts was further encouraged in the 1990s by the Alpha Course, an introduction to Christianity sponsored by the Anglican parish of Holy Trinity Brompton, in London, and its leader Nicky Gumble. The Alpha Course is estimated to have reached 13 million people across many denominations worldwide. These examples are within already established denominations so fall outside the Pentecostal movement as such, but they show the ability of Protestantism to grow and cross-fertilize sections of Roman Catholicism and other denominations in spontaneous, sometimes messy and creative ways.

Sectarianism

Christian Science was a very different movement. In 1875, Mary Baker Eddy of Boston published *Science and Health*, a text arguing that healing takes place through accepting the moral and spiritual teaching of Jesus. She believed that evil and sickness are 'unreal' and can be destroyed by the believer becoming aware of God's power and love. Her teaching created a devoted following and led to the founding of Christian Science churches, which were congregationally led and made a point of always reading and listening to sections of *Science and Health*. They spread to many parts of the English-speaking world and to Germany. Like the Seventh Day Adventists, the followers of Christian Science are seriously at odds with the rest of their society in some matters, while being highly respectable in others. They show how some groups within Protestantism evolved from being voluntary associations, which recognized the wider society as the primary community in which its members live, to being sects, which see the Church itself as the primary community and object of loyalty of its members, with restricted interaction with and interest in the wider community.

This sectarianism is seen most clearly in Charles Taze Russell (1852–1916) who founded the Jehovah's Witnesses in Pittsburgh in 1881. They were first known as the Watch Tower Bible and Tract Society and believed that Jesus was 'a perfect man' and had returned invisibly to earth in 1874 in order to prepare the world for the coming of the Kingdom of God after the battle of Armageddon. This was initially expected in 1914 and believers were to warn others so that they might get ready for the cataclysm. But only 144,000 from the whole of human history would be saved, a figure drawn from a literal reading of the book of Revelation. In the twentieth century, as the movement grew in many parts of the world, it became very strict in its discipline and in 'indifference' to the world. Jehovah's Witnesses frequently clashed with governments, and their members have become well known for doorstep evangelism and sale of their magazine *The Watchtower*. In their reluctance to mix with non-members, they demonstrate very clearly the difference between a communitarian sect and a communally-minded church. By the end of the twentieth century, it was estimated there were 4 million Jehovah's Witnesses around the world.

Protestant nationalism?

Other Protestant churches went in a very different direction. After the defeat of Napoleon, a number of Protestant monarchies gained control of the Protestant churches in their lands. In the Netherlands, King William I (1813–40) introduced a system of church government in which the state had considerable powers. He also allowed liberal values to thrive and took a broad approach to doctrinal beliefs. This was the period in which German biblical scholarship was beginning to undermine belief in the historical reliability of the Bible, and some Protestants were moving away from dogma to scepticism on issues like the authorship of the Pentateuch (i.e. that it was not written by Moses), the virgin birth and the miracles of Jesus. The Dutch Church provided a safe haven for those influenced by this modernism. But others, still firmly within the Calvinist tradition, were not happy, and in 1834 a conservative movement split from the state church to form the Calvinist Christian Reformed Church. Further opposition to modernism erupted in 1886, when Abraham Kuyper led another group out of the state Church. He was a Calvinist theologian, an anti-revolutionary but also, revealingly, a politician. He was still in favour of working with the state rather than separately from it, and he became leader of the Christian Democrat party and then Prime Minister in 1901. Protestant nationalism was still to the fore.

Further to the north, in Denmark the Lutheran Church was also under the state and dominated by the liberal minded. It was led by Hans Larsen Martensen, who had been influenced by Hegel and believed that society and Church together could assist the divine purpose in the world. But, as in the Netherlands, others thought differently and a revival movement was led by the poet and preacher N. F. S. Grundtvig (1783–1872). He was a nationalist, and he endeavoured to awaken the 'Danish Spirit' of the people by recalling their ancient

Norse myths and showing how they could inspire their Christian piety in the present. The year 1848, the 'year of revolutions' in Europe, then took place and had a dramatic impact in Denmark. The state Church was reconstituted as the Danish People's Church and Grundtvig helped with the founding of Folk High Schools for the education of children within this nationalistic milieu. One independently minded theologian was scathing in his criticism of this and of the Hegelian outlook of Martensen. This was Søren Kierkegaard (1813–55), whose extensive writings were little read in his life but who came to have a profound influence on Protestantism and wider intellectual life in the twentieth century.

The emergence of a nationalistic Protestantism gathered pace in the late nineteenth and early twentieth centuries. As the nation states of Europe became increasingly competitive in the scramble for Africa of the 1880s and then in the arms race of the early 1900s, so their established churches became more and more caught up within nationalism. A high point of this in England was when the Bishop of London, A. F. Winnington-Ingram, exchanged his clerical robes for an army uniform and became a passionate recruiting sergeant for the army at the start of the First World War. But others were less jingoistic and as the war unfolded many clergy had their views changed by the experience of being chaplains on the front line. Church leaders began to support the campaign to respect conscientious objection.

The supreme example of nationalistic Protestantism was the co-option of the German Lutheran Church by Hitler and the Nazis in the 1930s. They blended a crude version of German mythology with populist sentiments and anger at the treatment of their country by the victors of the First World War. Hitler was able to recruit a number of theologians and church leaders to his 'German Christian' movement, which then tried to remove all references to Jewish elements within Christianity. When he became chancellor in 1933, the German Christians became the dominant group within the German Evangelical Church (the official name of the Lutheran Church) and took control of its life.

This was the moment of greatest strength for Protestant nationalism but also the tipping point towards its collapse. A different group of church leaders and theologians were galvanized into action. They believed the idolatry inherent in Hitler's project was now apparent, and it was up to them to start a movement that would resist this amalgamation of Church and state. It was called the Confessing Church, and it has come to have a crucial importance not only for Protestantism but for Western Christianity as a whole. Led by Pastor Martin

Niemöller, it began by setting up alternative parishes and administrative structures for those 'Confessional' churches that rejected the nationalist theology of the German Christians. Then from 1934 to 1939, it became a focus for resistance to the Nazis. Many of its clergy and laity were forcibly conscripted into the army. During the war many would be sent to the concentration camps, including Niemöller himself. The defining moment for the Confessing Church was the issuing of the Barmen Declaration in 1934. This was drafted by a group of theologians led by Karl Barth and was approved by the Synod of Barmen. It set out the theological grounds for opposing the national Church and the regime behind it: the only object of loyalty for the Church was to be the Word of God.

This was a key moment for Protestantism, when it acknowledged that its faith meant it should not be amalgamated with a nation and its state. A degree of separation was required, which would allow people to make up their own minds and come freely to church or not. The Church was not to be a state institution but to remain a voluntary association, connected to society in certain ways but with its ultimate loyalty lying elsewhere.

Ecumenism

No account of Protestantism in the modern period would be complete without mentioning the Ecumenical movement, a broadly based movement to bring the churches and especially the Protestant churches together. It was given great impetus by the World Mission Conference in Edinburgh in 1910, when representatives of most of the Protestant denominations met together to see how they could work together in mission. The aim of the conference was 'the evangelization of the whole world in this generation', an over-ambitious aim but one that led to increasing contact between the churches at international level and to the founding of national councils of churches in various parts of the world. There were conferences about the common faith and order of the churches, and their life and work, notably in Stockholm in 1925 and Oxford in 1937. A provisional committee of a new World Council of Churches met in 1938, and its first assembly took place in Amsterdam in 1948 'as a fellowship of churches which accept our Lord Jesus Christ as God and Saviour'. This excluded the Jehovah's Witnesses and Unitarians but would later include most Orthodox churches. The Roman Catholic Church did not participate but sent observers, more enthusiastically after the Second Vatican Council (see p. 173). The word 'fellowship' gives the reason for the success of the WCC, which did not aim to unite churches but to provide a forum for them to meet and work together on common initiatives in the world. Significantly, though, the Protestant churches recognized their common approach to sacraments in the document *Baptism, Eucharist and Ministry* of 1982 (the so-called Lima Document). At the Canberra Assembly in 1991, though, they acknowledged that the churches would never be institutionally re-united and that sharing communion would only come on the basis of a 'unity in diversity'. This is reflected in the fact that the only place in the world where churches have re-united has been India, first in the Church of South India (1947), followed by the Church of North India and the Church of Pakistan. These churches are the exception that proves the rule, which is that the modern period has witnessed the eruption of Protestantism into a colourful diversity of traditions and denominations, a diversity that many now recognize as a strength because it reflects the diversity of the peoples of the world.

Serving the Needs of the World

Bonhoeffer would become a figurehead for a third major strand of modern Western church history, a strand that crosses over Protestant and Roman Catholic traditions. This grew out of a tendency within some churches, already noted, to want to serve the wider society, a communal mission (see pp. 173–4). That tendency became very clear at the start of the modern period with William Wilberforce's (1759–1833) campaign to abolish slavery. Acting as a member of the Church of England as well as an MP, and with the backing of the Evangelically inspired Clapham Sect, a group of clergy and lay people met in the rectory at Clapham in London. They organized foreign missions, the reform of working conditions in factories, the promotion of literacy through the Sunday School movement, and the abolition of the slave trade. Wilberforce showed a dogged determination to get the support he needed in parliament for the abolition of the slave trade, and this was achieved in 1807. In 1833, his campaigning resulted in the House of Commons voting for the abolition of the institution of slavery itself throughout the British Empire. Wilberforce embodied the communal mission of the churches like no other.

Within the British Isles a more pressing problem was the dire situation of the poor in almost every way. Disease, squalor, drunkenness, prostitution and hopelessness were the predominant features of life for the new urban poor. In response to this, William Booth (1829–1912), who had been a Methodist preacher, founded the Christian Mission to London's East End in 1865. This undertook evangelistic, social and rescue work. Booth's own commitment to the poor, to caring for both their spiritual and bodily needs, found rich expression in this initiative. In 1878, it was re-named the Salvation Army, and in 1880, it spread to the USA, Australia, Europe and elsewhere. Booth spent much of his life travelling and organizing the new churches which were called 'citadels', and preaching. In 1890, he published *In Darkest England and the Way Out*, in which he suggested creating farm colonies and rescue homes. He was not very knowledgeable of theology, but he had a good commercial sense and a passion for the work, which made the Salvation Army one of the most widespread and enduring of the new independent churches. What is important is that the social work was not seen as a means to a different end, that of evangelism and increasing church membership, but as an end in itself. In this way, it expressed very well the emerging sense in the nineteenth century of the Church having a call to serve the world.

Many other examples could be mentioned but one name stands out because of the way this person not only taught the Church to move in this direction but gave his life in a Nazi concentration camp because of what he believed. Dietrich Bonhoeffer (1906–45) was a German Lutheran pastor and theologian, who taught and published academic theology as well as ministered to Lutheran congregations in London and Barcelona. As the Nazis gained more and more of a stranglehold on Germany, Bonhoeffer believed he had no choice but to return to his homeland and minister to his people there. During the later stages of the war he became associated with the group that tried to assassinate Hitler, and he was arrested in 1943. While in prison, he wrote extensively, and his *Letters and Papers from Prison* were published after the war. He was executed by the Gestapo just before his camp was liberated by the Allies.

Within his *Letters and Papers* is a statement that sums up the new-found calling of the Church to serve the world:

The Church is her true self only when she exists for humanity. As a fresh start she should give away all her endowments to the poor and needy. The clergy should live solely on the free-will offerings of their congregations, or possibly engage in some secular calling. She must take part in the social life of the world, not lording it over men, but helping and serving them. She must tell men, whatever their calling, what it means to live in Christ, to exist for others. (Bonhoeffer 1971, pp. 382–3)

Vatican II and liberation theology

After the war, this sentiment would find significant expression in Roman Catholicism especially in the wake of the Second Vatican Council. It was called by the jovial and saintly Pope John XXIII (Pope 1958–63), and the announcement took everyone by surprise, because when he was elected, the 77-year-old John had been regarded as a safe pair of hands. John gave the bishops of the Church the task of renewing (*aggiornamento*) their common life. The calling of the Council revived the idea of conciliarism (see p. 118), the view that ultimate leadership of the Church was by councils of pope and bishops together. The Council met from 1962 to 1965 with 3,000 participants from all over the world, the largest church council in history. Officially, the Council was meant to elucidate the teaching of previous councils such at Trent and Vatican I. But after some struggle between reformers and the conservatives of the Curia (the Vatican's civil service), the bishops made some important modernizing decisions, such as revising the liturgy and putting it into the vernacular from Latin and bringing the altar to the centre of churches so that the people and priest gathered around it. They also adopted a new openness to other churches, stating that, while the Roman Catholic Church was the only legitimate church, other churches might also know Christ. There was regret at the bitterness of the division with Protestantism. Orthodoxy was also recognized as being close to Roman Catholicism, with Orthodox ordinations recognized as valid. Other religions were seen as embodying much that was good and the way was opened for inter-faith dialogue.

Most significantly, the council recognized that God was at work in the world as well as the Church, leading humanity forward in the development of an international order of peace and health. The document *Gaudium et Spes* set the tone:

The joys and hopes, the grief and anguish of the people of our time, especially of those who are poor or afflicted, are the joys and hopes, the grief and anguish of the followers of Christ as well. Nothing that is genuinely human fails to find an echo in their hearts ... they cherish a feeling of deep solidarity with the human race and with its history. (Vatican Council II 1996, p. 163)

Who would respond to this new openness to the world? The bishops of Latin America were one group as they faced the sharp divisions in their continent between rich and poor, with powerful elites ruling through military dictatorship and oppressing the majority poor who were struggling for justice and liberation. The bishops met together at a conference at Medellín in 1968 and stated 'we are on the threshold of a new epoch in this history of Latin America. It appears to be a time of zeal for full emancipation, of liberation from every form of servitude, of personal maturity and of collective integration.' Echoing *Gaudium et Spes* they then described a divine presence within this historical movement:

> We cannot fail to see in this gigantic effort toward a rapid transformation and development an obvious sign of the Spirit who leads the history of humankind and of the peoples toward their vocation. We cannot but discover in this force, daily more insistent and impatient for transformation, vestiges of the image of God in human nature as a powerful incentive. This dynamism leads us progressively to an even greater control of nature, a more profound personalization and fellowship, and an encounter with the God who ratifies and deepens those values attained through human efforts. (in Gutiérrez 1988, p. xvii)

This opened the way for the rise of liberation theology and a liberation church in the dioceses of Latin America. The leading theologian Gustavo Gutiérrez wrote that the bishops' words express 'so well both the historical situation of liberation theology and the perspective of faith in which it interprets this situation' (ibid., p. xviii). Now the people of God could stand alongside others who were fighting for the material liberation of the poor and underprivileged of the world. The coming of the kingdom of God was linked with political and economic emancipation of such oppressed peoples, and the churches should take real steps toward its realization.

For the liberation theologians of the 1970s and 1980s, the divine presence was especially manifest in the Base Christian Communities (BCCs), which had grown up across the continent during the previous decade. During the 1970s, it was estimated that there were some 40,000 of these, mostly in poor rural areas and on the outskirts of towns, co-ordinated by lay people and committed to celebration of the Word, shared prayer and mutual help, joining with others for the Eucharist, when the priest visited the area. The bishops at Medellín thought very highly of them:

> The 'grass-roots' community is the primary, fundamental core of the church. On its own level it must take responsibility for the riches of faith and for its propagation, as well as for the cult, which brings faith to expression. It is consequently the initial cell of the church's structure, the focus of evangelization, and at present the main point of departure for man's improvement and development. (in Moltmann 1992, p. 329)

A very different form of the Church from that of Vatican I is here being envisioned. The Church is no longer seen as a centralized society with local churches as outposts of this, at one remove from the secular communities of the world. Instead, grass-roots 'cells' are the 'primary, fundamental core of the Church' which serve something bigger than themselves, humanity's 'improvement and development'. They are formed to be a means of conveying something else, described in liberation theology as the coming of God's saving kingdom to the oppressed of the world. They can function independently, like a plant cell (and differently from 'cell groups' in the later Cell Church Movement, which are sub-divisions of larger churches: see Croft 2008). But they are not self-contained communities with minimal interest in what goes on beyond their four walls. They serve a greater good and, as liberation theology also showed, will work with others towards that end. They can perhaps be likened to yeast cells whose purpose is to leaven the surrounding dough.

The Roman Catholic hierarchy under Pope John Paul II would later turn against liberation theology and try to suppress it. But through the witness of martyrs such as Archbishop Oscar Romero in El Salvador, its influence spread beyond Latin America. It was taken up with enthusiasm in other parts of the world among Black and Hispanic communities in the United States and in certain churches in Africa, Asia and the South Pacific and among Christian feminists. And as the twentieth century drew to a close, it was possible to see the cell church form being adopted in other parts of the world, not least within the emerging church movement in North America, Europe and Australasia (see Gibbs and Bolger 2006). In Latin America, however, the Base Christian Communities have increasingly come under the influence of the Pentecostal movement (described on pp. 166–7), and by the end of the twentieth century were predominantly independent rather than Roman Catholic.

Self-understanding: Moltmann on 'Grass-roots Communities'

By the end of the twentieth century, Western churches could look back on two centuries of extraordinary growth, as the splits of the Reformation led to greater and greater diversification and growth around the world. Revivals and awakenings created an extraordinary energy and enthusiasm for mission. The historic denominations grew as well, creating new dioceses, synods and provinces in many continents. While the Roman Catholic Church initially committed itself to separation from surrounding communities, during the second half of the twentieth century it rediscovered a calling to serve the needs of the wider world and even to work with other churches and groups in serving these needs. Protestantism experienced a new diversity of forms, with nationalistic state churches at one extreme and various sects at the other, and with a whole range of voluntary associations in between, some with major commitments to their surrounding communities and others showing increasing manifestation of the Pentecostal gifts of the spirit. The nationalistic state churches rose and then fell in this period, though as the twentieth century came to a close a few still retained some lingering connections with their respective states.

Meanwhile a strange paradox developed in the religious life of Western Europe. By the end of the twentieth century, its people had, by and large, stopped going to church on a regular basis. Church attendances fell dramatically, especially from the 1960s onwards, as a culture of obligation gave way to a culture of consumerism and most people decided there were other ways they would prefer to spend a Sunday morning. However, many still retained a sense of being connected in some way to one or other of the churches, with the label 'Christian' (in Protestant countries) and 'Catholic' (in Roman Catholic countries) still being used of themselves by a majority of the population. Furthermore, attendance at special services, such as funerals, baptisms, carol services and nativities, showed no signs of diminishing. Many still held a faith in God and prayed on a regular basis. Church involvement in primary and secondary education and in health care, not least in the hospice movement of the late twentieth century, was valued and supported by the wider communities as much as ever. The secularization thesis, that there was an unstoppable 'de-Christianization' of European culture and life throughout this period, was also increasingly questioned among sociologists.

How, then, can we characterize the corporate form of the Church in this changing setting? The most widespread form, that of the voluntary association inherited from the Reformation period, was having to adapt. By the end of the twentieth century, it was having to adjust to reduced attendances at regular services and therefore to reduced membership lists. Voluntary organizations usually depend on a signed-up membership who pay a regular subscription and finance the employees, such as ministers. But as membership reduced so giving reduced and therefore the formal organization of the churches contracted, with the result that there were fewer and fewer paid ministers. A different kind of voluntary association was needed, one that did not attempt to be a separate organization within the wider community but would be an integral part of that community, though with a distinctive contribution. But how could it do this without being swallowed up by that community?

Both the Protestant and Roman Catholic traditions had begun to feel their way to a new form in the various campaigns for social reform in the nineteenth and twentieth centuries. In the twentieth century, this form came to clear expression in the late writings of Dietrich Bonhoeffer, whose death added to the sense of his prophetic witness. It then achieved widespread expression in the Base Christian Communities of Latin America. In their 'cell' structure they began to show how it is possible to be identified with a community, through being at the service of its needs, while also making a distinctive contribution through its commitment to the coming of God's kingdom. The one is integral to the other. This cell form of church life can be seen as a distinctive contribution of the twentieth-century Church to Christian history as a whole.

In his widely read volume *The Church in the Power of the Spirit*, first published in 1975, Jürgen Moltmann was one of the first to recognize the significance of the Base Christian Communities for the wider Church and especially for Western Christianity, and so his observations can conclude this chapter. Following the bishops at Medellín, he called them 'grass-roots communities' and described how they had grown up almost simultaneously in different countries and denominations but that their centre of gravity was Latin America. After quoting the words of the bishops printed above, Moltmann began to draw out the inherent structure of these 'cell' churches:

> The characteristics of such communities are hard to sum up, because they vary so much. But the following seem to be essential to all of them:
>
> 1 The voluntary association of members in a Christian fellowship.
> 2 The fellowship of a manageable size, in which life in mutual friendship and common devotion to a specific task is possible.
> 3 The awakening of creative powers in every individual and the surrender of privileges that members bring with them.
> 4 Autonomy in forming the spiritual life of the community and its life of fellowship.
> 5 Common concentration on special Christian tasks in society, whether it be in the field of evangelization, or the liberation of the under-privileged and oppressed.
> 6 The deliberate return to a simple Christo-centricism in the devotional life and to a reflection of new Christian practice in theology. (Moltmann 1992, p. 329)

Moltmann adds that these groups have usually been led by lay people and have included prayer, preaching and self-help. 'In place of "the church for the people" we have the beginnings of "the church of the people", which lives, suffers and acts among the people themselves and with them' (ibid. p. 330). They are 'a prophetic leaven' for the renewal of Church and society, like the yeast that leavens the dough. Moltmann compares them to earlier Reformed Protestant churches in the impact they can have on society at large:

> Just as in the seventeenth century the Calvinist 'right to community' (compared with the state and the state church) provided motive power for the democratic development of the political polity, so the 'grass-roots' communities among the people can provide impulses for a fundamental and democratic social reconstruction. (ibid., p. 329)

In all of this, have we not moved into the domain of Cameron's fourth organizational form, the 'third-place meeting'? In her definition, such a church occurs 'within a public space', is 'constrained by the limits of that space' and has 'a shared aim which can be changed by agreement' (see p. 4). While Moltmann describes cell churches as 'voluntary associations', it is clear that they are rooted within something else, which is the shared life of the whole society that they serve, a society caught up in struggles and conflicts for justice and liberation. The cell church is also 'constrained', this time by the political and economic realities of that society, and must work within those constraints, sometimes paying a heavy price in terms of state opposition and persecution. Furthermore, the members of cell churches have a shared aim, clear to all, of serving the coming of God's kingdom of justice and peace for all. In these three ways, then, they show that they are not so much Cameron's second organizational form of voluntary associations, which have a definite membership and set procedures to run themselves by, as the less formal and more outward looking 'third-place meeting'.

It is fascinating and remarkable to observe that, after all the evolution and development of the Church through two millennia of history, it seems now to have recovered a form not unlike that of the apostolic Church, which could also be described as a third-place meeting (see pp. 29–30). Does this mean that as the twentieth century gave way to the twenty-first century, the Church had begun to regain something of its primitive passion and sense of what it should be?

Discussion Questions

Should churches endeavour to become self-sufficient communities?

Can churches ever be nationalist?

What are the strengths and weaknesses of cell churches?

Bibliography and Further Reading

Bettenson, Henry and Chris Maunder (eds) (2011), *Documents of the Christian Church*, 4th edn, Oxford: Oxford University Press.

Bonhoeffer, Dietrich (1971), *Letters and Papers from Prison*, enlarged edn, London: Fontana.

Croft, Steven (2008), *Ministry in Three Dimensions*, London: Darton, Longman and Todd.

Croft, Steven (ed.) (2010), *The Future of the Parish System*, London: Church House Publishing.

Dulles, Avery, SJ (1988), *Models of the Church*, 2nd edn, New York: Gill and Macmillan.

Gibbs, Eddie and Ryan K. Bolger (2006), *Emerging Churches: Creating Christian Community in Postmodern Culture*, London: SPCK.

Grass, Tim (2008), *SCM Core Text Modern Church History*, London: SCM Press.

Gutiérrez, Gustavo (1988), *A Theology of Liberation*, revised edn, London: SCM Press.

Knight, Frances (2008), *The Church in the Nineteenth Century*, London: I. B Tauris.

MacCulloch, Diarmaid (2009), *A History of Christianity: The First Three Thousand Years*, Chs 22–5, Harmondsworth: Allen Lane.

Moltmann, Jürgen (1992), *The Church in the Power of the Spirit*, 2nd edn, London: SCM Press.

Vatican Council II: the Basic Sixteen Documents (1996), ed. Austin Flannery OP, Dublin: Dominican Publications.

10

Local Church History

In the final pages of his acclaimed survey of Christian history, Diarmaid MacCulloch states that 'this book has no ending, because, unlike Jesus Christ, historians in the Western secular tradition stemming from the Enlightenment do not think in terms of punchlines to the human story. This history can [only] draw attention to what has gone before: an extraordinary diversity called Christianity' (MacCulloch 2009, p. 1015). This Studyguide, examining one aspect of that involved and involving story, can agree that there can be no conclusion, because the story is still ongoing and 'it would be very surprising if this religion, so youthful, yet so varied in its historical experience, had now revealed all its secrets' (ibid., p. 1016). Secondly, it can also agree with MacCulloch's use of the phrase 'extraordinary diversity' to describe what has been revealed. For these pages began with the question 'what kind of body is the Church?', and its journey through Christian history has revealed not one but six answers to this question. At some points, the Church has been seen to be an arm of the state, a kind of public utility providing religious validation and support for rulers and their populations in different times and regions. This was especially the case in the early medieval period when tribal kings directed and extended the life of the Church in central and northern Europe. At other points, the church became a series of voluntary associations, with clear membership and set procedures for governing its own life. This became the case in the Hellenistic period, when after the break with Judaism the Church had to function within Graeco-Roman society and was required to formalize and regularize its own life. It was even more the case within the Protestant churches of the post-Reformation period, where demarcation from the rest of society became more and more pronounced and membership became more clearly defined.

At other points, church organization was much less formal and regulated, with the Church functioning as a kind of friendship group within a wider community. This was the case for the earliest expressions of Pietism, which were informal devotional groups of believers gathering to pray and read their bibles together. More commonly, the meetings of Christians developed a certain degree of order and leadership. The meetings took place within the setting of a wider society which imposed its own constraints on the life of the Church, sometimes very harshly. The Apostolic Church was an example of such 'third-place meetings', where the Christians remained as much part of the wider Jewish community as any other Jews, though they had the clear aim of preparing that society for the return of the messiah. Twentieth-century cell churches, such as the Base Christian Communities of Latin America, can also be seen as a recent and arresting expression of this organizational form.

At other points of history, under the powerful influence of the monastic movement, the Western Church became a resourcing network, with a number of centres across the continent and with the shared aim of praying for the souls of the faithful. This was especially the case in the medieval period, when a succession of monastic orders extended their influence across Europe, with large abbeys, monastic houses and local churches providing access points within every community, and local lords and kings becoming benefactors of this impressive structure. At other times, though less often than might be expected, the Church evolved into a series of self-sufficient communities, largely disinterested in what was around except when the need arose to recruit new members. Some Protestant sects have provided examples of this, such as the Amish of Pennsylvania and the Mormons and, more extremely, the Jehovah's Witnesses. The documents of the First Vatican Council also exhibited tendencies in this direction.

One very important point from the end of the first chapter needs to be recalled, that the characteristic beliefs and practices of each era are not limited to that era but continue to be expressed in later eras. This means that each organizational form is not limited to the period in which it has been studied. We have already begun to find examples of some forms in more than one period, and this could be extended. While a certain form may be typical of a certain period, it can usually be found, to a lesser extent, in other periods. Monastic networks, for example, are still in existence today and provide support and leadership for monks and nuns around the world, though they can no longer be seen as defining the nature of the Church as a whole. Similarly, some churches still retain links with their respective states, and function as arms of the state when it comes to marrying or burying its citizens. One form, as has been argued, will be predominant in each era, and will ultimately define the Church of that era, but other forms can also usually be found, leading to a complex and sometimes confusing picture.

A case study

But what does this all mean for the local church and, in particular, for church life in our own community wherever that may be. As this Studyguide draws to a close, we can ask how this broad history expresses itself in the place where we live and worship. And, in particular, returning to the question of organizational form and recalling that many of the forms are still in play in our own era, we can ask *which* of the major forms of Christian history can be found in our own local church now?

It is not easy to answer this question as churches will often show evidence of a number of different forms, with the predominant one not always obvious. To make headway a case study can be presented, from an actual community in the north of England that I know well, and with it some distilling of whatever forms of organization are within it. This type of approach can then be applied to other churches in different settings.

With the case study a general sketch can be presented before investigating its forms of organization. The church in question serves the central area (parish) of a medium-sized town. The population lives in terrace housing near the town centre, detached suburban housing further out and a poorer housing estate on the edge of the town. There are two church-supported primary schools (one for five to seven-year-olds, and one for eight to eleven-year-olds), in which the clergy and a team of lay helpers have involvement. There is also a high school and some busy doctors' surgeries near the church. Most employment is in light industry and the service sector. There is a nursing home in which a weekly communion service is celebrated. The population is almost entirely white British and mostly of long-standing residence. There is a strong local voluntary sector, represented by active cubs and scouts, sports clubs, brass bands and an annual gala.

The church is near the town centre though separated from it by a busy road. It is a large Victorian structure, built to be the established church of the town, though never as well supported as the Methodist churches of the town, which have now combined and have a more visible building next to the bus station. In recognition of the smaller congregation that now attends the church, it was re-ordered a few years ago, with the west end converted into a modern meeting room, kitchen, parish office, etc. The east end has retained a fine Edwardian reredos and stained-glass window. In the centre, on a platform that extends the sanctuary into the nave, with seating set around in a slight semi-circle, a striking free-standing nave altar provides a focus for the building. The worship at the church is mainly Eucharistic, with a small choir, servers, and a music group which leads all-age worship once a month. There is a usual Sunday attendance of around 80, mostly older adults with a handful of young families and with a few people with learning disabilities from a care home next door. Many of the regulars are active in local groups, including joint activities with other local churches, and give generously to local and national charities.

The church is also used by the wider community for baptisms, weddings and funerals. These occasionally fill the church and are one of the ways the church is at the service of the wider community. Another way is through support of the two primary schools: many of the school governors are drawn from the congregation; the pupils come into church on a regular basis; the church runs a number of after-school clubs in the schools. It also runs a small youth club in the church for children who have recently moved to the high school.

What kind of organization is this not untypical Church of England church? First impressions will be of a traditional 'parish church', a church created to administer rites of passage to the population at large and to provide the Sunday services of the established church. The suggestion of it being a public utility is supported by the fact that the church was built with money supplied by the state at the end of the Napoleonic Wars to many such industrial towns. It was built to be a 'preaching box', a large structure with a gallery and as many pews as possible, so that the whole population could be accommodated. It was the venue of the annual Lord Mayor's service (when the town had its own civic council), at which councillors and other local dignitaries would occupy the most prominent pews and the church would be filled with uniformed organizations and other local organizations. Furthermore, not so very long ago, much of the clergy's working time was taken up with preparing families for the occasional offices of baptisms, weddings and funerals. A large proportion of the population came to the church for these rites. Some of the vicars were also local magistrates, fulfilling duties in the local courts alongside their religious duties. In many ways, therefore, the church showed that it was working in alliance with the state and could even be regarded as an arm of the state in recognition of its right to marry and bury its citizens.

But is it still possible to describe this church as a public utility? A number of features suggest not. The clergy still spend time preparing and conducting the occasional offices, but the number of these has reduced. Only a minority of babies born in the parish are baptized in the parish church, and even fewer couples get married there. Most funeral services now take place at the local crematorium, with the clergy leading only a handful of those. Those who come to the church generally do so because of a family connection with the place. Secondly, with the re-ordering of the church the amount of seating has been greatly reduced, with enough for the regular Sunday congregation and some extras, but not for the general population at large which, anyway, has greatly increased since the church was built. The Lord Mayor no longer exists and so the symbolically important Lord Mayor's service no longer takes place. Thirdly, the financing of the church and its clergy has changed over the years. The amount that the national church contributes has reduced and the amount that the regular congregation contributes has greatly increased, resulting in a level of contributions that roughly matches the cost of the clergy time the congregation receives. In earlier times, the church had access to funds which the clergy distributed among the poor of the parish. Now the church council spends a large amount of time raising funds to pay its way and maintain the building. This, then, shows that the life and activity of the church is much more focused on the regular congregation than it used to be. Finally, and as a result of this, the leadership of the church is now vested not just in the clergy but in a wider team of laity who not only belong to the church council but provide the financial and human resources to maintain the building, lead fundraising activities and assist with pastoral care. This in turn means that the clergy spend a much greater proportion of their time overseeing and supporting this team rather than being out and about in the wider community. Again, a greater focus on the regular congregation is apparent in the organization of the church.

In all these ways, the church has moved from being predominantly a public utility to being a voluntary association, with a membership list, elected officers and its own funding. In a more deliberate way than before, the church exists for the sake of its members and their spiritual and social needs. While this membership is open to all, there is now a definite sense of needing to sign up and cross a line when coming into the church.

But does this analysis fully capture what is now happening in the church? The sketch above contains a number of features which might point in a different direction. These include the fact that the clergy and a sizeable team of laity spend a large amount of time in the two local schools, leading worship, as governors and as leaders of daily after-school clubs. Secondly, clergy and laity spend time each week in the local care home, leading worship for residents who will never come to the church. Thirdly, clergy and laity spend time in the town centre with the shop keepers and business leaders, offering support and taking part in special markets and meetings. Fourthly, some members of the church make a point of meeting with and liaising with other churches in the town, joining forces with events and projects where possible. With all these forms of outreach there is neither financial gain nor any significant benefit for the Sunday morning congregation, and indeed these activities can take clergy and laity away from congregational activities and fellowship in the church. It must be noted that this kind of non-productive outreach is not typical of voluntary associations, which generally have a form of organization geared towards the benefit of their own members.

What other organizational form does all this reveal? It cannot be a third-place meeting, because the church itself does not meet in a public space such as a café or pub but in its own building. It still invests a large proportion of its time and money in maintaining this building and the congregational activities, which shows how important the church itself remains. Yet, these activities are combined with the extensive outreach work described above. Such a dual focus recalls the fifth organizational form, the network resource, which is organized both to build up and strengthen 'the resource' itself, in this case the faith and discipleship of the congregation, and to allow its flow through 'the network' to others, in this case the wider community of the parish. A network resource does not seek to bring the network *into* the resource (if that were ever possible), but to allow the resource to flow out through the network. Nevertheless, it must ensure that the resource is in good enough shape to be able to flow through the network, so all the while it must be built up and strengthened. In the same way, this church does not attempt to bring the population of the parish into the church, but rather to ensure the congregation is in good enough spiritual shape to allow its life of prayer and discipleship to be of benefit to the wider population. So, for example, Sunday services seek to encourage and equip the congregation, so that they may pass on an awareness of God and prayerfulness to others during the week, such as the children who attend the after-school clubs.

At this point in history, then, in response to dramatic changes in the social and cultural life of the surrounding parish, it is possible to see this local church evolving in its organizational life. It started out in the nineteenth century as a public utility, providing the essential services of the occasional offices, covering the entire population (insofar as they allowed it to do so) and without a membership but having legal officers (the vicar and churchwardens). In the twentieth century, however, as this establishment role diminished in response to social and cultural changes, it became more obviously a voluntary association, having a definite membership who took up more and more of the clergy time, and developed more effective procedures for the members to run the association themselves. This was caused by, and helped to encourage, greater congregationalism, in which the life of the church was increasingly focused on the needs and wishes of the congregation itself, who largely paid for what they received.

Now, though, a different form of the church may be emerging, one focused on the congregation *and* on the spiritual needs and hunger of the wider population. Church life is providing support to a group of 'regulars' who not only attend its services but have a shared aim of awakening a 'God consciousness', to use Schleiermacher's phrase (pp. 155–6), in the wider population, and this in conjunction with other local churches around the town. In this the church is becoming a 'network resource' for this larger undertaking and so returning to a form of organization not unlike that of the monastic movement of the medieval period, with the 'regulars' now fulfilling the role of the monks and nuns. In different language, they could be seen as discovering a vocation to be yeast that leavens the dough of the wider population, and church life as the place that nurtures that yeastiness. Correspondingly, the success of church life could now be assessed not on the size or financial strength of the regular congregation, but on the level of its impact on the wider population.

Why is this happening? One reason must be the social and cultural changes already mentioned, which mean that the general population as a rule do not participate in church life. But another is a growing perception, generated especially by contact with the school children and with the elderly people in the care home, that God is at work in the community as well as in the church and that the congregation find blessings and grace when they encounter him out there. In theological language, this is the perception that God's mission is present in the world, as the *missio Dei*, and the church is invited to participate in that mission. Then, as it rediscovers the presence of God in schools and homes and elsewhere, it can put into words and symbols what is happening and invite others to participate as well. In this manner, it becomes a network resource, fed by God's loving mission in the world and, in turn, helping others to be part of that mission. In these kinds of ways it shows the truth of MacCulloch's statement, that Christianity has not yet revealed all its secrets.

Discussion Questions

Look at the recent history of your local church and the major features of its evolving life and assess which organizational forms have been present within it?

Which form is now predominant? Why do you think this?

What difference does this awareness make?

Bibliography and Further Reading

Cameron, Helen (2010), *Resourcing Mission: Practical Theology for Changing Churches*, London: SCM Press.

MacCulloch, Diarmaid (2009), *A History of Christianity: The First Three Thousand Years*, Harmondsworth: Allen Lane.

Further Reading

General Works

Ashwin-Sjiekowski, Piotr (2010), *SCM Studyguide Early Christian Doctrine and the Creeds*, London: SCM Press.

Backhouse, Stephen (2011), *The Compact Guide to Christian History*, Oxford: Lion Hudson.

Bettenson, Henry and Chris Maunder (eds) (2011), *Documents of the Christian Church*, 4th edn, Oxford: Oxford University Press.

Cameron, Euan (2005), *Interpreting Christian History: the Challenge of the Churches' Past*, Oxford: Blackwell.

Chadwick, Henry (ed.) (2010), *Not Angels, but Anglicans: A History of Christianity in the British Isles*, revised updated edn, Norwich: Canterbury Press.

Cross, F. L. and E. A. Livingstone (eds) (2005), *The Oxford Dictionary of the Christian Church*, 4th edn, Oxford: Oxford University Press.

Gilley, Sheridan and W. J. Sheils (eds) (1994), *A History of Religion in Britain: Practice and Belief from Pre-Roman Times to the Present*, Oxford: Blackwell.

Hastings, Adrian (1999), *A World History of Christianity*, London: Cassell.

Hill, Jonathan (2007), *The History of Christianity*, Oxford: Lion Hudson.

Küng, Hans (1995), *Christianity: Its Essence and History*, London: SCM Press.

MacCulloch, Diarmaid (2009), *A History of Christianity: The First Three Thousand Years*, London: Allen Lane.

MacCulloch, Diarmaid (2012), *Christian History: An Introduction to the Western Tradition*, London: SCM Press.

Mullin, Robert Bruce (2008), *A Short World History of Christianity*, Louisville, KY: Westminster John Knox Press.

Pecknold, C. C. (2010), *Christianity and Politics: A Brief Guide to the History*, Eugene, OR: Cascade Books.

The New SCM Dictionary of Church History, (2008), Robert Benedetto (ed.), London: SCM Press.

Williams, Rowan (2005), *Why Study the Past? The Quest for the Historical Church*, London: Darton, Longman and Todd.

Wilken, Robert (2013), *The First Thousand Years: A Global History of Christianity*, New Haven: Yale University Press.

Early Church

Brown, Peter (2003), *The Rise of Western Christendom: Triumph and Diversity 200–1000*, Oxford: Blackwell.

Brox, Norbert (1994), *A History of the Early Church*, London: SCM Press.

Chadwick, Henry (1967), *The Early Church*, London: Penguin.

Collins, John N. (2009), *Diakonia: Re-interpreting the Ancient Sources*, Oxford: Oxford University Press.

Evans, G. R. (2004), *The First Christian Theologians: An Introduction to Theology in the Early Church*, Oxford: Blackwell.

Frend, W. H. C. (1984), *The Rise of Christianity*, London: Darton, Longman and Todd.

Hall, Stuart G. (1991), *Doctrine and Practice in the Early Church*, London: SPCK.

Hazlett, Ian (ed.), (1991), *Early Christianity: Origins and Evolution to AD 600*, Nashville, TN: Abingdon Press.

Kelly, J. N. D. (2000), *Early Christian Doctrines*, London: Continuum.

Miles, Margaret (2004), *The Word Made Flesh: A History of Christian Thought*, Oxford: Wiley-Blackwell.

Stevenson, J. and W. H. C. Frend (1987), *A New Eusebius: Documents Illustrating the History of the Church to AD336*, London: SPCK.

Stevenson, J. and W. H. C. Frend (1989), *Creeds, Councils and Controversies: Documents Illustrating the History of the Church AD337–461*, London: SPCK.

Wilken, Robert (2013), *The First Thousand Years: A Global History of Christianity*, New Haven: Yale University Press

Young, Frances with Andrew Teal (2010), *From Nicaea to Chalcedon*, 2nd edn, London: SCM Press.

Medieval Church

Bede (1992), *Saint Bede the Venerable 673–735: Bede's Ecclesiastical History of the English People*, eds Bertram Colgrave and R. A. B. Mynors, Oxford: Clarendon Press.

Benedict (1990), *The Rule of Saint Benedict*, trans. Abbot Parry OSB with commentary by Esther de Waal, Leominster: Gracewing.

Burton, Janet (2011), *The Cistercians in the Middle Ages*, Woodbridge: The Boydell Press.

Clark, James G. (2011), *The Benedictines in the Middle Ages*, Woodbridge: The Boydell Press.

Evans, G. R. (ed.) (2001), *The Medieval Theologians*, Oxford: Blackwell.

Frank, Wilhelm Isnard (1995), *A History of the Medieval Church*, London: SCM Press.

Herrin, Judith (1989), *The Formation of Christendom*, London: Fontana.

Logan, F. Donald (2002), *A History of the Church in the Middle Ages*, London: Routledge.

Ozment, Stephen (1980), *The Age of Reform 1250–1550*, New Haven: Yale University Press.

Miles, Margaret (2004), *The Word Made Flesh: A History of Christian Thought*, Oxford: Wiley-Blackwell.

Robson, Michael (2006), *The Franciscans in the Middle Ages*, Woodbridge: The Boydell Press

Southern, R. W. (1970), *Western Society and the Church in the Middle Ages*, London: Penguin.

Reformation

Althaus, Paul (1972), *The Ethics of Martin Luther*, Philadelphia: Fortress.

Bagchi, D. and D. Steinmetz (eds) (2004), *The Cambridge Companion to Reformation Theology*, Cambridge: Cambridge University Press.

Bossy, John (1985), *Christianity in the West 1400–1700*, Oxford: Oxford University Press.

Cameron, Euan (2012), *The European Reformation*, 2nd edn, Oxford: Oxford University Press.

Gordon, Bruce (2009), *Calvin*, New Haven: Yale University Press.

Janz, Dennis R. (2002), *A Reformation Reader: Primary Texts with Introductions*, new edn, Minneapolis: Augsburg Fortress Press.

Lindberg, Carter (1995), *The European Reformations*, Oxford: Blackwell.

Lindberg, Carter (ed.) (2001), *The Reformation Theologians: An Introduction to Theology in the Early Modern Period*, Oxford: Blackwell.

Loyola, Ignatius (1914), *The Spiritual Exercises of St Ignatius of Loyola*, trans. Fr E. Mullan SJ, New York: P. J. Kenedy & Sons.

MacCulloch, Diarmaid (2003), *Reformation: Europe's House Divided*, Harmondsworth: Allen Lane.

McGrath, Alister (1999), *Reformation Thought: An Introduction*, 3rd edn, Oxford: Blackwell.

Methuen, Charlotte (2011), *Luther and Calvin: Religious Revolutionaries*, Oxford: Lion Hudson.

Miles, Margaret (2004), *The Word Made Flesh: A History of Christian Thought*, Oxford: Wiley-Blackwell.

Trent (1848), *The Council of Trent: The canons and decrees of the sacred and oecumenical Council of Trent*, ed. and trans. J. Waterworth, London: Dolman.

Modern Church

Bebbington, David (1989), *Evangelicalism in Modern Britain: A History from the 1730s to the 1980s*, London: Routledge.

Brown, Callum (2001), *The Death of Christian Britain: Understanding Secularisation 1800–2000*, London: Routledge.

Chadwick, Owen (1971), *The Victorian Church*, 2 vols, London: SCM Press.

Davies, Noel and Martin Conway (2008), *World Christianity in the 20th Century*, London: SCM Press

Grass, Tim (2008), *Modern Church History*, London: SCM Press.

Hastings, Adrian (2001), *A History of English Christianity 1920–2000*, 4th edn, London: SCM Press.

Hastings, Adrian (ed.) (1991), *Modern Catholicism: Vatican II and After*, London: SPCK.

Hempton, David (2005), *Methodism: Empire of the Spirit*, New Haven: Yale University Press.

Hempton, David (2011), *The Church in the Long Eighteenth Century*, London: I. B. Tauris.

Knight, Frances (2008), *The Church in the Nineteenth Century*, London: I. B Tauris.

Livingston, James C. (2006), *Modern Christian Thought*, 2 vols, Minneapolis: Fortress Press.

Noll, Mark A. (2004), *The Rise of Evangelicalism*, Leicester: Intervarsity Press.

Rack, Henry (1989), *Reasonable Enthusiast: John Wesley and the Rise of Methodism*, Peterborough: Epworth Press.

Welch, Claude (1972), *Protestant Thought in the Nineteenth Century*, 2 vols, New Haven: Yale University Press.

Worrall, B. G. (1988), *The Making of the Modern Church*, London: SPCK.

Vatican Council II: the Basic Sixteen Documents (1996), ed. Austin Flannery OP, Dublin: Dominican Publications.

Glossary

Albigensians A term applied in the late twelfth and early thirteenth century to the people of South West France who lived near and around the city of Albi and who in their beliefs were Cathars (see below). Pope Innocent III authorized a Crusade against them, which led to a long period of brutal warfare in which the French monarchy and Catholic forces were in the end victorious in 1229. From 1233 the Inquisition continued to repress the Albigensians.

Alexandria An Egyptian coastal city with many cults and which was important to the growth of the early Church. It was a centre of Hellenistic culture and philosophy and home to one of the greatest libraries of the ancient world. It was also home to a large Jewish population whose leading philosopher was Philo. Christianity grew within this Jewish community and some of its churches nurtured Gnosticism. It also produced a succession of remarkable theologians, including Clement of Alexandria, Origen and Athanasius, as well as Arius the father of Arianism.

Anabaptists A sect of radical Protestant reformers dating from the 1520s who believed that baptism should only be administered to believing adults. The sect followed the ideas of reformers such as Zwingli but took their ideas to an extreme. They not only rejected infant baptism but advocated the complete separation of church and state. Many of them were persecuted and executed. Some branches of the Baptist tradition continue to follow their ideas, not least the Mennonites.

Apologists A group of early Christian writers who between c.120–220 addressed the task of making a reasoned defence and recommendation of the Christian faith to educated outsiders. They included Justin Martyr, Athenagoras and Tertullian. They sought to dispel misunderstanding and slanders about Christianity and show that Christians were loyal subjects of the Roman Empire and that their faith was in accord with Greek philosophy.

Arianism An influential outlook in the early Church which denied the divinity of Christ. It originated with the Alexandrian priest Arius (c.250–c.336) and maintained that the son of God was created by the Father from nothing and was therefore not coeternal with the Father, nor of the same substance. This outlook was condemned as a heresy by the Council of Nicea in 325 and again at Constantinople in 381. While it was forced out of the Roman Empire it retained a following among the Germanic tribes until the conversion of the Franks to Catholicism in 496.

Arminianism The doctrine of the Dutch Protestant theologian Jacobus Arminius, 1560–1609, who rejected the Calvinist doctrines of predestination and election and taught that the sovereignty of God is compatible with human free will. This implied that justification was open to everyone, not just those who had been predestined to be justified. His teachings had a considerable influence on John Wesley and the Methodist movement.

Augsburg Confession A statement of Lutheran confessional theology, drawn up mainly by Philipp Melanchthon, 1497–1560, and approved by Luther before being presented to the Emperor Charles V at Augsburg on 25 June 1530. The emperor rejected the confession but it became a defining document for Lutheran churches and was influential on other reformers including Archbishop Thomas Cranmer.

Book of Concord This was a collection of key Lutheran documents that were published in Dresden in 1580. It arose out of disagreements within Lutheranism over the proper interpretation of the Augsburg Confession (which was included in the book, along with Luther's Small Catechism). It represents a definitive collection of the principal confessional documents of Lutheranism.

Bull (papal) A written mandate of the pope. They used to be sealed with the pope's signet-ring but since 1878 only the most important ones are sealed in this way.

Cartesianism The philosophical outlook of René Descartes, 1596–1650, the French philosopher, scientist and mathematician widely acknowledged as one of the chief architects of the modern age. He taught that all observed phenomena are ultimately to be explained by the interaction of particles and in particular by their size, shape and motion. He also taught a radical dualism in which the mind is separate from the physical world that it perceives. The only secure knowledge comes from an introspection that states 'I think therefore I am' (in Latin *cogito ergo sum*).

Cathars Members of a movement in the medieval church which taught a form of Manichaean dualism, a view that the material world was evil and the spiritual domain was pure. The movement originated in the tenth century in the Balkans (among the

Bogomils) and then in France around the city of Albi, where followers were called Albigensians (see above). Here it was ruthlessly suppressed but later appeared in Germany and Italy in the twelfth century, where the term Cathars (from the Greek 'katharos', meaning pure) was used of its followers.

Chalcedon A former city on the Bosphoros in Asia Minor, now a district of Istanbul. The fourth ecumenical council met here in 451, which condemned Nestorius and the Monophysite view of Eutyches that Christ had one nature that was 'not consubstantial with humanity'. Instead, the Council affirmed that Christ is 'one Person in two Natures': the Divine which is of the same substance as the Father; and the human, which is of the same substance as humanity. These are united unconfusedly, unchangeably, indivisibly, inseparably. Many churches, especially those to the east known as the Oriental Orthodox Churches, did not accept this formula.

Cistercians Members of a monastic order founded in 1098 at Citeaux (Latin *Cistercium*) near Dijon in France. The order was founded for the strict observance of the Rule of St Benedict. Cistercian houses for both monks and nuns spread throughout Europe in the twelfth and thirteenth centuries. Those who continue to follow the rule strictly are known as Trappists.

Cluny A town in Burgundy in eastern France where a monastic order was founded in 910 to keep the rule of St Benedict. The order spread far and wide across Europe, becoming very influential and wealthy in the eleventh and twelfth centuries.

Conciliarism A movement in the late-medieval Western church which argued that supreme authority in the church lies not with the pope or kings but with general councils of leading bishops. Hugh of Pisa, John of Paris and Marsiglio of Padua were proponents of conciliarism, as was Nicholas of Cusa. The schism between the popes at Avignon and those in Rome demonstrated the need for a general council, which the Council of Constance (1414–18) partially fulfilled. When a unified papacy was restored at Rome from 1417 conciliarism was gradually undermined, contributing eventually to the need for the Reformation.

Confessing Church The group of German Reformed and Lutheran Christians who were opposed to the German Christian Church movement sponsored by the Nazis between 1933 and 1945. Its first leader was Martin Niemöller and at the Synod Barmen in May 1934 it issued the Barmen Declaration, drafted by a group of theologians including Karl Barth and Dietrich Bonhoeffer, which gave the theological reasons for opposing Nazi control of the church. Many of the leaders were persecuted until the outbreak of war when open resistance came to an end.

Congregationalism A form of self-government by independent churches that has its roots in sixteenth-century England. Congregationalists were originally known as Independents and a group of them known as the 'Pilgrim Fathers' emigrated to the Netherlands and then to America during the reign of Charles I. Others came to form the backbone of Cromwell's army during the English civil war. After the restoration of the monarchy and episcopacy in 1660 Congregationalists along with others became known as 'dissenters'.

Conventuals A branch of the Franciscan order in the medieval period that disagreed with the 'Spirituals' who wanted a strict adherence to the rule of St Francis of Assisi. The Conventuals allowed monks to accumulate property and they adapted Francis' rule for life in large monasteries.

Council Within church history these are gatherings of the bishops of the church to decide on matters of doctrine and church order. The first ecumenical council was under the chairmanship of the layman the Emperor Constantine.

Crusades Military expeditions made by Western European Christian kings and armies, from the eleventh to the thirteenth centuries, to recover Jerusalem and the Holy Land from Saracen Muslims. They were initially successful but then failed to stop Muslim resurgence and re-capture of the Holy Land. The fourth crusade was diverted to Constantinople, where the crusaders brutally sacked the city.

Desert Fathers Hermits who took their inspiration from St Anthony of Egypt who in the deserts of Egypt and Syria lived lives of discipline, prayer and fasting in order to combat demons and Satan. They lived alone but would sometimes group together in colonies. They came to Western Europe in this form, through the encouragement of Martin of Tours among others.

Docetism The belief that Christ's body was not human but either a phantasm or of a real but purely spiritual substance. This implied that his sufferings were only apparent. In the early Church this belief was held by the Gnostics.

Dominicans An order of preaching friars founded by Dominic in 1215–16. Members were also called Black Friars because of the colour of their cloaks. They were mendicants (relying on alms) and were devoted to renewing the church through preaching in the towns and villages of medieval Europe. Some became scholars, such as St Thomas Aquinas. They later became officers of the Inquisition.

Donatism The teaching of the Donatists, who were a Christian group in North Africa led by Donatus (d.355) who were opposed to the election of Caecilian as bishop of Carthage. (When a Roman official, Caecilian had previously persecuted the church.)

Donatism held that only those who led a blameless life could belong to the church, and their churches broke away from the Catholic Church. Augustine of Hippo vigorously opposed their teaching.

Ecclesiology The theology of the nature and structure of the church. In the nineteenth century the word was also used to describe the study of church building and decoration.

Ecumenism Work for the full visible unity of the Christian church, overcoming historic divisions between denominations and their doctrines.

Edict of Milan A document from Emperor Licinius to provincial governors in the Eastern Roman Empire in 313. It arose from an agreement with Emperor Constantine at Milan that there should be freedom of worship for all, including Christians, and the restitution of possessions lost by the churches since the persecution of 303.

Enlightenment A European intellectual movement of the late seventeenth and eighteenth centuries, heavily influenced by the thinking of seventeenth-century philosophers and scientists such as Descartes, Locke and Newton, and at heart being a belief in human reason as the key to knowledge and progress. It included a new belief in religious tolerance and a distrust of superstition.

Filioque A Latin phrase meaning 'and from the Son'. It was inserted into the Nicene Creed from about the fourth century especially in the Western church, to assert the doctrine of the procession of the Holy Spirit from the Father 'and from the Son'. This inclusion became one of the main reasons the Eastern Church (later known as Eastern Orthodox churches) separated itself from the Western Church from 1054.

Friars Monks who belong to orders (such as the Franciscans and the Dominicans) that live out their vocation in the world, depending on alms as mendicants, rather than in monasteries set apart from the world.

Gallicanism A movement in the French Roman Catholic Church that asserted its freedom from the ecclesiastical authority of the papacy in Rome. It reached the peak of its influence in the seventeenth century.

German Christians Lutheran and Reformed church members who, during the Hitler regime, tried to bring about a synthesis of Nazism and Christianity. Some tried to eradicate everything Jewish from Christianity, including the OT, Paul and Augustine of Hippo's theology of original sin. With the support of the regime they came to control more than half of German Protestant churches up to the end of the Second World War.

Gnosticism A movement that became very influential in the second-century Church. It was heavily influenced by Greek philosophy and some pagan myths, seeing a sharp separation between the material world, which is corrupt, and the divine spiritual world. Access to the spiritual world is gained through secret knowledge (Greek: 'gnosis') which is handed on by those who know it. The material world is controlled by the demiurge or creator god, and the spiritual world by the supreme but remote divine being. Christ was an emissary of this being, bringing 'gnosis' to those to whom he chose to reveal it.

Hussites Followers of a reforming and nationalist movement begun by Jan Hus (1372–1415), a Czech philosopher and priest. After Hus's execution his followers took up arms against the Holy Roman Emperor and demanded a set of reforms that anticipated the Reformation. One group of extreme Hussites were defeated but another moderate group succeeded in 1436 in establishing a Czech church independent of the Catholic Church. One section, the Bohemian Brethren, would eventually become the Moravian Church.

Inquisition An ecclesiastical court established by Pope Gregory IX around 1232 for the detection of heretics. It was active in northern Italy and southern France, becoming notorious for the use of torture. Heretics who refused to recant would be handed over to civil authorities to be burnt at the stake. In 1542 it was reinstituted to fight Protestantism. The Spanish Inquisition was a separate body formed in 1478 to root out heresy among Jewish and Muslim converts to Christianity. It operated with great severity and was not dissolved until the early nineteenth century.

Jamnia A city south of Joppa in Palestine to which Jewish religious leaders went after the fall of Jerusalem in 70AD. In some ways they replaced the Sanhedrin and they held regular synods. A synod in the year 100 may have settled the limits of the OT canon.

Jesuits An order of priests founded in 1534 by Ignatius Loyola, Francis Xavier and others to do missionary work throughout the world. The order tried to oppose the Reformation in Europe with uncompromising zeal. It was persecuted in some countries but grew to become one of the largest and most influential religious orders in the Catholic Church, not least through its educational work around the world. Jesuits swear a special oath of loyalty to the pope.

Liberation theology A movement among both academic theologians and local churches that has its roots in the 1960s in the Roman Catholic Church in Latin America. Under the influence of Marxism as well as the Bible it recovered a sense of God's preferential option for the poor, re-thinking Christian faith and life from this perspective. Liberation is seen as much about social, political and economic realities as spiritual realities. It has influenced churches in many parts of the world and was criticized and restricted by Pope John Paul II.

Lollards Followers of the philosopher and reformer John Wycliffe (*c.*1329–84), who believed that the church should follow scripture rather than the church hierarchy and should help people to imitate Christ. Lollards attacked many church practices including clerical celibacy, transubstantiation, indulgences, pilgrimages and the monastic orders. They were responsible for one of the first translations of the Bible into English. The word 'lollard' came from the Dutch word for mumbler. They did not receive widespread support among the nobility and were often persecuted, but they influenced Jan Hus in Prague and were still to be found in Tudor England. They anticipated many Reformation beliefs.

Manicheism A dualistic religious outlook with Christian, Gnostic and pagan elements, founded in Persia in the third century by Manes (c.216–276). It believed that while all matter was evil, a particle of divine 'light' could be found within every person, which a strict ascetic way of life could release. Manicheism spread widely through the Roman Empire and into Asia. It was persecuted but survived.

Methodism A movement for Christian revival that began in the Church of England under the influence of John and Charles Wesley. It was influenced by Arminian ideas of universal access to salvation and started as religious meetings to guide and encourage a fervent personal faith in Christ with hymn singing and social welfare. It spread throughout the British Isles and North America, especially among the working class. After the death of John Wesley it formally separated from the Church of England in 1791. In the nineteenth century it divided over doctrinal questions but re-united again in the twentieth century. It remains one of the largest Protestant denominations around the world.

Monasticism The life of the monastic orders, which look to Anthony of Egypt, Martin of Tours and Benedict of Nursia as it founders, and spread across the Eastern and Western church in many different forms. In the early Middle Ages monasticism was largely responsible for the spread and growth of Christianity in the West. Through the mendicant friars, especially Dominicans and Franciscans, it became a major force in the Reformation period for the spread of Catholicism around the world.

Montanism A movement founded in Phrygia in Asia Minor by Montanus in the second century. It reacted against the way the church was becoming influenced by Greaco-Roman culture in the urban centres and wanted a stricter adherence to the principles of primitive Christianity. It was an apocalyptic movement, believing in the imminent return and outpouring of the Holy Spirit, which had already begun to be poured into its own prophets and prophetesses. In north Africa the theologian Tertullian became a Montanist, calling for stricter fasting and penitence.

Moravians Members of a Lutheran church who under the influence of Pietism took personal devotion very seriously. They were founded in 1722 by emigrants from Moravia in Bohemia, who brought Hussite views with them. They made a profound impression on John Wesley. The Moravian church spread around the world and is still active today.

Mormonism The outlook of the Church of Jesus Christ of Latter Day Saints, which was founded in New York State in 1830 by Joseph Smith. It is a millenarian religious movement, believing that Christ will return soon. It follows the Bible and the Book of Mormon, which tells a story about a group of Hebrews who emigrated to America around 600AD. Smith claimed to have found and translated the Book of Mormon by divine revelation. He also instituted polygamy. In 1847 the movement moved its headquarters to Salt Lake City in Utah and has spread widely across the globe since then.

Neoplatonism A religious and philosophical worldview originating with the philosopher Plotinus. The ideas of Plato were fused with Eastern mysticism. It became the dominant philosophy of the pagan world until the early sixth century. A dualistic worldview presented the human soul as being able to gain knowledge of the transcendent and immaterial One, escaping the imperfect material world, through ascetic virtue and sustained contemplation.

Nicea An ancient city in Asia Minor, the site of the Emperor Constantine's summer palace and location of the Council of Nicea in 325 which condemned Arianism and adopted the Nicean formula describing Christ as 'begotten of the Father, the only begotten; that is, of the essence of the Father, God of God, Light of Light, very God of very God, begotten, not made, being of one substance with the Father; by whom all things were made both in heaven and on earth …'

Nonconformity A term used of Protestants who refused to conform to the Established Church (the Church of England) after the restoration of the monarchy and the episcopacy in 1660. They refused to use the Book of Common Prayer and worshipped as independent churches, such as the Congregationalists, Baptists, Quakers and, from the end of the eighteenth century, the Methodists.

Pentecostalism A renewal movement that began in the early twentieth century among independent churches (starting in Los Angeles) inspired by the description of the coming of the Holy Spirit at Pentecost in Acts 2.1–4. Worship involves spontaneous 'speaking in tongues' which are generally unintelligible utterances arising from intense emotion and religious experience, with prophecy, healings and exorcism. By the second half of the twentieth century the movement had spread around the world, being especially strong in Latin America and parts of sub-Saharan Africa, and in the form of the Charismatic movement had gained a large following in some historic denominations.

Pietism A movement originating in Frankfurt around 1670 for the renewal of Lutheranism, with devotional circles for prayer and Bible study. There was special emphasis on personal devotion to Christ focused on his suffering and death on the cross. Pietism was spread around the world by the Moravian church and influenced John Wesley and the Methodist movement.

Presbyterianism A form of Protestant church government in which the local church is governed by presbyters or elders (including lay elders who are elected). The system was first put forward by John Calvin who in 1541 set up the first Presbyterian church court in Geneva. He believed his system to be based on the account of the early Church in the book of Acts. Christ, rather than the pope or a monarch, was the head of the church and all other members were spiritually equal under him. This system is followed by Church of Scotland and other Reformed churches across Europe and around the world. (But the Church of Scotland retains the monarch as an honorary head.) There are also regional and national courts in Presbyterianism.

Puritans Protestants who from the reign of Elizabeth I onwards thought that the English reformation had not gone far enough and wanted to remove all elements of Catholicism not found in scripture. At first they campaigned to remove statues, vestments and organs, and from 1570 started to attack the institution of episcopacy, wishing to substitute the Presbyterian system of church government by elders. They were oppressed under James I and Charles I but gained pre-eminence during the Civil War. They then fragmented into sects and after the restoration of the monarchy and episcopacy in 1660 they left the Church of England and became known as dissenters or nonconformists.

Quakers Members of the Society of Friends, a body founded by George Fox around 1650. The term 'quaker' is thought to come from the way they would sometimes quake (have fits) in worship. Central to their belief is the doctrine of the 'Inner Light', concerning Christ's direct working in the soul. This led them to reject all set liturgical forms and ritual in worship, with no priests or minister, and meetings were held in silence until a member felt stirred to speak. They were persecuted by the authorities but refused to meet in secret and wore plain clothes. Many emigrated and the state of Pennsylvania was founded by Quakers. They refused to take up arms or to swear oaths. They are found in many parts of the world.

Qumran The site of some ruins at the NW end of the Dead Sea. It was near here in 1947 that the 'Dead Sea scrolls' were found, with further finds in later years. At the time of Jesus it was probably home to an ascetic sect who expected the coming of the messiah to liberate Israel. It later became a Roman military outpost before their assault on the Zealots in their hill top fortress of Masada between 70 and 74AD.

Reformation The sixteenth-century movement, instituted by Martin Luther around 1517, to reform the beliefs and practices of the Catholic Church. The campaign for reform led to the creation of Protestant Churches, first in Germany and then in Switzerland and across northern Europe, with the backing of many of the monarchs. Its roots go back to the fourteenth century with groups such as the Lollards and Hussites attacking the church for its wealth and hierarchical structure. Many historians now regard the 'Counter-Reformation', within countries still loyal to the papacy, as part of a European-wide movement of change and renewal in the churches. Religious divisions became political divisions, however, leading to war in both the sixteenth and seventeenth centuries.

Renaissance A revival of interest in the art and literature of ancient antiquity, leading in Western Europe to a widespread and profound revival of art, literature and scholarship, from the fourteenth to the sixteenth century.

Schism The separation of a church into two churches, or the secession of a group over doctrinal or disciplinary or other matters.

Schmalkaldic League A league of Protestant princes and cities formed in Schmalkalden in 1531 in response to Charles V's rejection of the Augsburg Confession and of Protestantism in the Holy Roman Empire generally. The League united Lutherans and Zwinglians and by 1537 included 35 states. It was destroyed by Charles in 1547.

Scholasticism A method of scholarly enquiry which developed in the new schools and universities of Western Europe from the eleventh century onward. It posed questions to ancient texts and through the application of logic sought to reveal their underlying agreement, seeking to attain what the scholastics saw as the one inner truth of things. It flourished until the sixteenth century when it came under severe criticism from Humanist scholars, who preferred a more literary and historical approach to ancient literature.

Septuagint A Greek version of the Old Testament (Hebrew Bible) including the Apocrypha, made for the use of Jewish communities in Egypt whose native language was Greek, between the third and second century BC. Its name comes from the belief that it was produced by about 70 scholars. The early Church used the Septuagint as its Bible, and it is still the standard version of the OT in the Greek Orthodox Church.

Spirituals A branch of the Franciscan order in the medieval period who wanted a strict adherence to the rule of St Francis of Assisi. They opposed the Conventuals who allowed monks to accumulate property and who adapted Francis' rule for life in large monasteries.

Theatines A religious order founded in Rome in 1524 that aimed to turn the Church away from grave abuses and scandals that were then widespread. They were not allowed to have any property and had to observe a strict and austere way of life. Their distinctive dress was a habit with white socks. The order spread from Italy to Spain and Central Europe. They contributed to the Counter-Reformation.

Ultramontanism A movement in the Roman Catholic Church in northern Europe in the nineteenth century aimed at restoring the authority of the papal curia which was 'ultramontane' (literally 'over the mountain'), i.e. over the Alps in Rome. It campaigned for the centralisation of the RC church as opposed to the de-centralisation of authority in national and diocesan structures (opposing Gallicanism among other movements). Its greatest triumph was the declaration of papal infallibility by the First Vatican Council in 1870.

Unitarians A religious body that believes God is not a trinity but one being and upholds freedom from formal dogma or doctrine. It dates from the Reformation period, in which Unitarian communities became established in the sixteenth and seventeenth centuries in Poland, Hungary and England, while in the twentieth century it grew in the United States.

Vulgate The Latin version of the Bible translated mainly by Jerome in the late fourth century (finished around 405), containing a version of the OT translated directly from the Hebrew. In 1546 the Council of Trent declared that the Vulgate was to be the sole Latin source for the Bible.

Waldensians The followers of a strict religious sect founded in southern France around 1173, by Peter Valdes, a merchant of Lyons. The sect suffered persecution throughout the medieval period. After the Reformation it survived as a Protestant sect and can still be found in northern Italy and North America.

Index